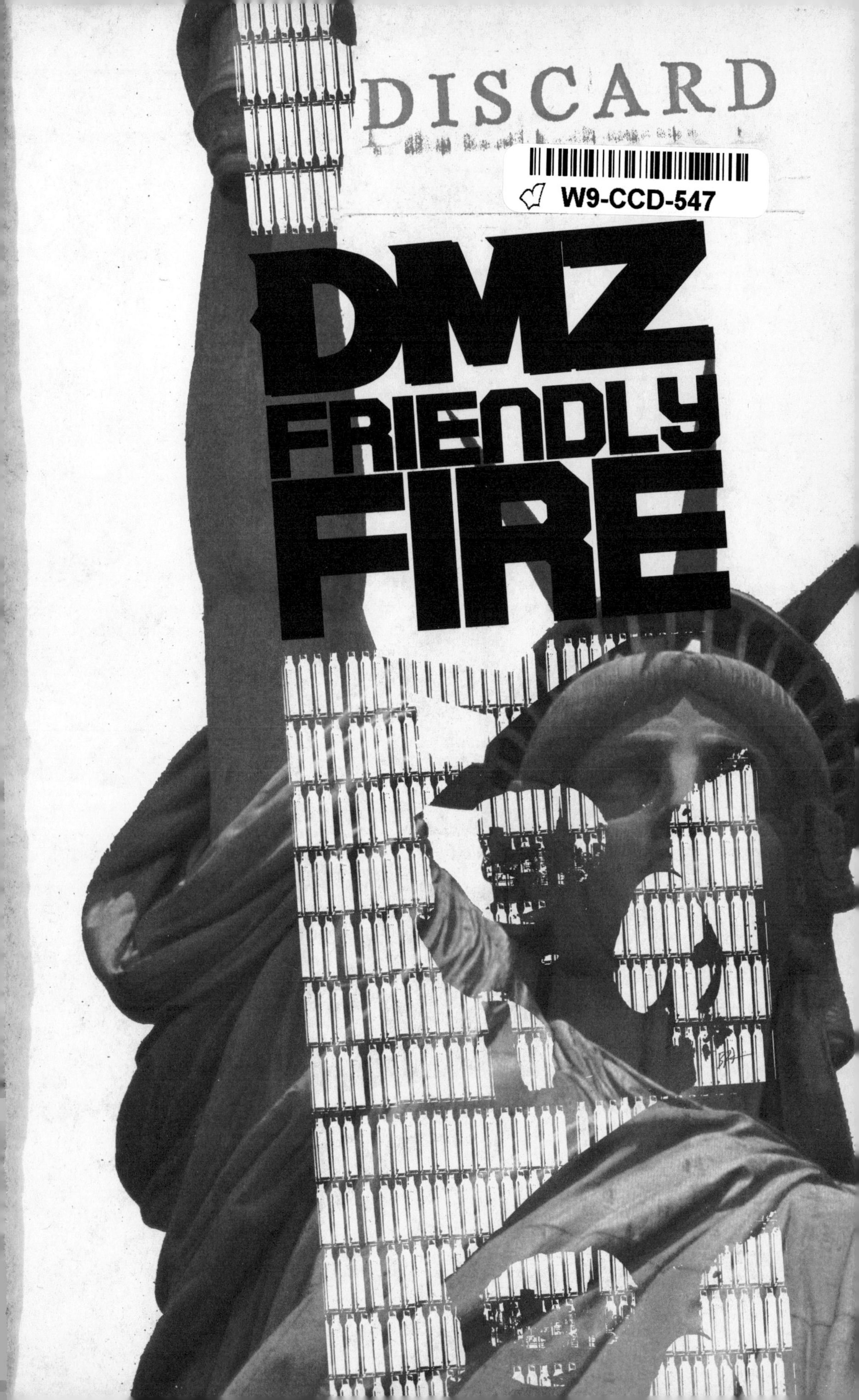
DMZ
FRIENDLY
FIRE

Cover illustration and logo design by Brian Wood
Publication design and additional photography by Amelia Grohman

DMZ: FRIENDLY FIRE
Published by DC Comics. Cover, introduction and compilation
Copyright © 2008 DC Comics. All Rights Reserved.

Originally published in single magazine form as DMZ 18-22. Copyright © 2007 Brian Wood and Riccardo Burchielli.
All Rights Reserved. VERTIGO and all characters, their distinctive likenesses and related elements featured in this publication are
trademarks of DC Comics. The stories, characters and incidents featured in this publication are entirely fictional. DC Comics does
not read or accept unsolicited submissions of ideas, stories or artwork.

DC Comics
1700 Broadway, New York, NY 10019
A Warner Bros. Entertainment Company
Printed in Canada. Second Printing.
ISBN: 978-1-4012-1662-7

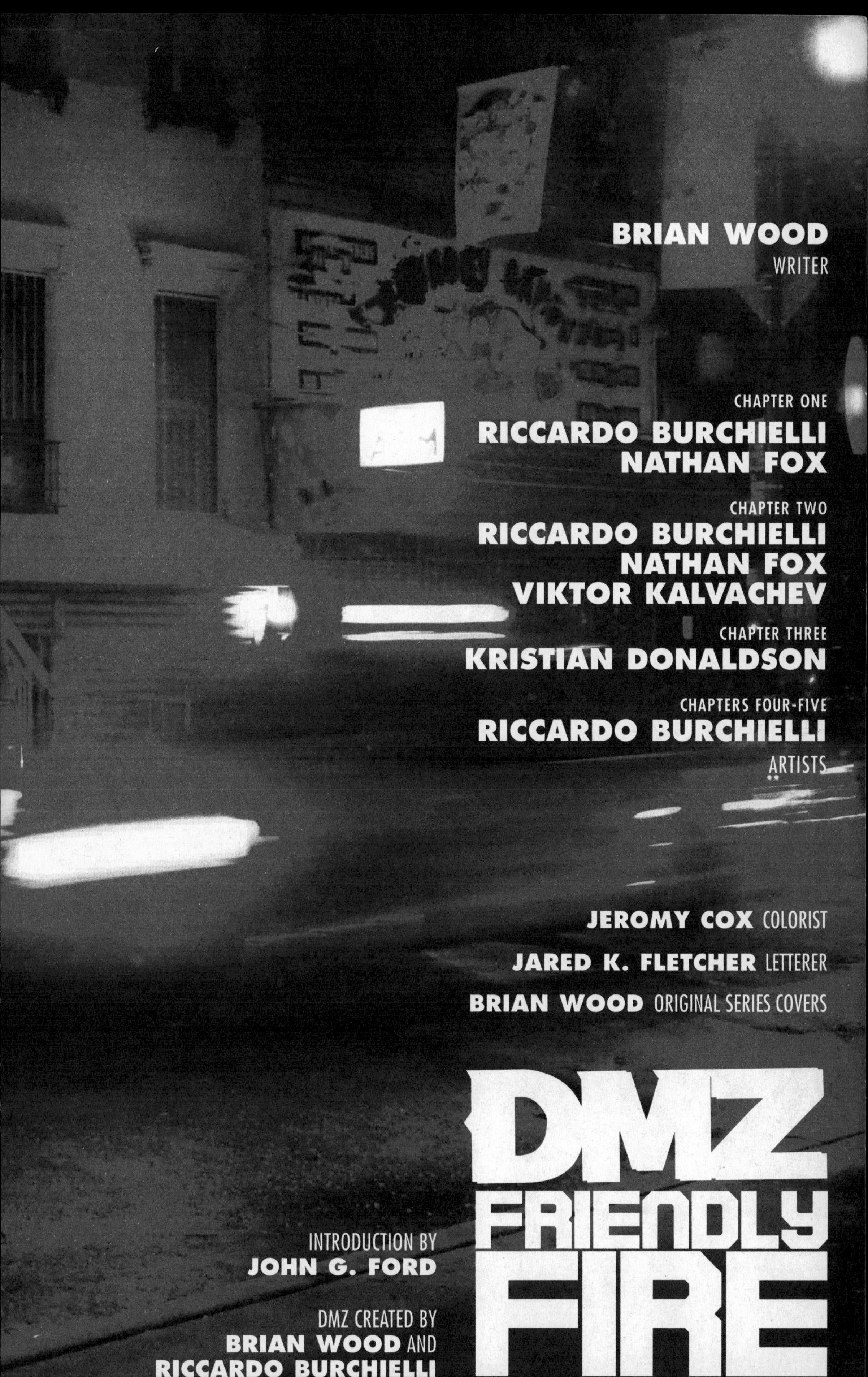

BRIAN WOOD
WRITER

CHAPTER ONE
RICCARDO BURCHIELLI
NATHAN FOX

CHAPTER TWO
RICCARDO BURCHIELLI
NATHAN FOX
VIKTOR KALVACHEV

CHAPTER THREE
KRISTIAN DONALDSON

CHAPTERS FOUR-FIVE
RICCARDO BURCHIELLI
ARTISTS

JEROMY COX COLORIST

JARED K. FLETCHER LETTERER

BRIAN WOOD ORIGINAL SERIES COVERS

DMZ
FRIENDLY FIRE

INTRODUCTION BY
JOHN G. FORD

DMZ CREATED BY
BRIAN WOOD AND
RICCARDO BURCHIELLI

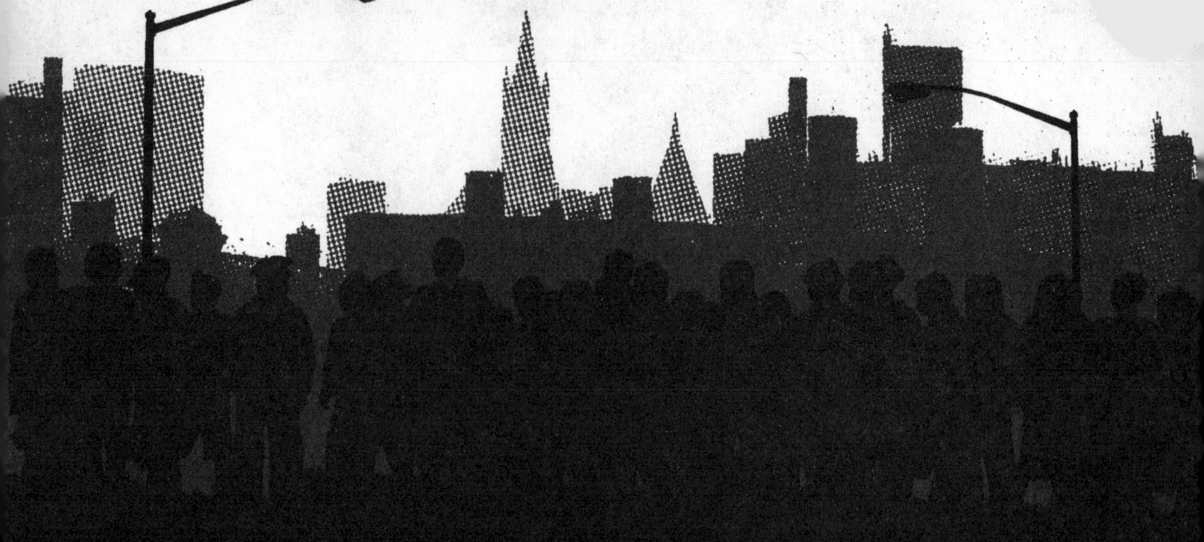

FRIENDLY FIRE IS AN OXYMORON.

Trust me, there is no such thing. This is a cute little term that can be used in polite company. Ask any soldier what it means and they'll tell you it means "fucked up." Man, let me tell you, that is *exactly* what it means. When someone higher than you in the food chain screws the pooch and you get placed in a bad situation with no support, you won't be thinking in polite terms. After serving a tour in Afghanistan and another in Iraq, I've seen firsthand what happens when something goes horribly wrong and the policy makers start thinking "exit strategy."

When I first picked up an issue of DMZ I was mesmerized. I was thinking, *"Finally*, some-one out there gets it. At last, someone had the stones to put something on the market that resonated with me and the other grunts, something real and hard and ugly." DMZ is *Black Hawk Down* meets Black Flag, and nothing is sugar coated. This is *war* and all bets are off.

Some friends of mine sent me a few early issues of DMZ while I was in Northern Iraq and Kurdistan, but I'd missed a lot of the series. First thing I did when I got back state-side was get caught up, and lo and behold I picked with up the *Friendly Fire* storyline. Man…breathtaking. Here we have a PFC Nobody from the Midwest whose options are revolution or jail and not much else. But hey, if he joins up maybe he'll get to make something of himself, maybe learn a trade, and if he's really lucky—money for college.

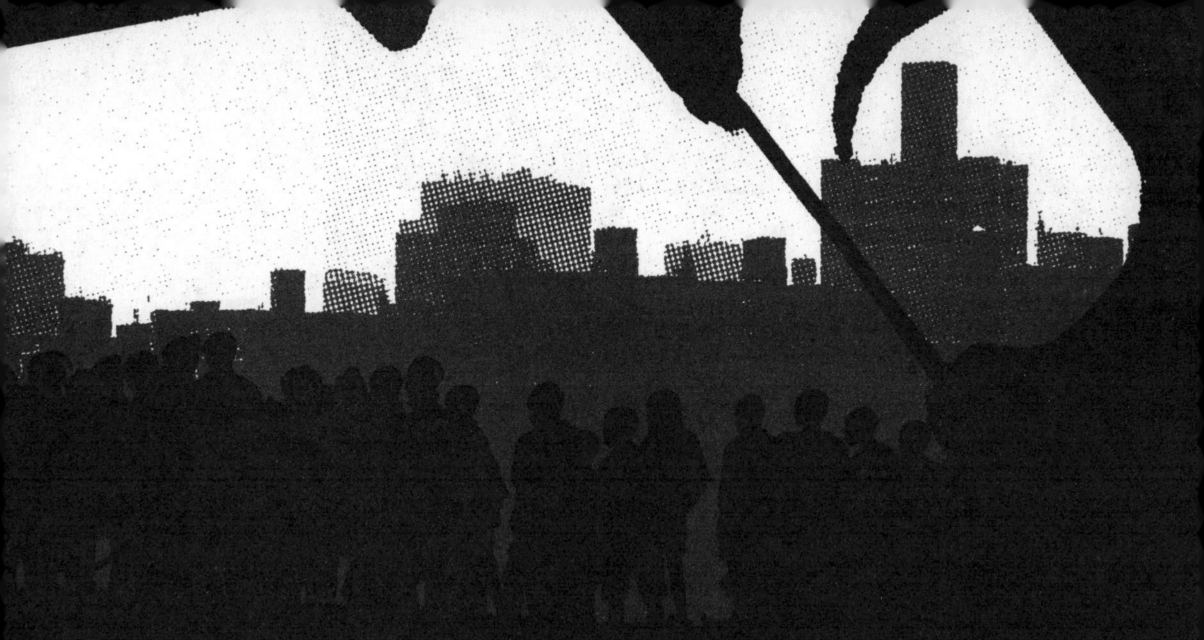

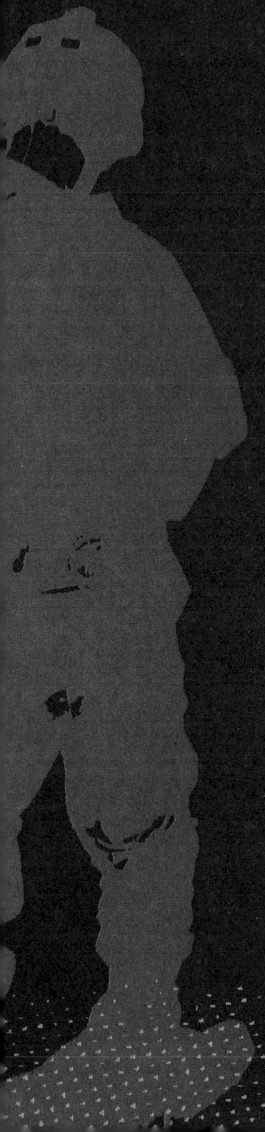

Now put him in a bad situation — scratch that, a *nightmare* situation, with minimum support, poor leadership, and the ever-present reality of punishment for any and every action. Shit goes down and he's the one left holding the bag: game over, man. Set up for failure from Day One.

You don't think this goes down? Go to war and then disagree with me.

Now comes damage control. Those in charge have "careers" to think about, promotions to deserve, asses to cover. Coming forward and admitting the system is broken or that the military is hurting is not an option. There's too much at stake for those in charge. This is timeless, this is historic, and it could happen to anybody, military or not.

Declaring war will not be a declining trend. Defense spending is one of the only things keeping our economy alive. When DMZ happens I just hope I get to choose sides. And trust me, ain't nothing going to be "friendly" about that.

SGT. JOHN G. FORD
U.S. ARMY
OCTOBER 2007

John G. Ford is a veteran of the Navy and the Army, having been deployed to Afghanistan, South America and Iraq. Still in the reserves, he is a full-time student. He is married and has two wonderful children.

THE WORLD OF DMZ

In the near future, America's worst nightmare has come true. With military adventurism overseas bogging down the Army and National Guard, the U.S. government mistakenly neglects the very real threat of anti-establishment militias scattered across the 50 states. Like a sleeping giant, Middle America rises up and violently pushes its way to the shining seas, coming to a standstill at the line in the sand — Manhattan, or as the world now knows it, the DMZ.

CAST:

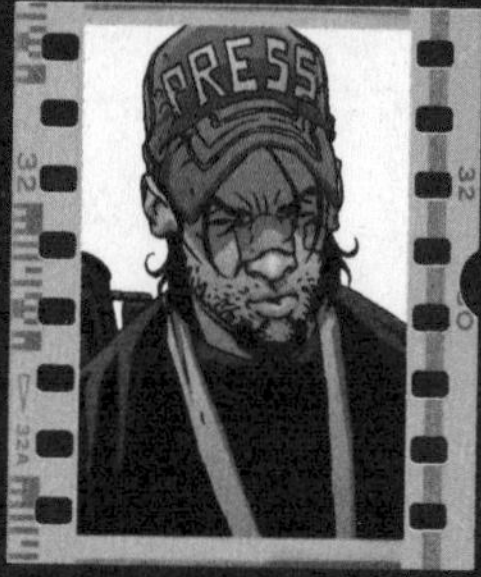
PRESS

MATTY ROTH

A recent college grad from Long Island, Matty shows up for the first day of his internship and finds himself alone and stranded in the DMZ. He steps into the role of journalist, despite not really being trained as one. He struggles constantly to maintain objectivity and negotiate the politics on the ground, and finds himself frequently caught in the middle or worse, being used by one side against the other.

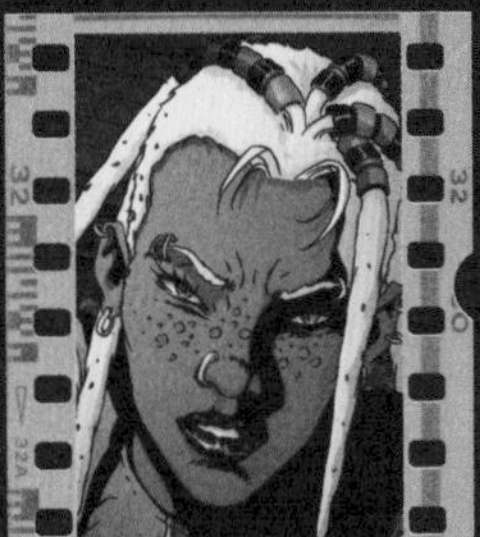

ZEE HERNANDEZ

Native New Yorker and med student, Zee is a trusted figure in the city, making house calls on local clinics and securing medical supplies on the black market. She took Matty in and under her protection initially out of pity but has since grown to respect him, if only grudgingly. She acts as Matty's guide in the city, a consultant on the intricacies of the block-by-block politics, and as a trusted friend when he's down on his luck.

Zee herself opted to stay in the city at the start of the war when everyone who could was being evacuated. She's chosen this life, to help the ones who never had a choice of their own.

WILSON

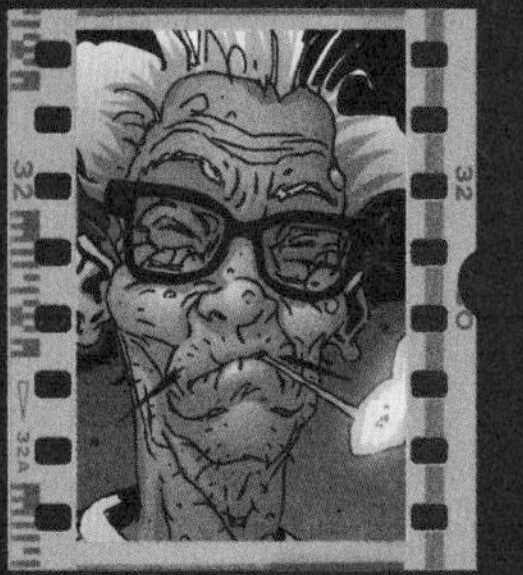

Matty's neighbor and drinking buddy, Wilson is full of surprising revelations. With an army of armed "grandsons" at his disposal and the casual confidence that comes with being untouchable, Wilson's status as a local mob boss is gradually being revealed.

VIKTOR FERGUSON

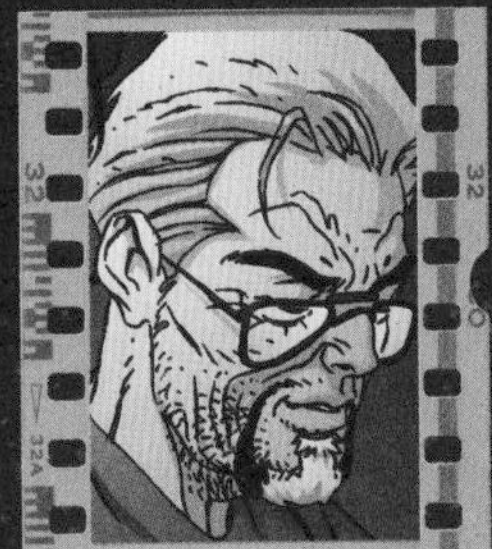

An award-winning journalist, Viktor was captured by the FSA and used as a bargaining chip before eventually being executed by his own side in an elaborate cover-up operation. Viktor played a key role in securing Matty's cred and place in the DMZ.

JAMAL GREENE

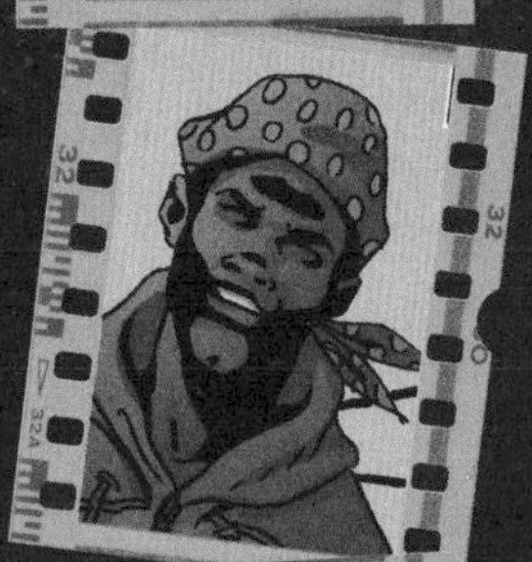

Jamal is an architecture student, stranded in the DMZ at the start of the war. He's built a community of people with similar skills who take it upon themselves to maintain key infrastructures in the city. A friend to Zee and Matty, he helps out when he can but prefers to stay neutral. In the past, Matty pushed his luck with Jamal and it's unclear if Jamal will be willing to help him again.

AMINA

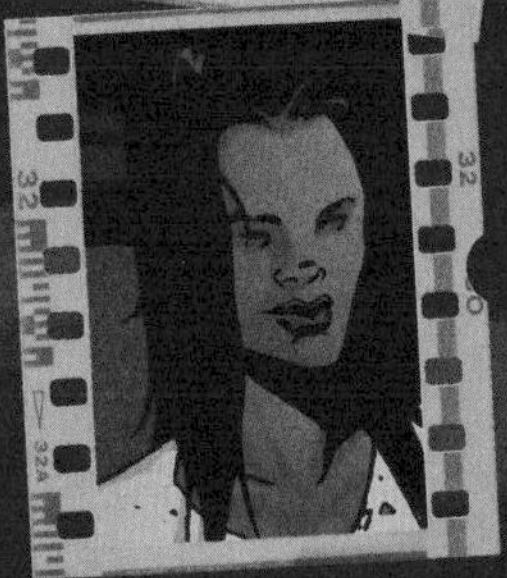

Amina is a young girl who got caught up in Matty's undercover sting operation. She was tasked by a terrorist cell to bomb a U.N. press conference, but Matty intervened and saved her life. Despite his best intentions, this left Amina adrift, with no friends and no place to call home.

KELLY CONNOLLY

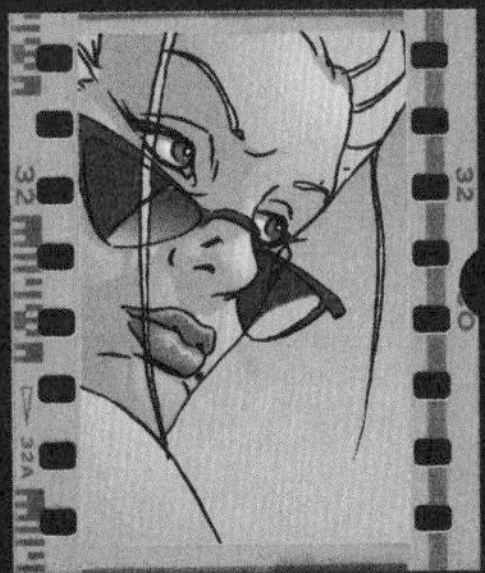

Foreign correspondent for Independent World News, Kelly has helped Matty and Zee in the past. She and Matty have a physical relationship as well as a professional one, but they only see each other infrequently.

ENTITIES:

LIBERTY NEWS / THE UNITED STATES OF AMERICA

What is left of the United States has merged with its biggest supporter in the media, Liberty News, to the point that the two are indistinguishable. Matty's father sits on the board of Liberty News and from time to time arranges things for his son, including the internship that got Matty stranded in the DMZ in the first place.

THE FREE STATES OF AMERICA

The opposition forces, born out of the separatist militia movement in the Midwest. The FSA gained a lot of momentum early on, tapping into the anger and alienation felt by many Americans at their government's increasing tendency to pay more attention to other parts of the world, rather than address their needs. The FSA is more an idea than an organized army, and their supporters are mixed into the population as a whole, nearly impossible for the USA to identity and neutralize.

INDEPENDENT WORLD NEWS

The counterbalance to Liberty News, IWN reports on the war when they can gain access, which isn't very often. They remain an alternative for Matty to file the stories that Liberty won't touch.

TRUSTWELL, INC.

A reconstruction/security firm, equal parts Halliburton and Blackwater. Despite the public relations disaster they recently suffered, they a remain major player in the war.

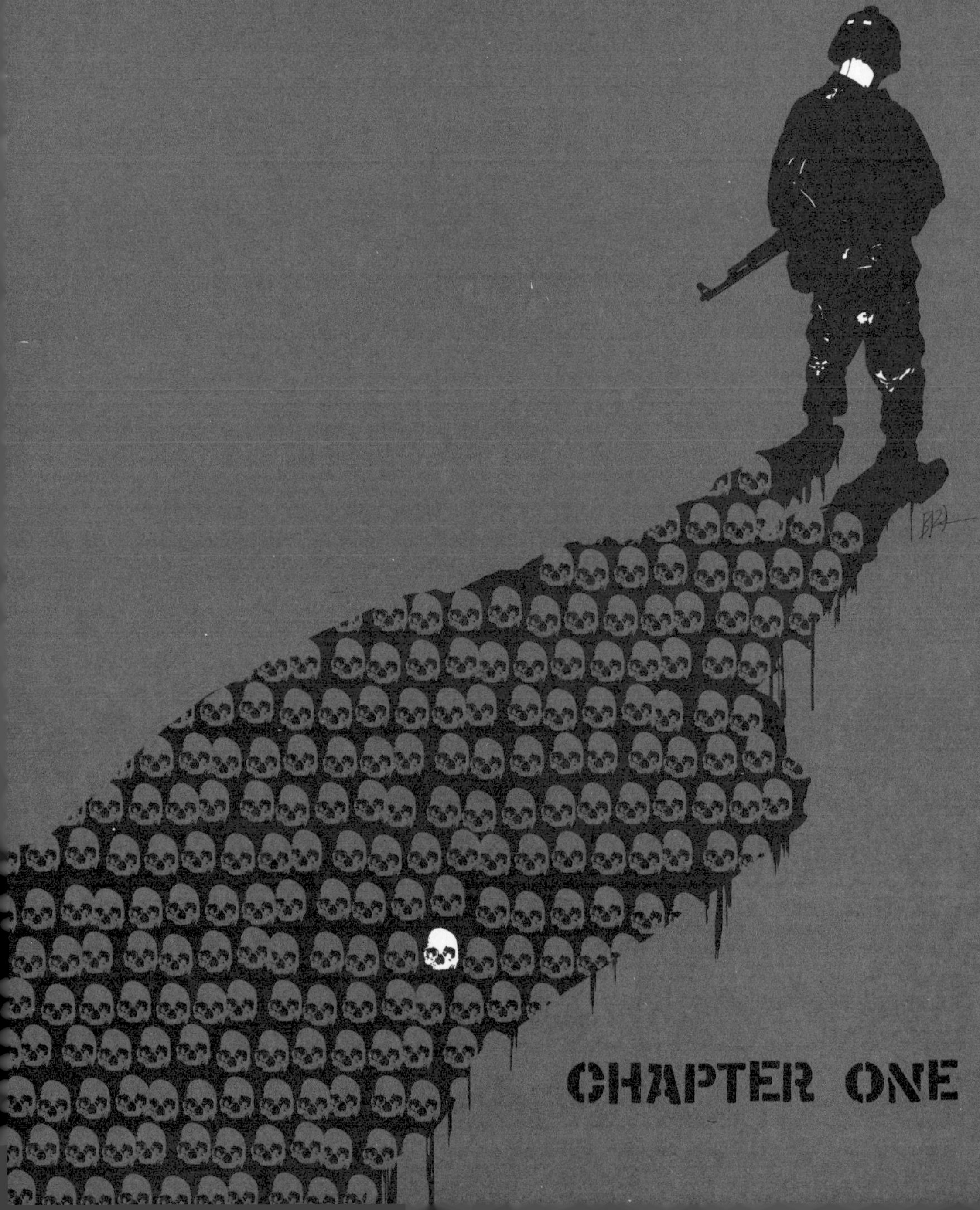

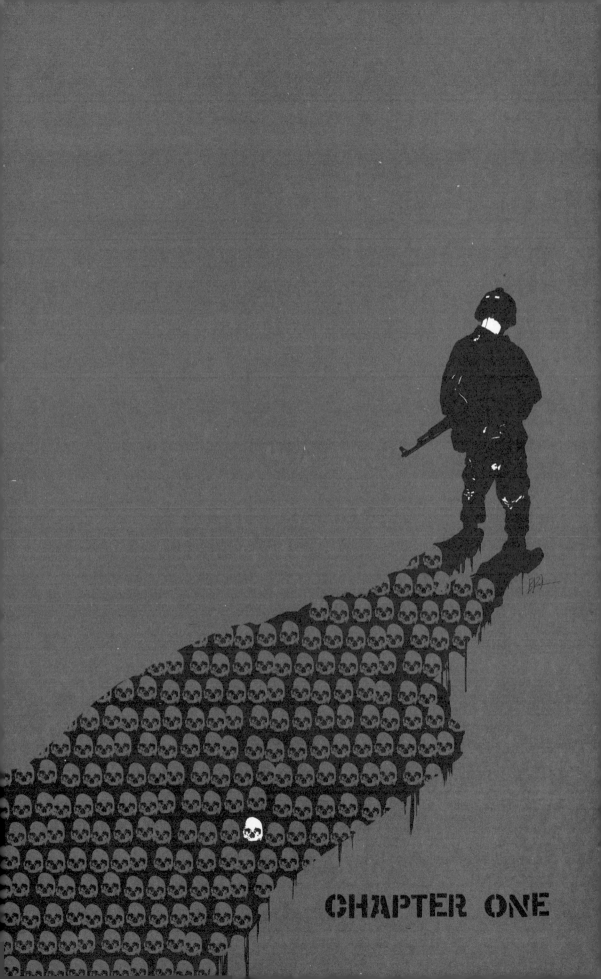

CHAPTER ONE

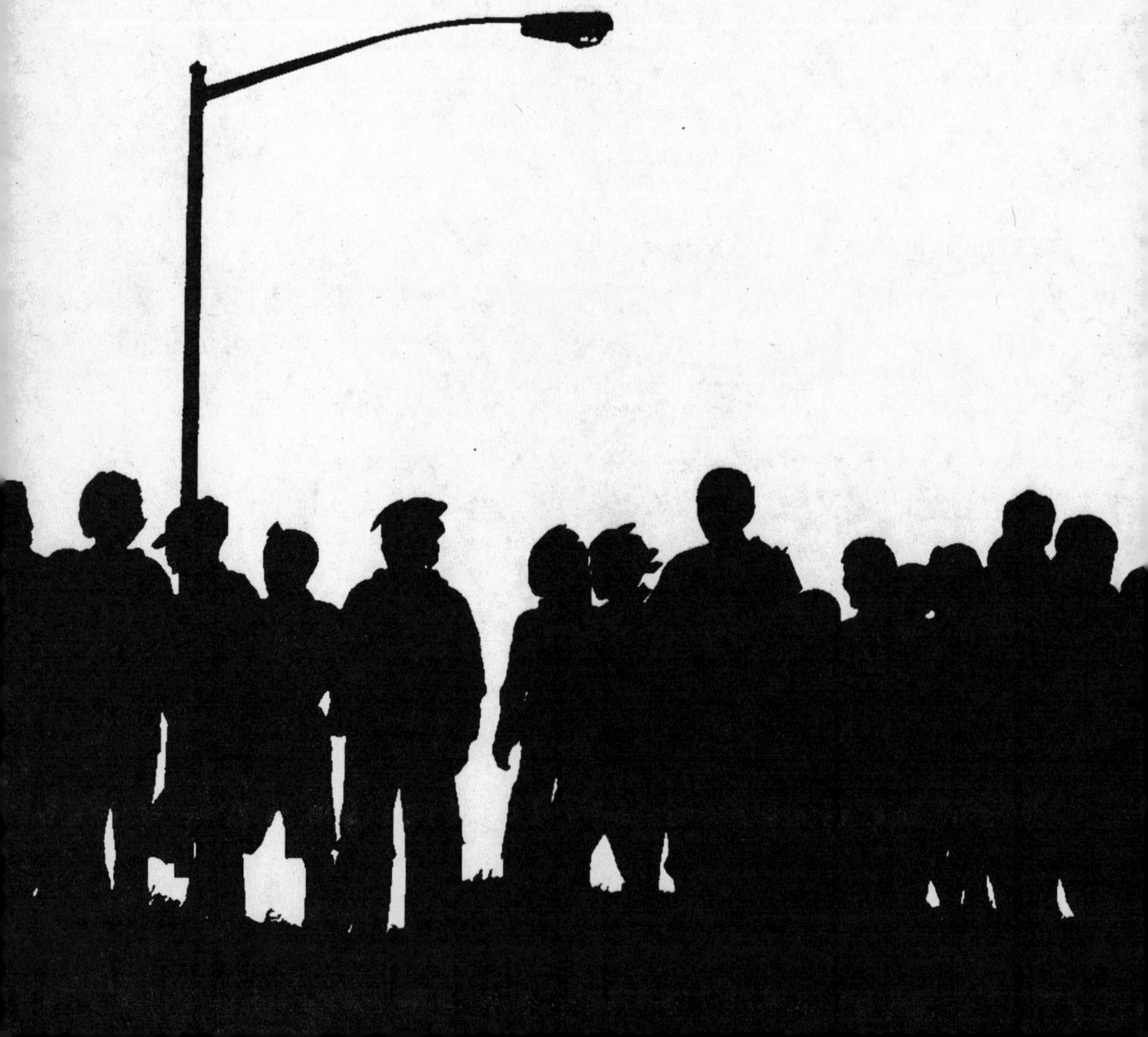

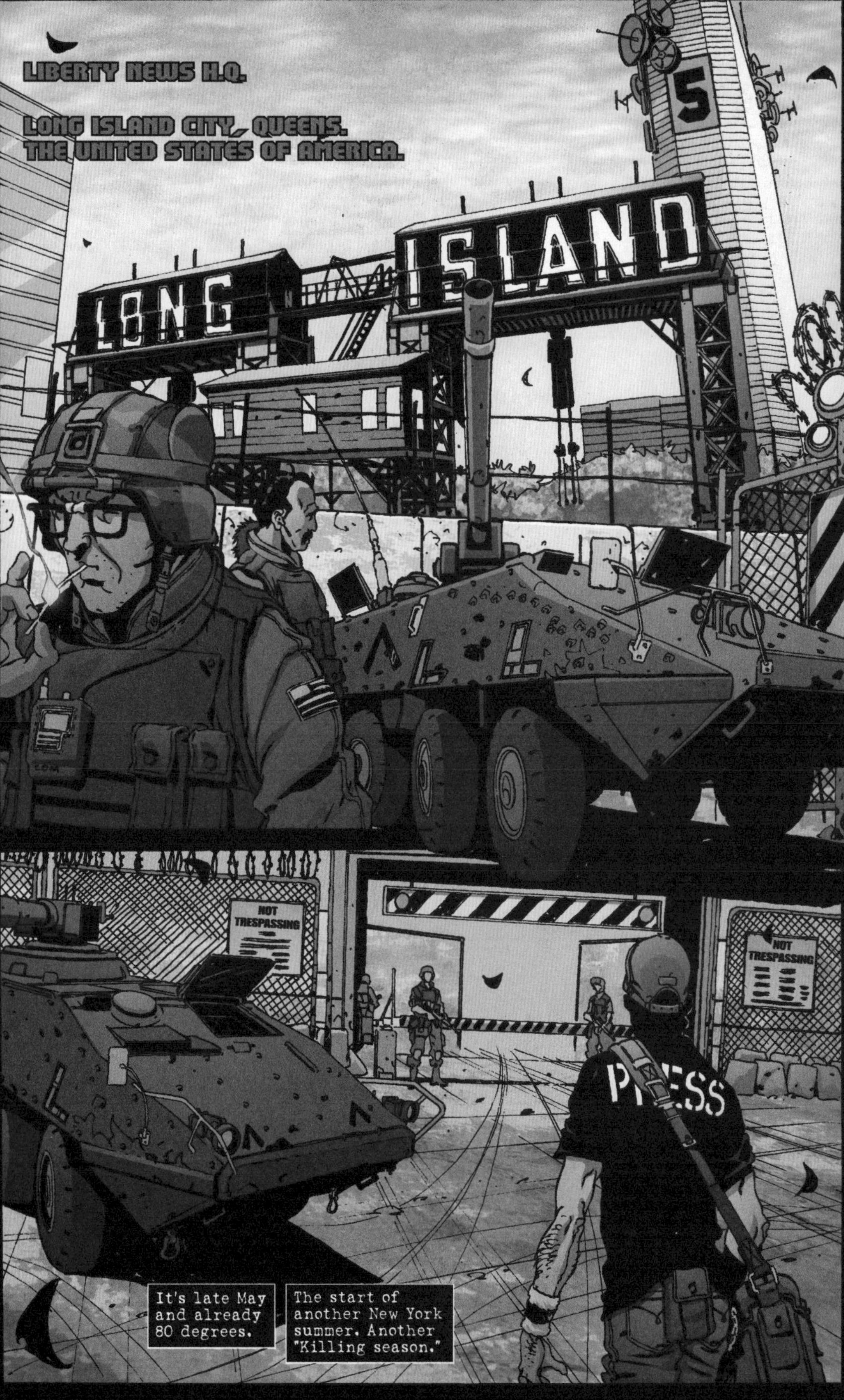
LIBERTY NEWS H.Q.
LONG ISLAND CITY, QUEENS.
THE UNITED STATES OF AMERICA.
LONG ISLAND
5
NOT TRESPASSING
NOT TRESPASSING
PRESS
It's late May and already 80 degrees.
The start of another New York summer. Another "Killing season."

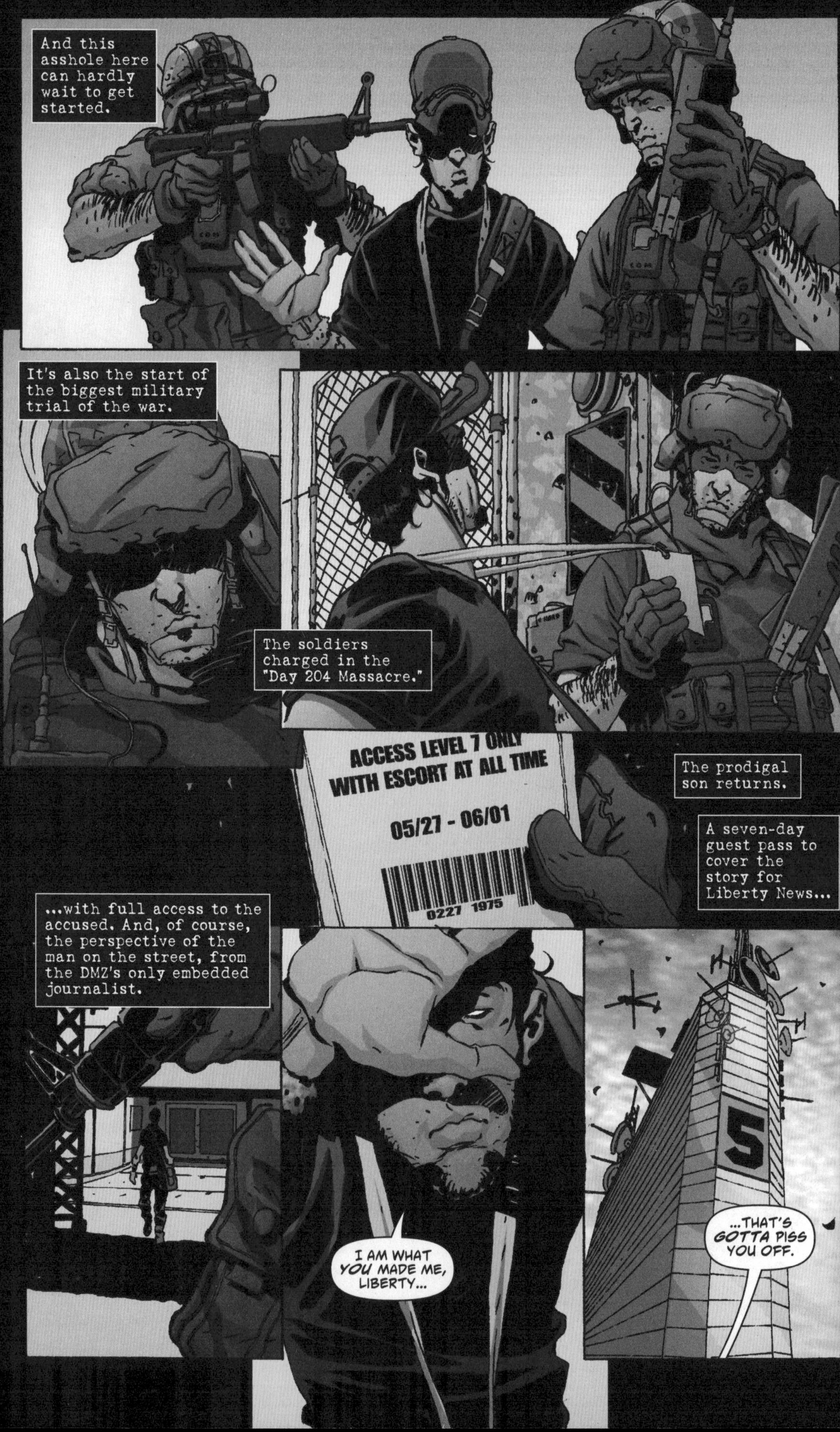
And this asshole here can hardly wait to get started.
It's also the start of the biggest military trial of the war.
The soldiers charged in the "Day 204 Massacre."
ACCESS LEVEL 7 ONLY WITH ESCORT AT ALL TIME
05/27 - 06/01
0227 1975
The prodigal son returns.
A seven-day guest pass to cover the story for Liberty News...
...with full access to the accused. And, of course, the perspective of the man on the street, from the DMZ's only embedded journalist.
I AM WHAT YOU MADE ME, LIBERTY...
...THAT'S GOTTA PISS YOU OFF.

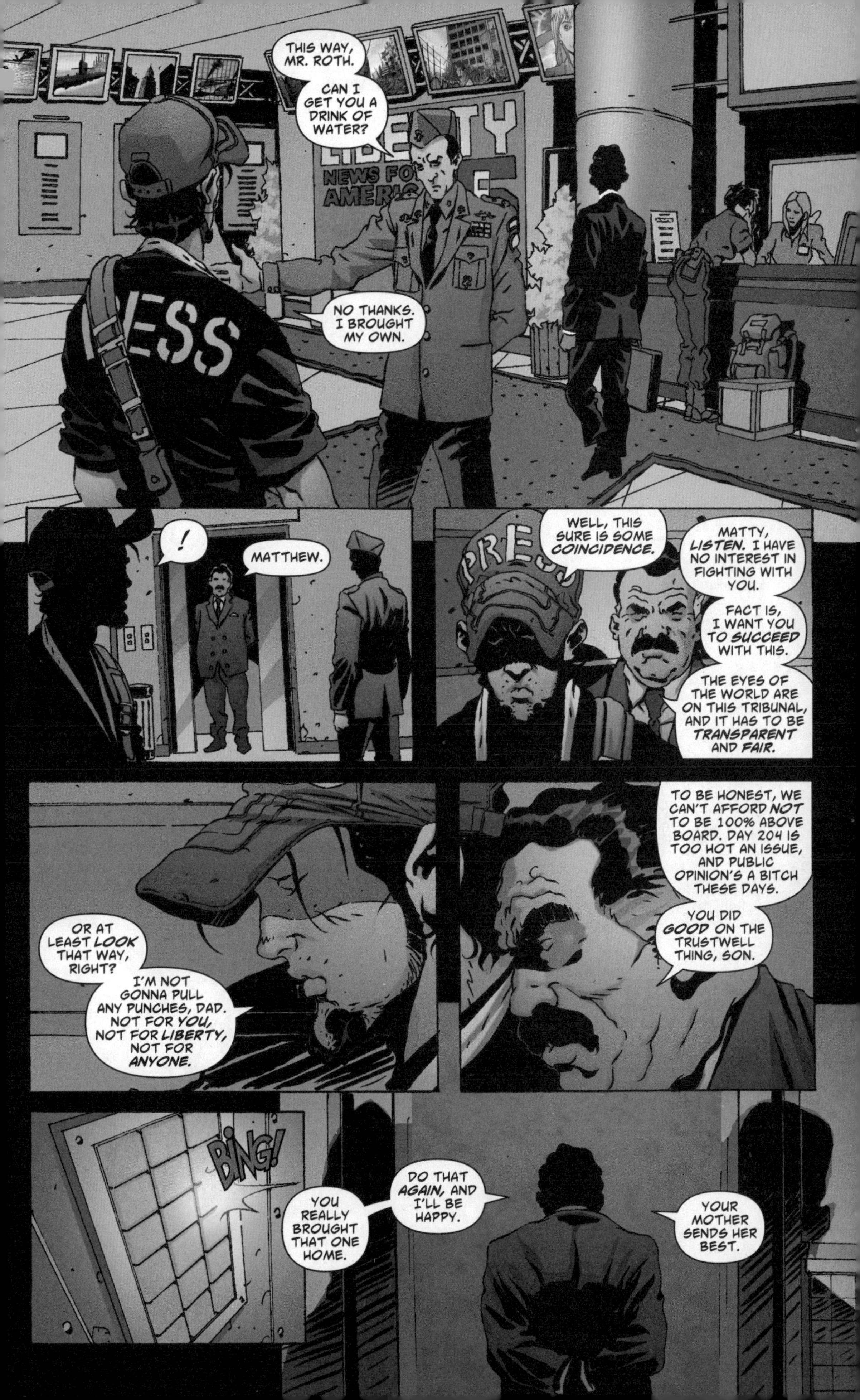
THIS WAY, MR. ROTH.
CAN I GET YOU A DRINK OF WATER?
NO THANKS. I BROUGHT MY OWN.
!
MATTHEW.
WELL, THIS SURE IS SOME COINCIDENCE.
MATTY, LISTEN. I HAVE NO INTEREST IN FIGHTING WITH YOU.
FACT IS, I WANT YOU TO SUCCEED WITH THIS.
THE EYES OF THE WORLD ARE ON THIS TRIBUNAL, AND IT HAS TO BE TRANSPARENT AND FAIR.
TO BE HONEST, WE CAN'T AFFORD NOT TO BE 100% ABOVE BOARD. DAY 204 IS TOO HOT AN ISSUE, AND PUBLIC OPINION'S A BITCH THESE DAYS.
YOU DID GOOD ON THE TRUSTWELL THING, SON.
OR AT LEAST LOOK THAT WAY, RIGHT?
I'M NOT GONNA PULL ANY PUNCHES, DAD. NOT FOR YOU, NOT FOR LIBERTY, NOT FOR ANYONE.
BING!
YOU REALLY BROUGHT THAT ONE HOME.
DO THAT AGAIN, AND I'LL BE HAPPY.
YOUR MOTHER SENDS HER BEST.

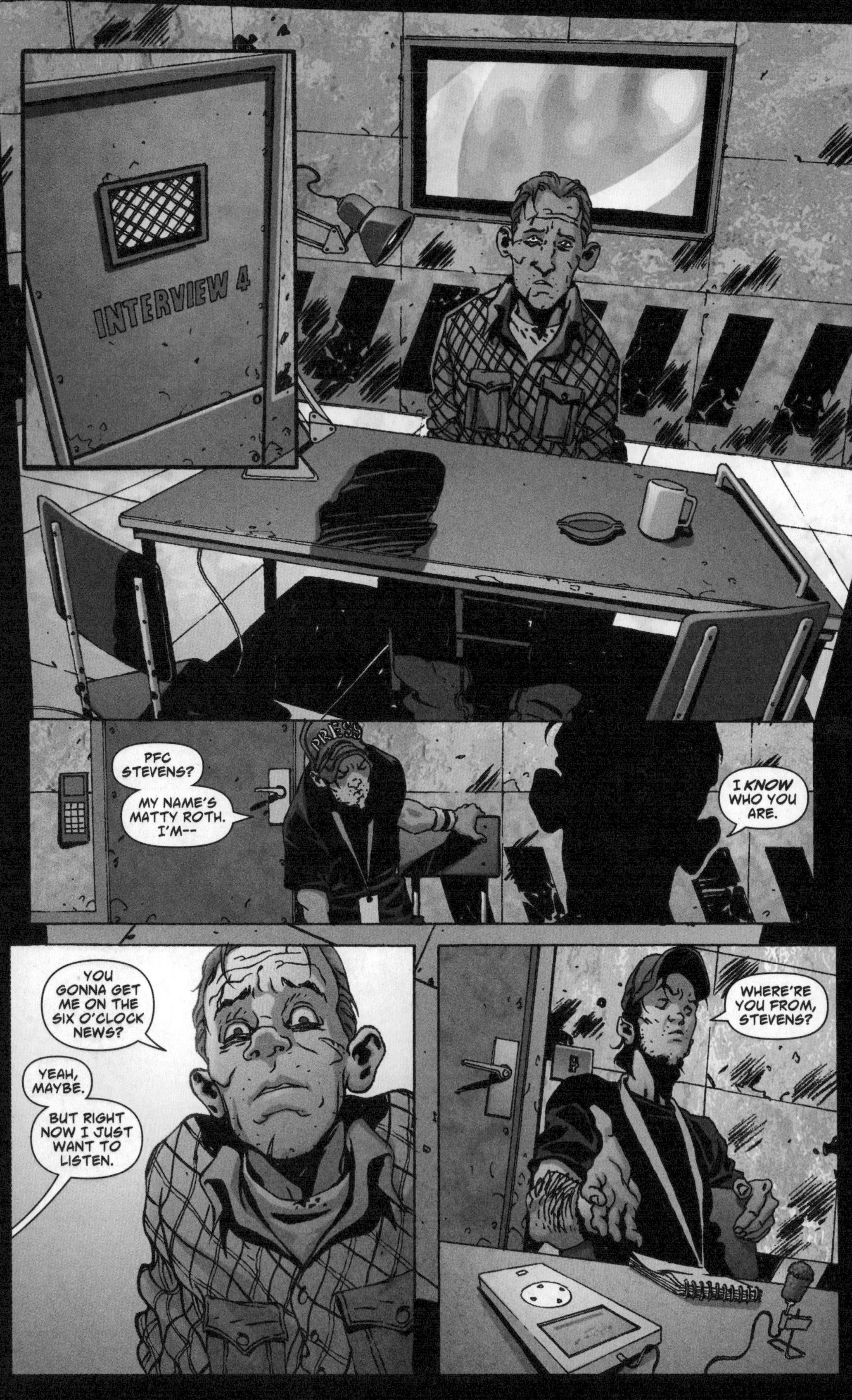
INTERVIEW 4
PFC STEVENS?
MY NAME'S MATTY ROTH. I'M--
PRESS
I KNOW WHO YOU ARE.
YOU GONNA GET ME ON THE SIX O'CLOCK NEWS?
YEAH, MAYBE.
BUT RIGHT NOW I JUST WANT TO LISTEN.
WHERE'RE YOU FROM, STEVENS?

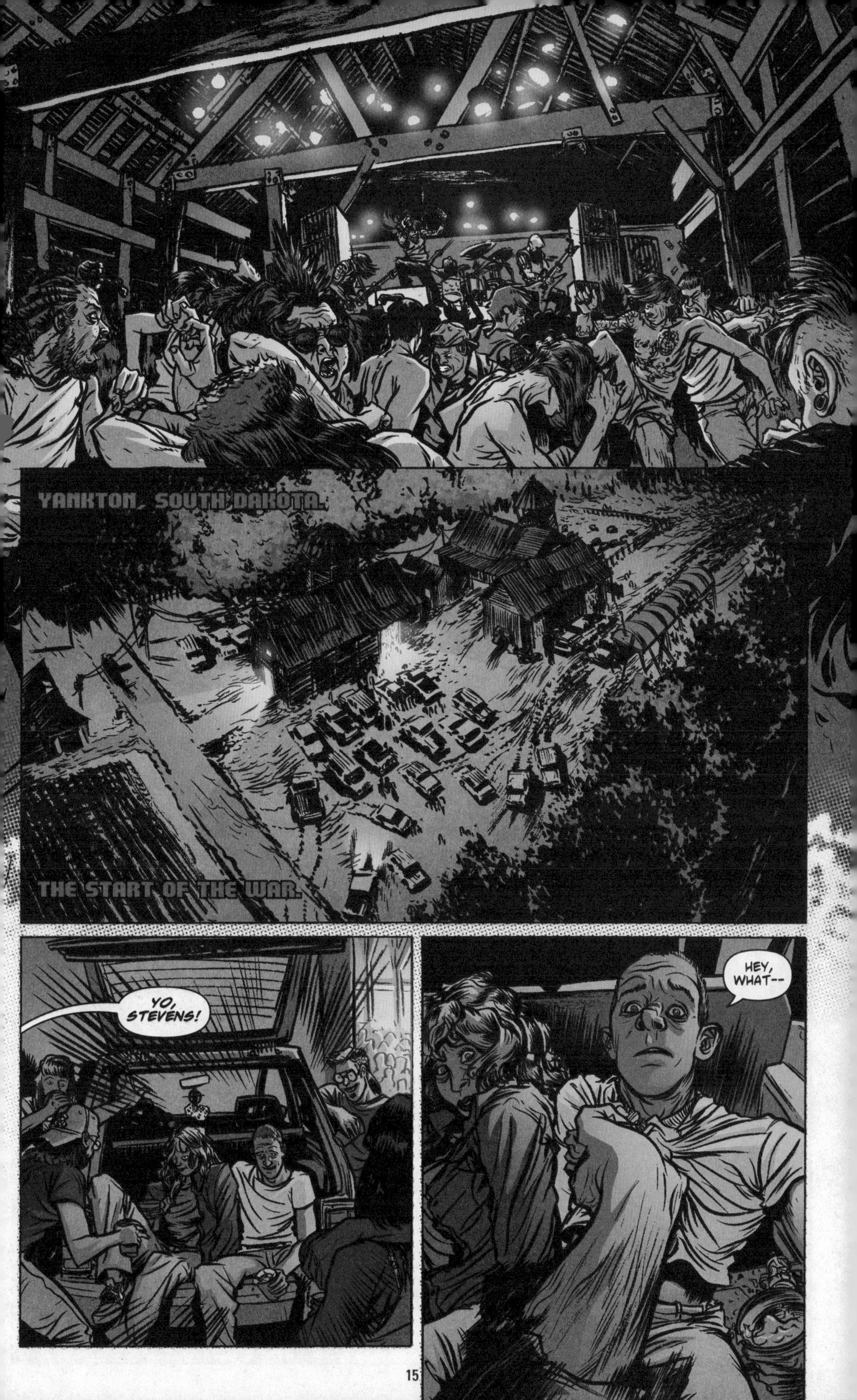
YANKTON, SOUTH DAKOTA.
THE START OF THE WAR.
YO, STEVENS!
HEY, WHAT--

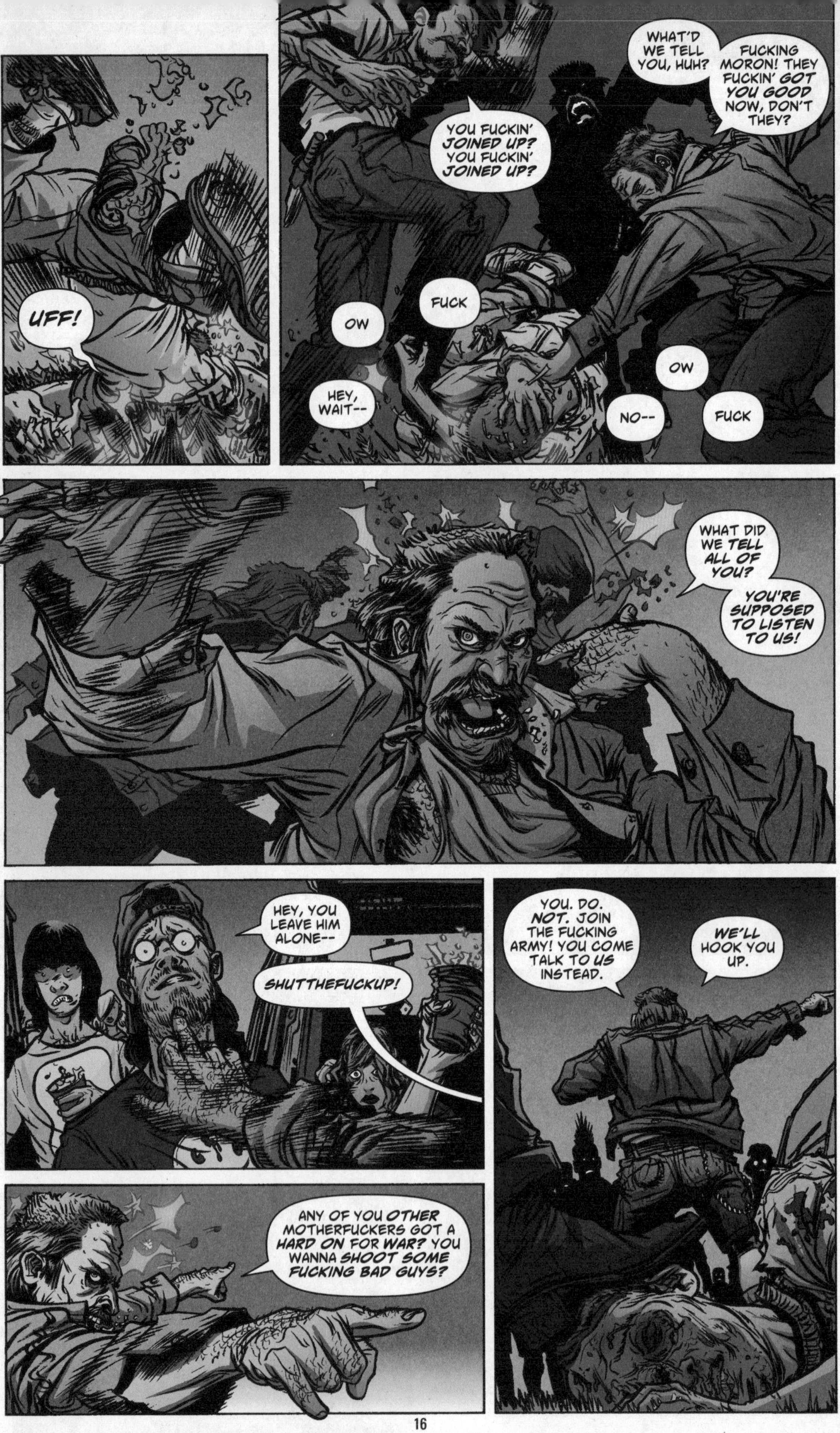
UFF!
WHAT'D WE TELL YOU, HUH?
FUCKING MORON! THEY FUCKIN' GOT YOU GOOD NOW, DON'T THEY?
YOU FUCKIN' JOINED UP? YOU FUCKIN' JOINED UP?
FUCK
OW
HEY, WAIT--
OW
NO--
FUCK
WHAT DID WE TELL ALL OF YOU?
YOU'RE SUPPOSED TO LISTEN TO US!
HEY, YOU LEAVE HIM ALONE--
SHUTTHEFUCKUP!
ANY OF YOU OTHER MOTHERFUCKERS GOT A HARD ON FOR WAR? YOU WANNA SHOOT SOME FUCKING BAD GUYS?
YOU. DO. NOT. JOIN THE FUCKING ARMY! YOU COME TALK TO US INSTEAD.
WE'LL HOOK YOU UP.

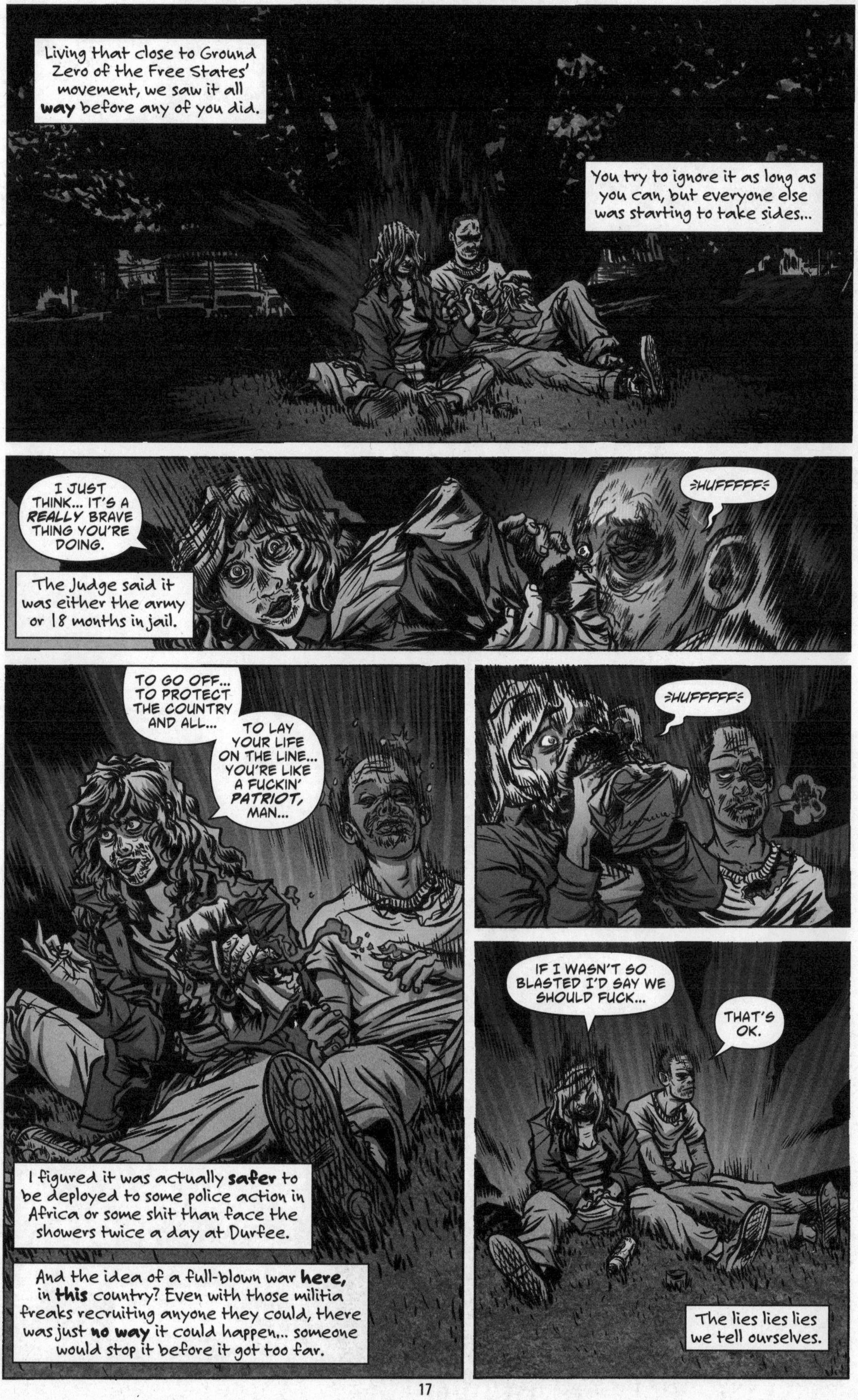

Living that close to Ground Zero of the Free States' movement, we saw it all **way** before any of you did.
You try to ignore it as long as you can, but everyone else was starting to take sides...
I JUST THINK... IT'S A *REALLY* BRAVE THING YOU'RE DOING.
The Judge said it was either the army or 18 months in jail.
HUFFFFF
TO GO OFF... TO PROTECT THE COUNTRY AND ALL...
TO LAY YOUR LIFE ON THE LINE... YOU'RE LIKE A FUCKIN' *PATRIOT*, MAN...
I figured it was actually **safer** to be deployed to some police action in Africa or some shit than face the showers twice a day at Durfee.
And the idea of a full-blown war **here**, in **this** country? Even with those militia freaks recruiting anyone they could, there was just **no way** it could happen... someone would stop it before it got too far.
HUFFFFF
IF I WASN'T SO BLASTED I'D SAY WE SHOULD FUCK...
THAT'S OK.
The lies lies lies we tell ourselves.

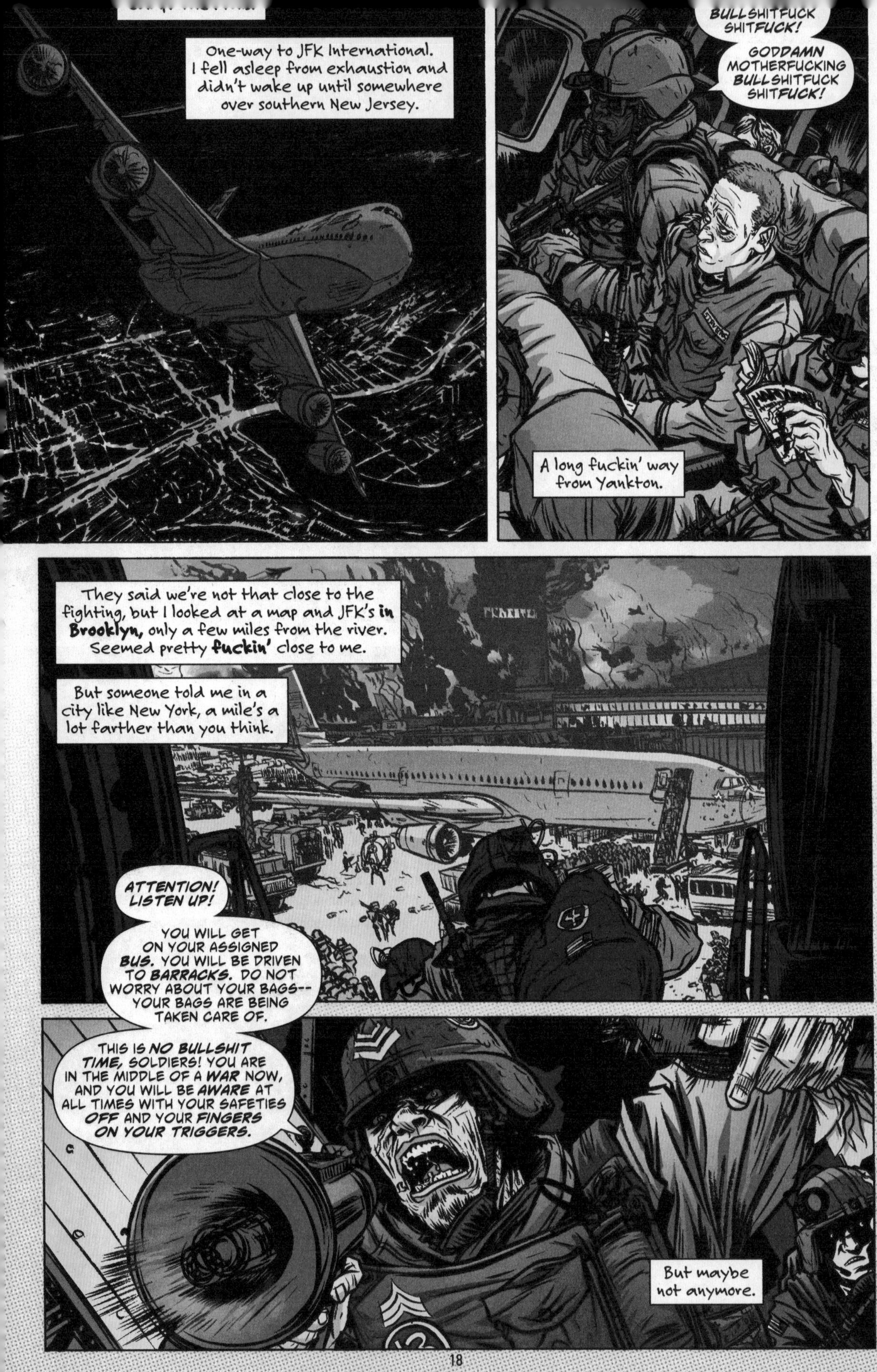
One-way to JFK International. I fell asleep from exhaustion and didn't wake up until somewhere over southern New Jersey.
BULLSHITFUCK SHITFUCK!
GODDAMN MOTHERFUCKING BULLSHITFUCK SHITFUCK!
A long fuckin' way from Yankton.
They said we're not that close to the fighting, but I looked at a map and JFK's in Brooklyn, only a few miles from the river. Seemed pretty fuckin' close to me.
But someone told me in a city like New York, a mile's a lot farther than you think.
ATTENTION! LISTEN UP!
YOU WILL GET ON YOUR ASSIGNED BUS. YOU WILL BE DRIVEN TO BARRACKS. DO NOT WORRY ABOUT YOUR BAGS-- YOUR BAGS ARE BEING TAKEN CARE OF.
THIS IS NO BULLSHIT TIME, SOLDIERS! YOU ARE IN THE MIDDLE OF A WAR NOW, AND YOU WILL BE AWARE AT ALL TIMES WITH YOUR SAFETIES OFF AND YOUR FINGERS ON YOUR TRIGGERS.
But maybe not anymore.

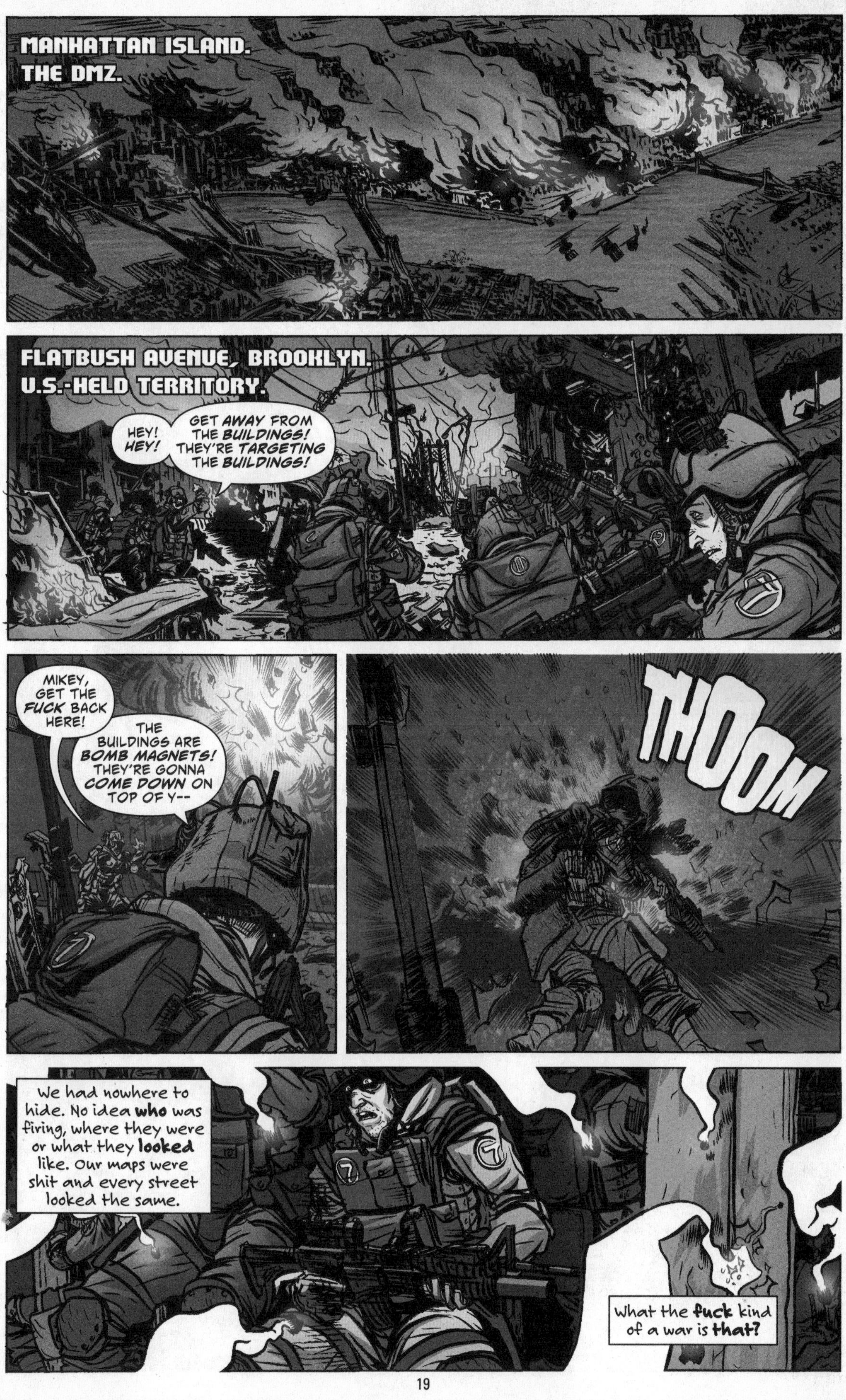
MANHATTAN ISLAND.
THE DMZ.
FLATBUSH AVENUE, BROOKLYN.
U.S.-HELD TERRITORY.
HEY! HEY!
GET AWAY FROM THE BUILDINGS! THEY'RE TARGETING THE BUILDINGS!
MIKEY, GET THE FUCK BACK HERE!
THE BUILDINGS ARE BOMB MAGNETS! THEY'RE GONNA COME DOWN ON TOP OF Y--
THOOM
We had nowhere to hide. No idea who was firing, where they were or what they looked like. Our maps were shit and every street looked the same.
What the fuck kind of a war is that?

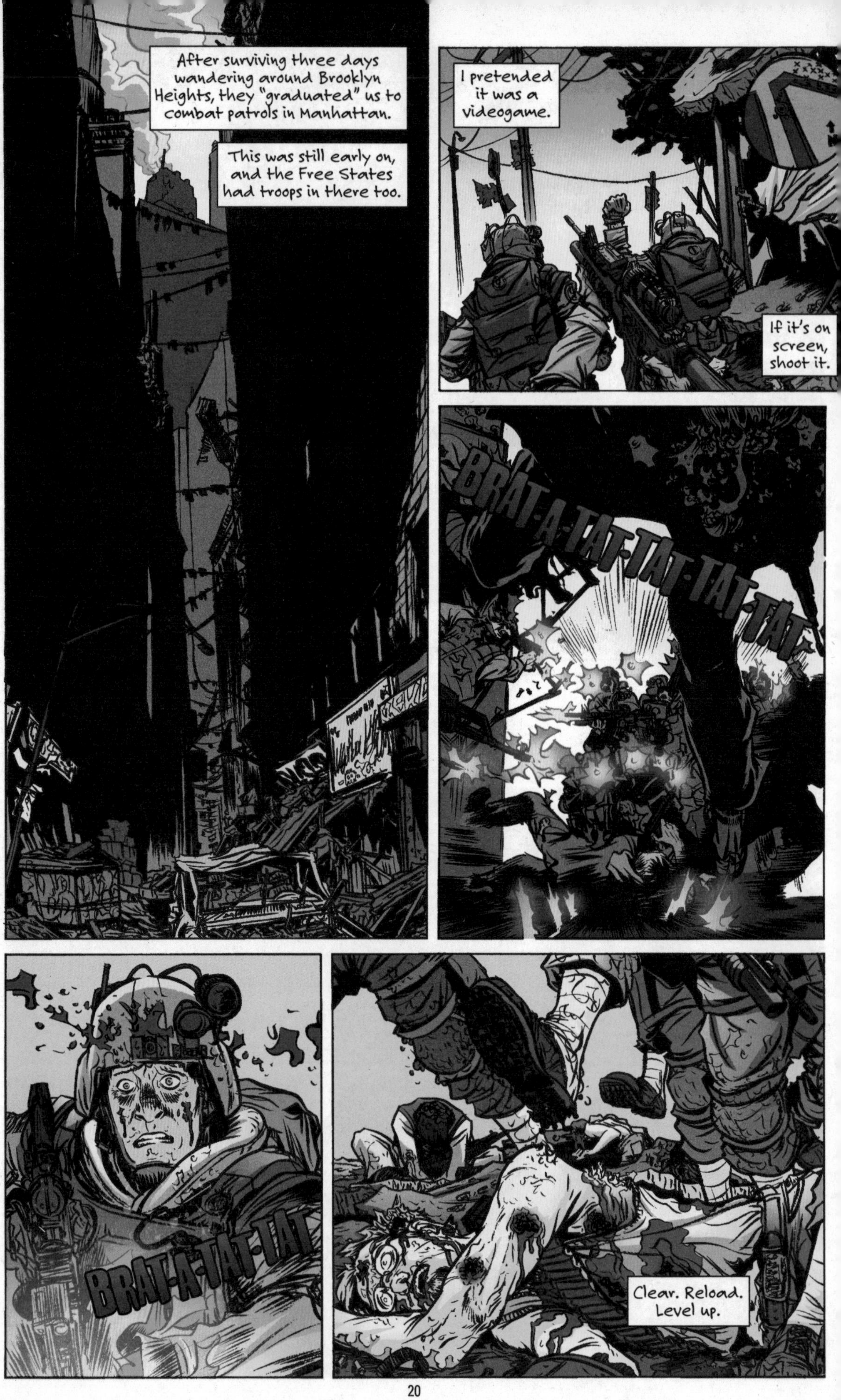
After surviving three days wandering around Brooklyn Heights, they "graduated" us to combat patrols in Manhattan.
This was still early on, and the Free States had troops in there too.
I pretended it was a videogame.
If it's on screen, shoot it.
BRAT-A-TAT-TAT-TAT-TAT
BRAT-A-TAT-TAT
Clear. Reload. Level up.

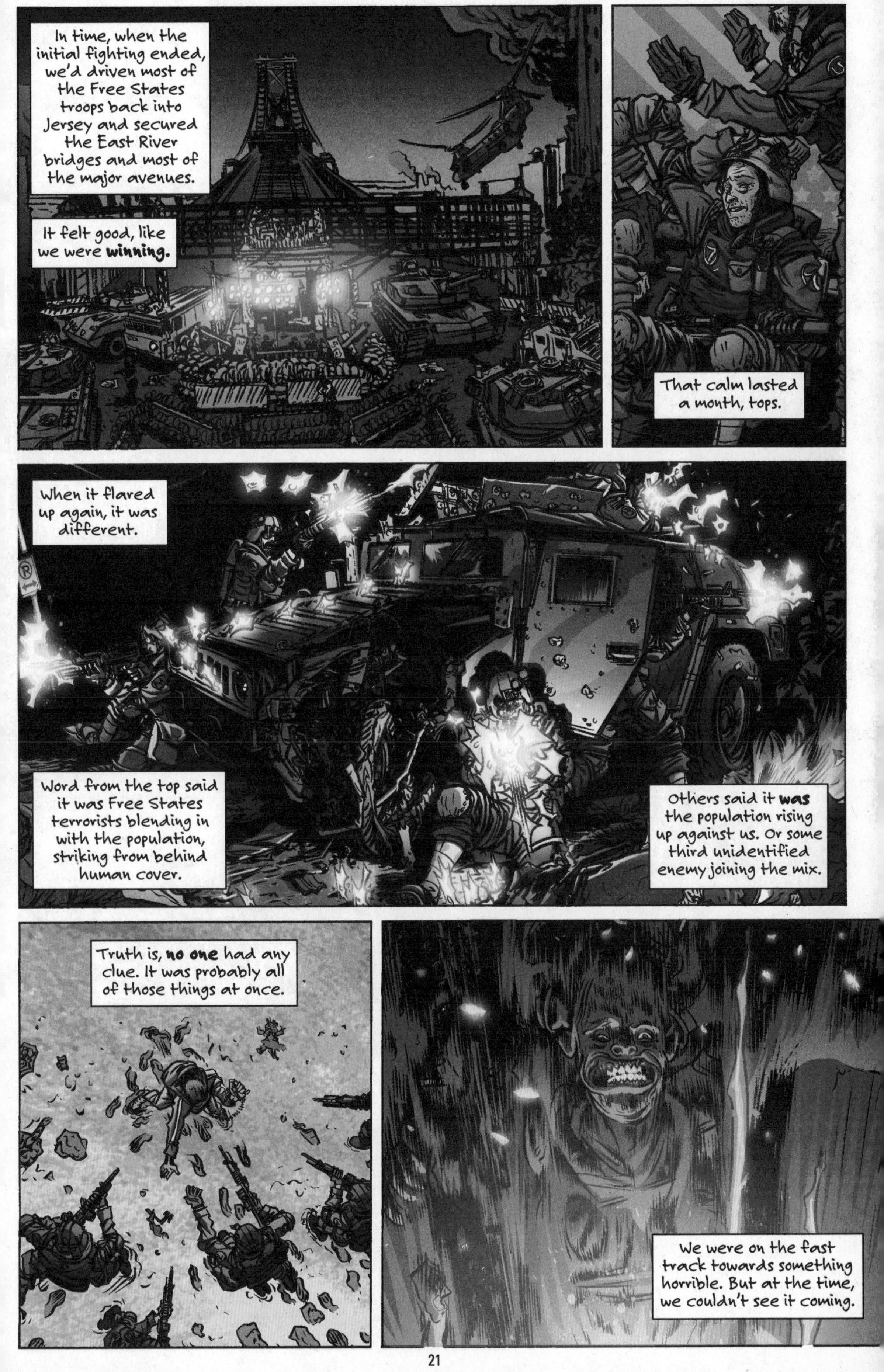
In time, when the initial fighting ended, we'd driven most of the Free States troops back into Jersey and secured the East River bridges and most of the major avenues.
It felt good, like we were **winning.**
That calm lasted a month, tops.
When it flared up again, it was different.
Word from the top said it was Free States terrorists blending in with the population, striking from behind human cover.
Others said it **was** the population rising up against us. Or some third unidentified enemy joining the mix.
Truth is, **no one** had any clue. It was probably all of those things at once.
We were on the fast track towards something horrible. But at the time, we couldn't see it coming.

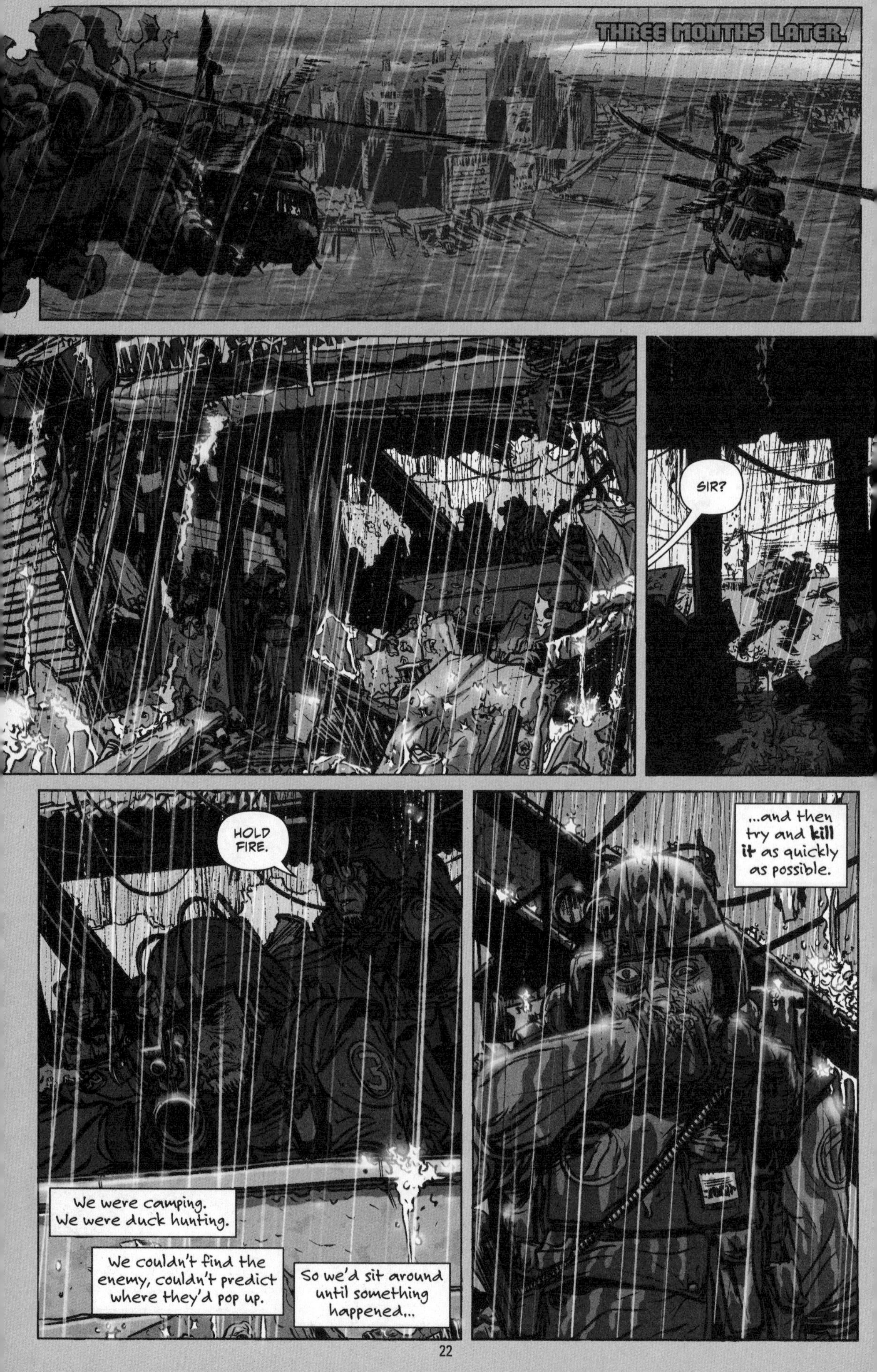
THREE MONTHS LATER.
SIR?
HOLD FIRE.
We were camping. We were duck hunting.
We couldn't find the enemy, couldn't predict where they'd pop up.
So we'd sit around until something happened...
...and then try and **kill it** as quickly as possible.

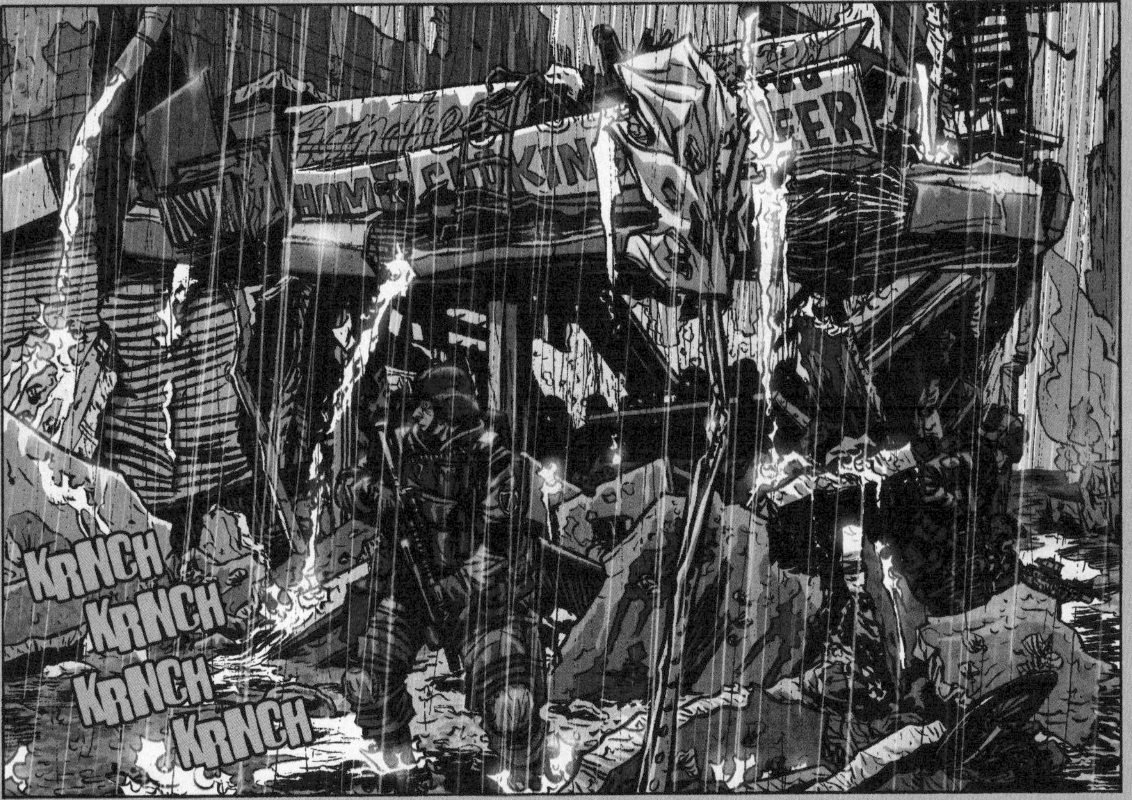
KRNCH
KRNCH
KRNCH
KRNCH

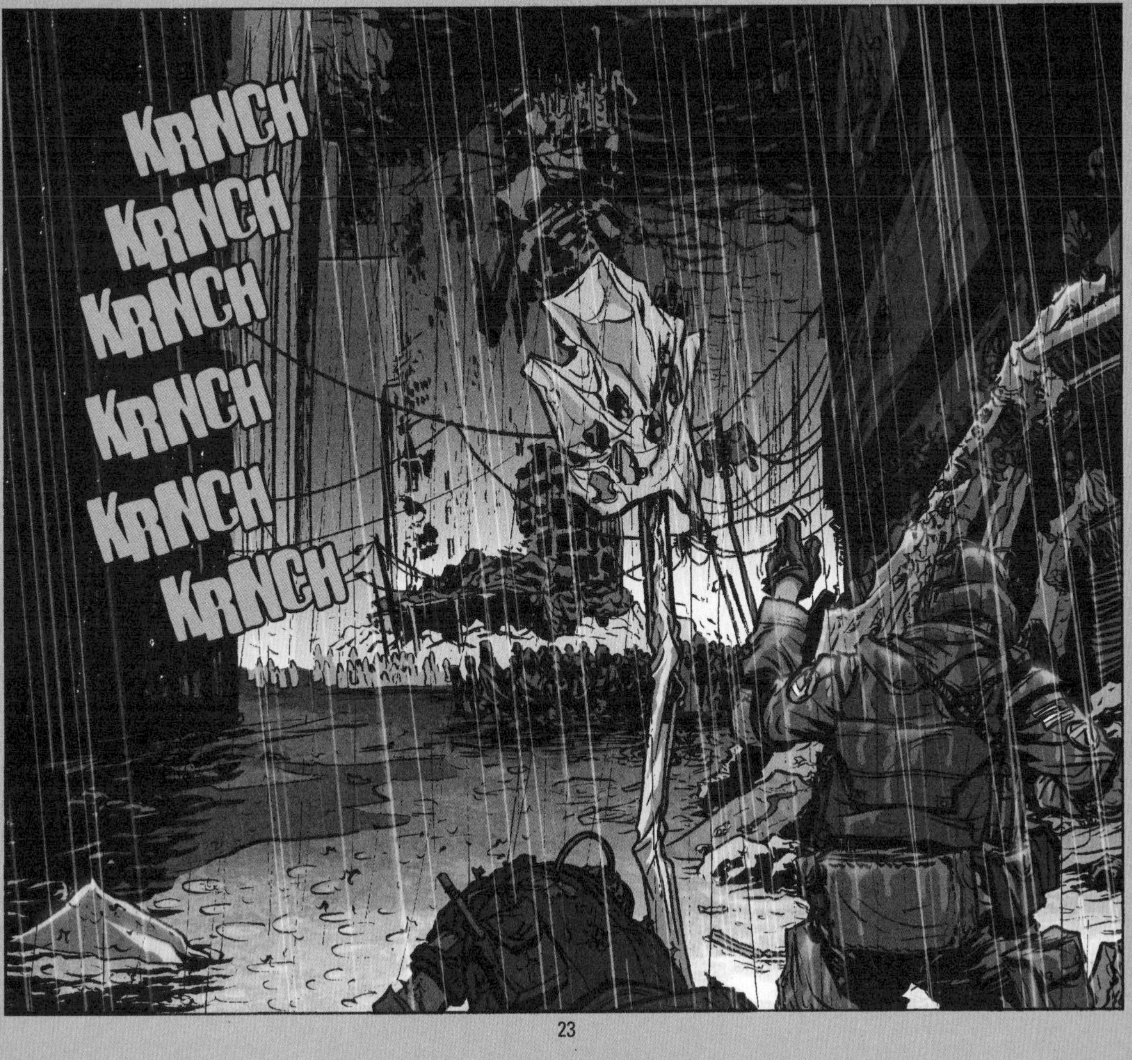
KRNCH
KRNCH
KRNCH
KRNCH
KRNCH
KRNCH

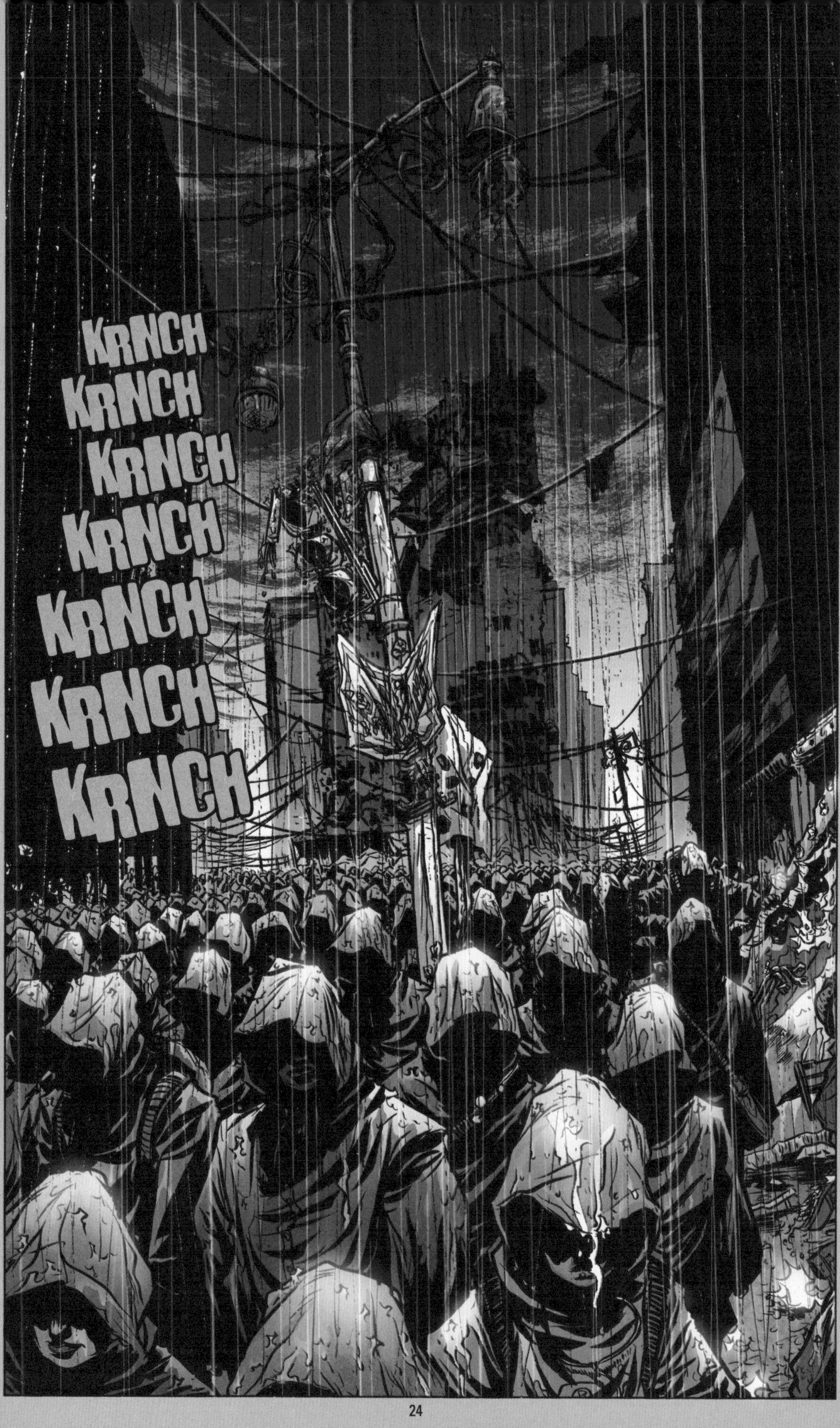
KRNCH
KRNCH
KRNCH
KRNCH
KRNCH
KRNCH
KRNCH

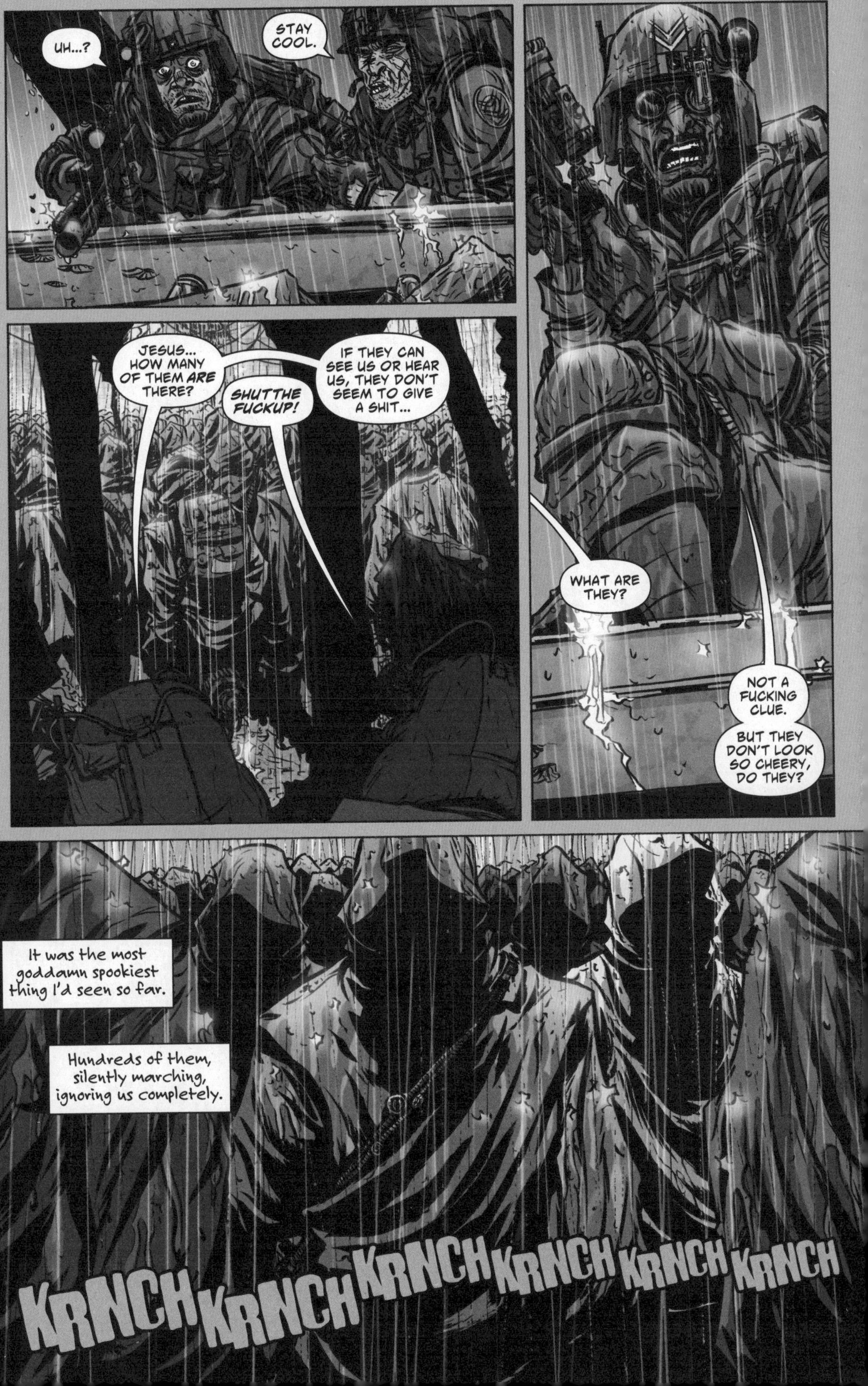

UH...?
STAY COOL.
JESUS... HOW MANY OF THEM ARE THERE?
SHUT THE FUCKUP!
IF THEY CAN SEE US OR HEAR US, THEY DON'T SEEM TO GIVE A SHIT...
WHAT ARE THEY?
NOT A FUCKING CLUE.
BUT THEY DON'T LOOK SO CHEERY, DO THEY?
It was the most goddamn spookiest thing I'd seen so far.
Hundreds of them, silently marching, ignoring us completely.
KRNCH KRNCH KRNCH KRNCH KRNCH KRNCH

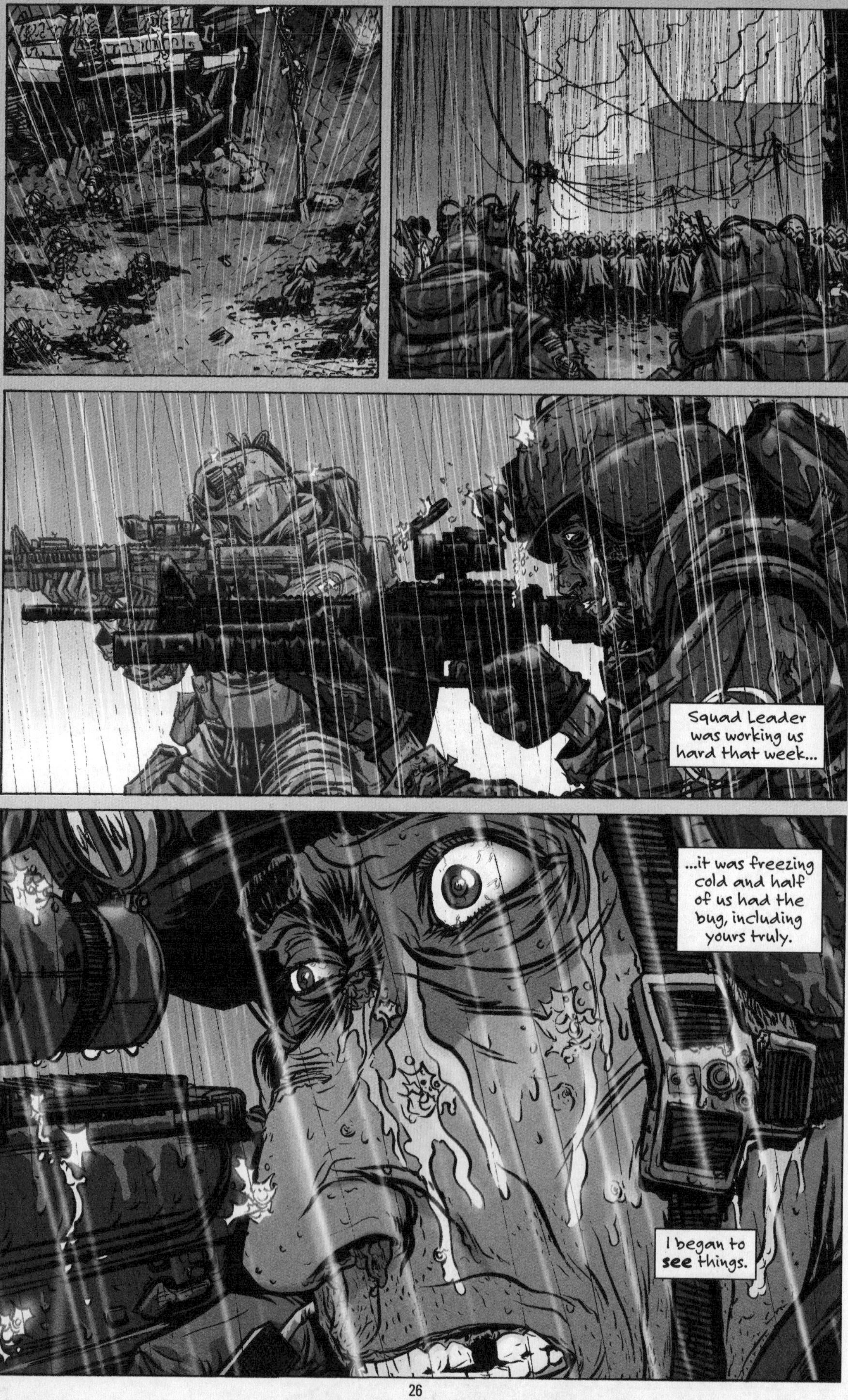
Squad Leader was working us hard that week...
...it was freezing cold and half of us had the bug, including yours truly.
I began to **see** things.

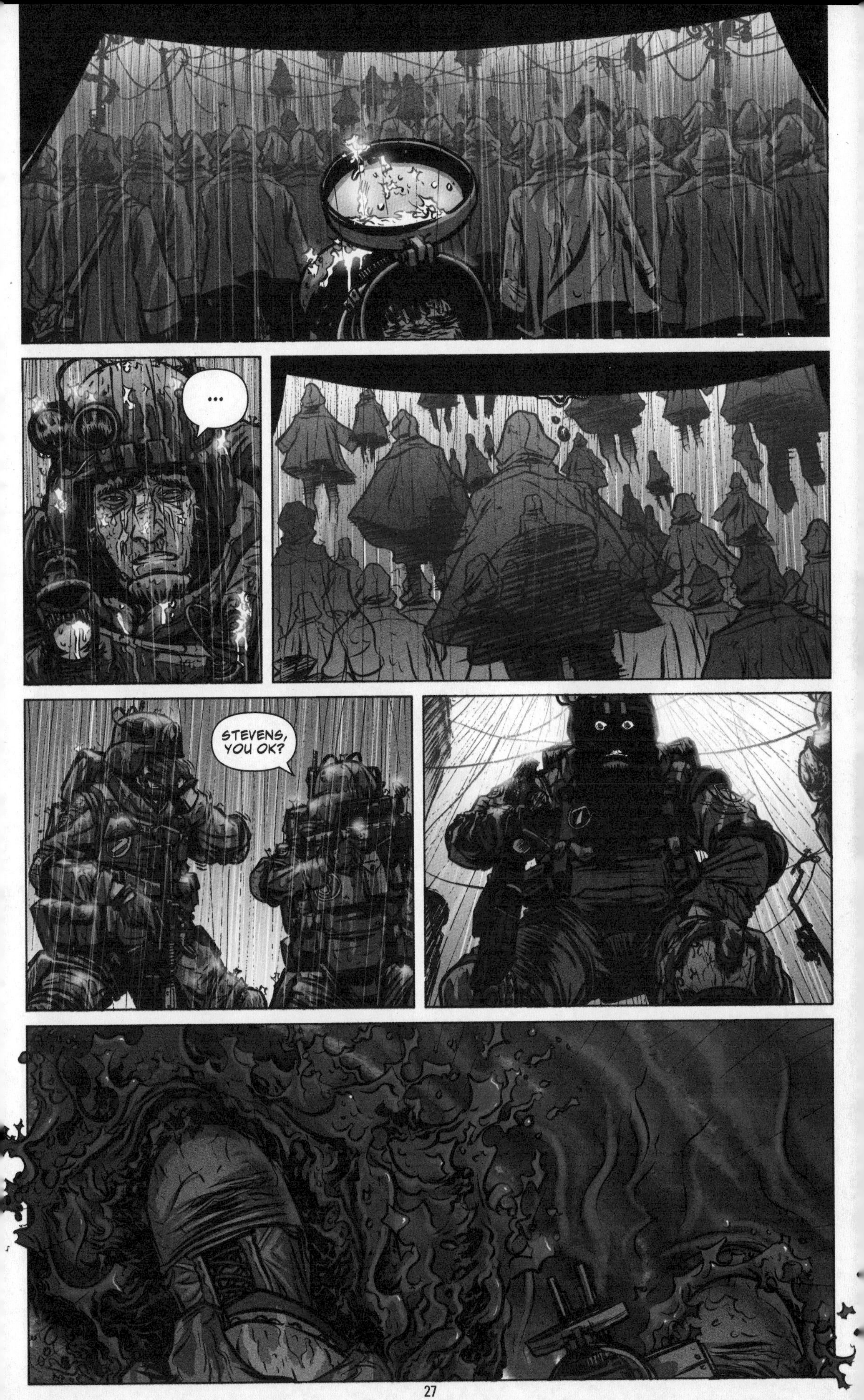
...
STEVENS, YOU OK?

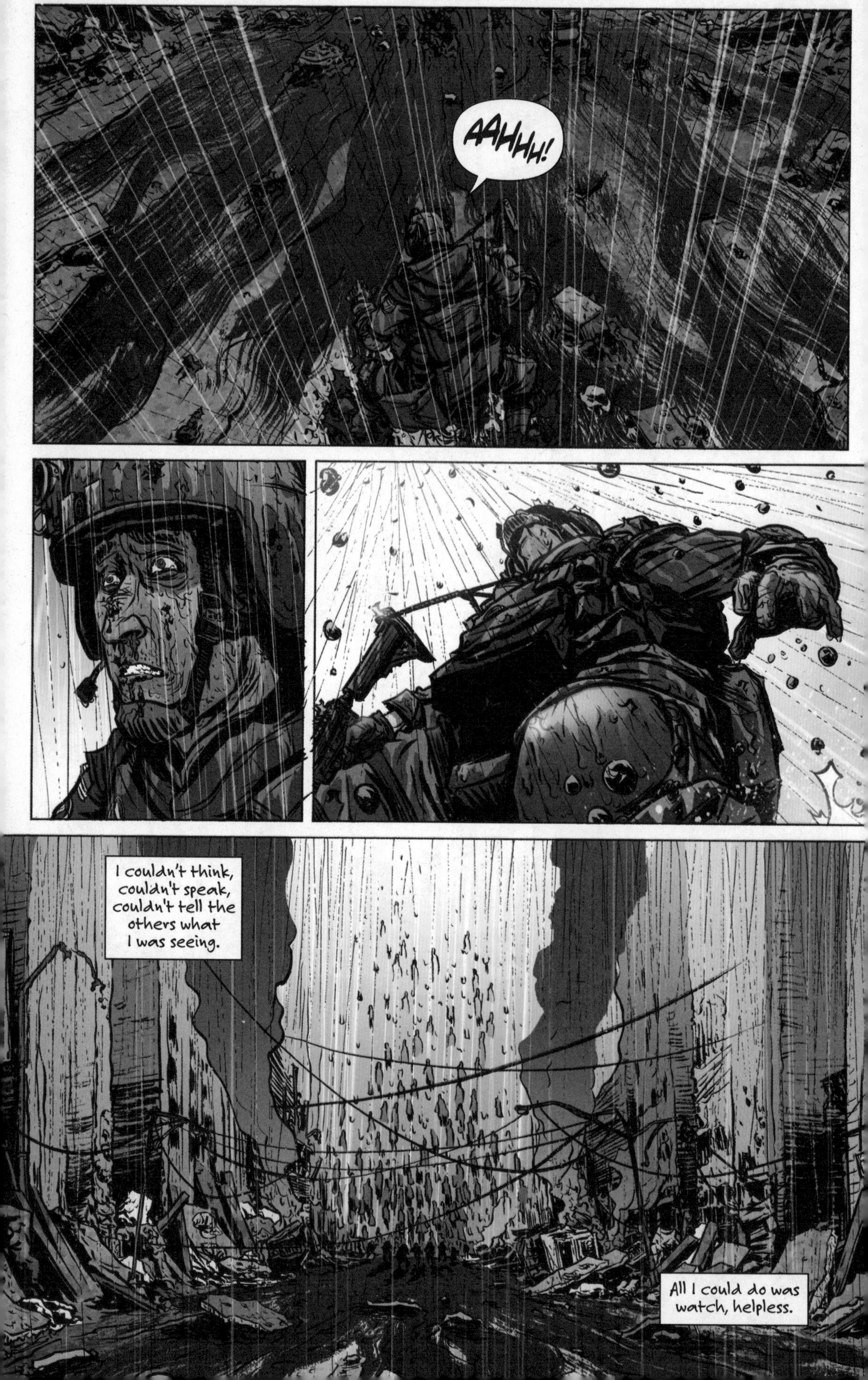
AAHHH!
I couldn't think, couldn't speak, couldn't tell the others what I was seeing.
All I could do was watch, helpless.

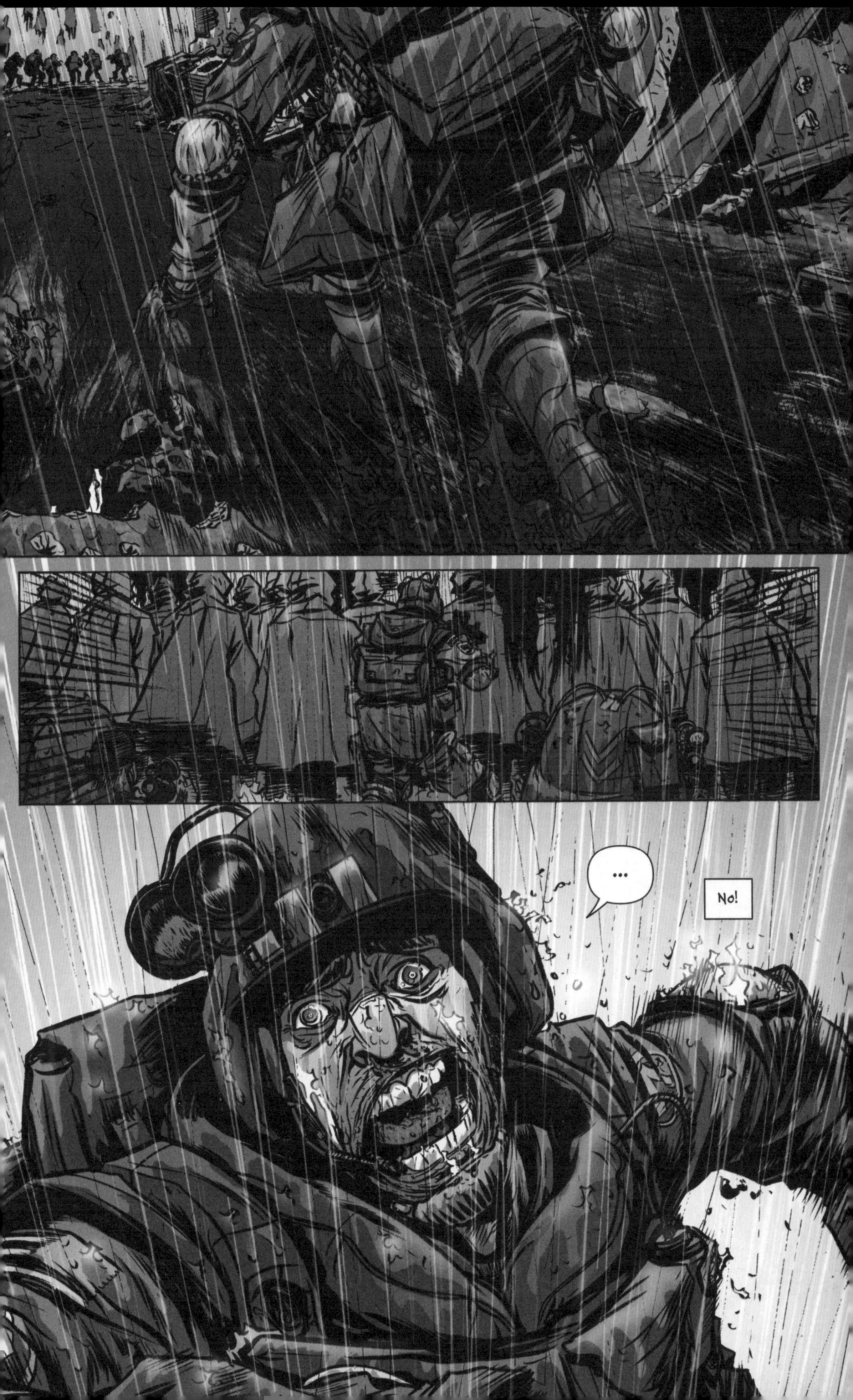
...
No!

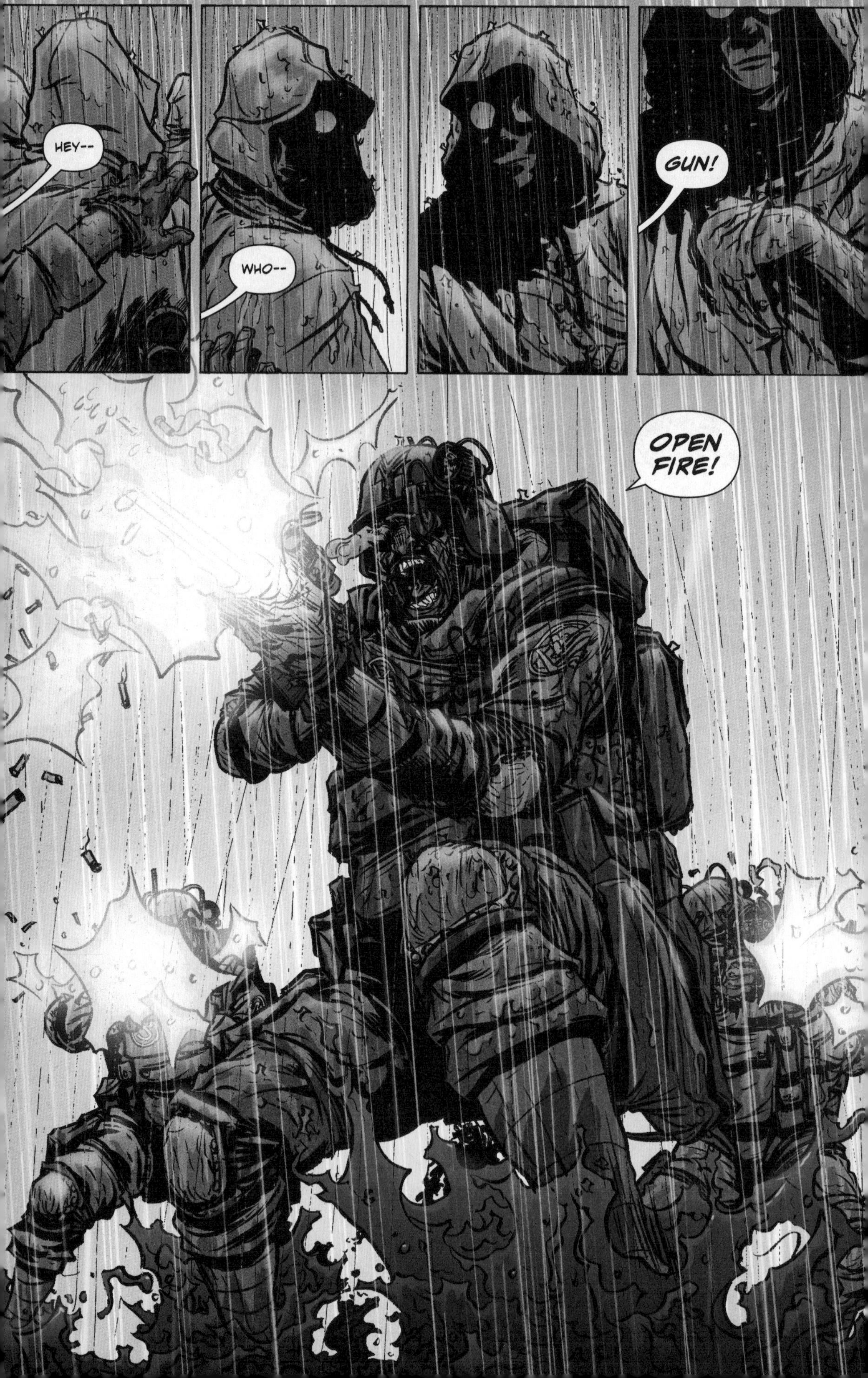
HEY--
WHO--
GUN!
OPEN FIRE!

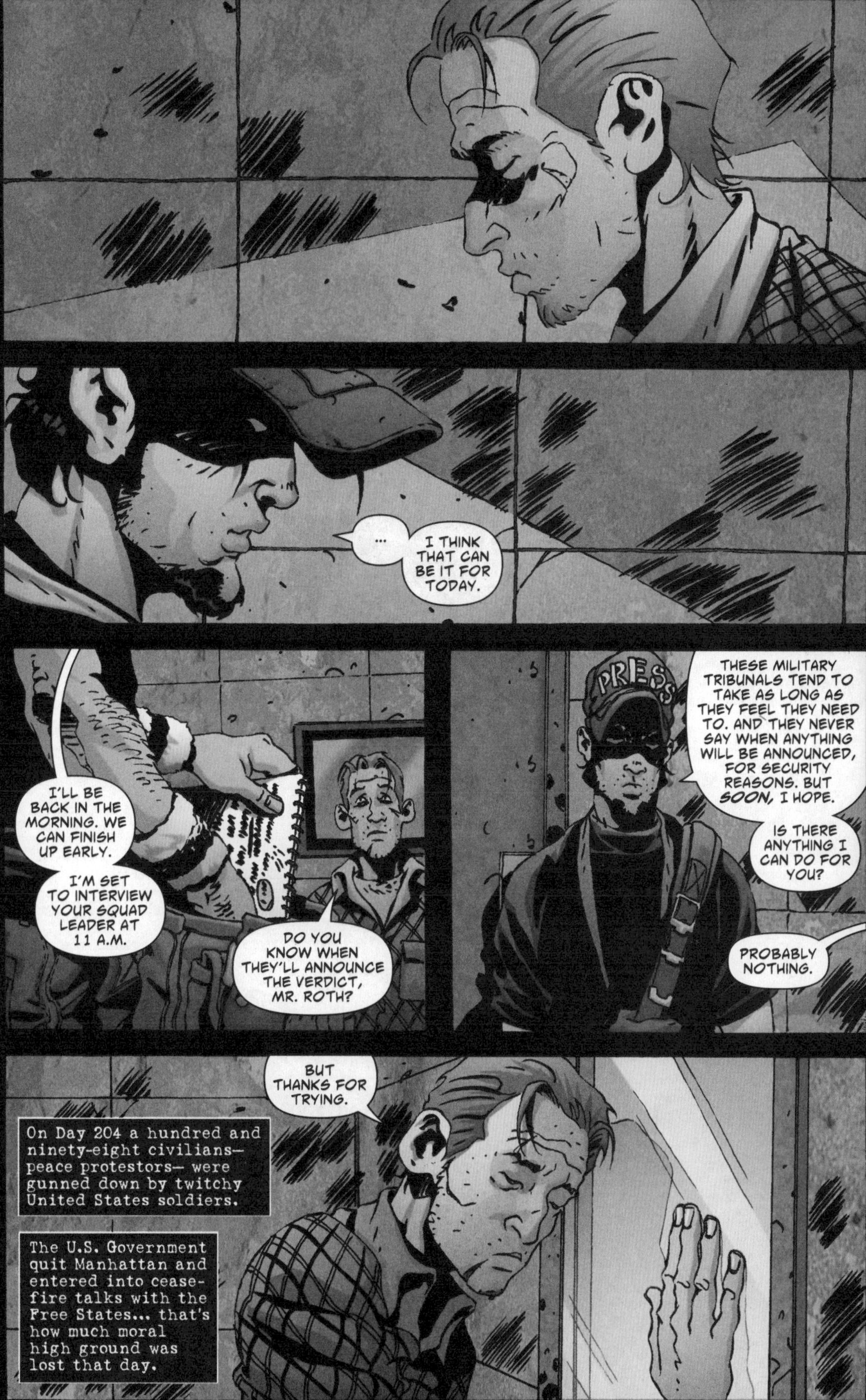
... I THINK THAT CAN BE IT FOR TODAY.
I'LL BE BACK IN THE MORNING. WE CAN FINISH UP EARLY.
I'M SET TO INTERVIEW YOUR SQUAD LEADER AT 11 A.M.
DO YOU KNOW WHEN THEY'LL ANNOUNCE THE VERDICT, MR. ROTH?
PRESS
THESE MILITARY TRIBUNALS TEND TO TAKE AS LONG AS THEY FEEL THEY NEED TO. AND THEY NEVER SAY WHEN ANYTHING WILL BE ANNOUNCED, FOR SECURITY REASONS. BUT SOON, I HOPE.
IS THERE ANYTHING I CAN DO FOR YOU?
PROBABLY NOTHING.
BUT THANKS FOR TRYING.
On Day 204 a hundred and ninety-eight civilians— peace protestors— were gunned down by twitchy United States soldiers.
The U.S. Government quit Manhattan and entered into cease-fire talks with the Free States... that's how much moral high ground was lost that day.

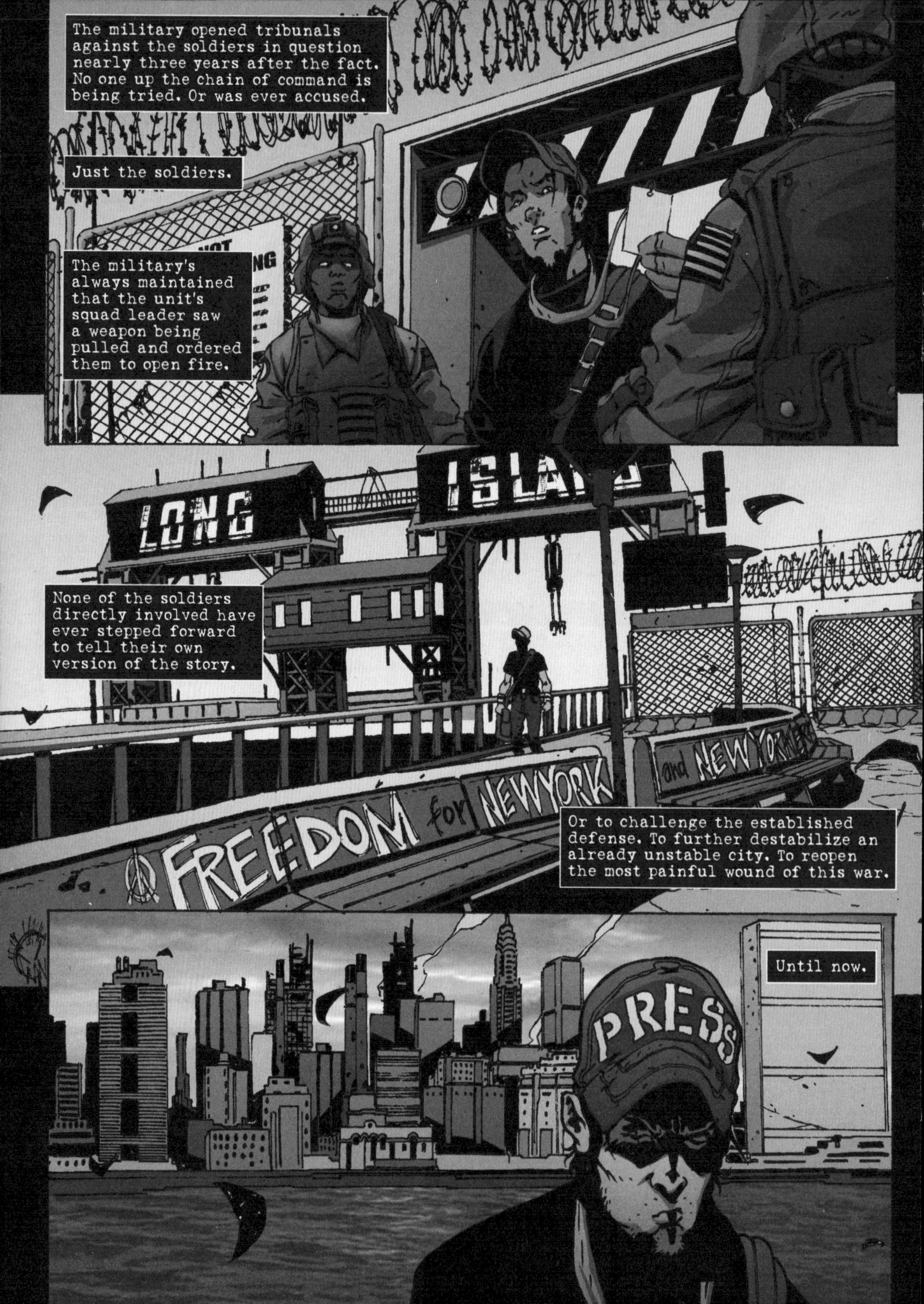
The military opened tribunals against the soldiers in question nearly three years after the fact. No one up the chain of command is being tried. Or was ever accused.
Just the soldiers.
The military's always maintained that the unit's squad leader saw a weapon being pulled and ordered them to open fire.
LONG
ISLA
None of the soldiers directly involved have ever stepped forward to tell their own version of the story.
FREEDOM for NEWYORK
and NEW YORKERS
Or to challenge the established defense. To further destabilize an already unstable city. To reopen the most painful wound of this war.
Until now.
PRESS

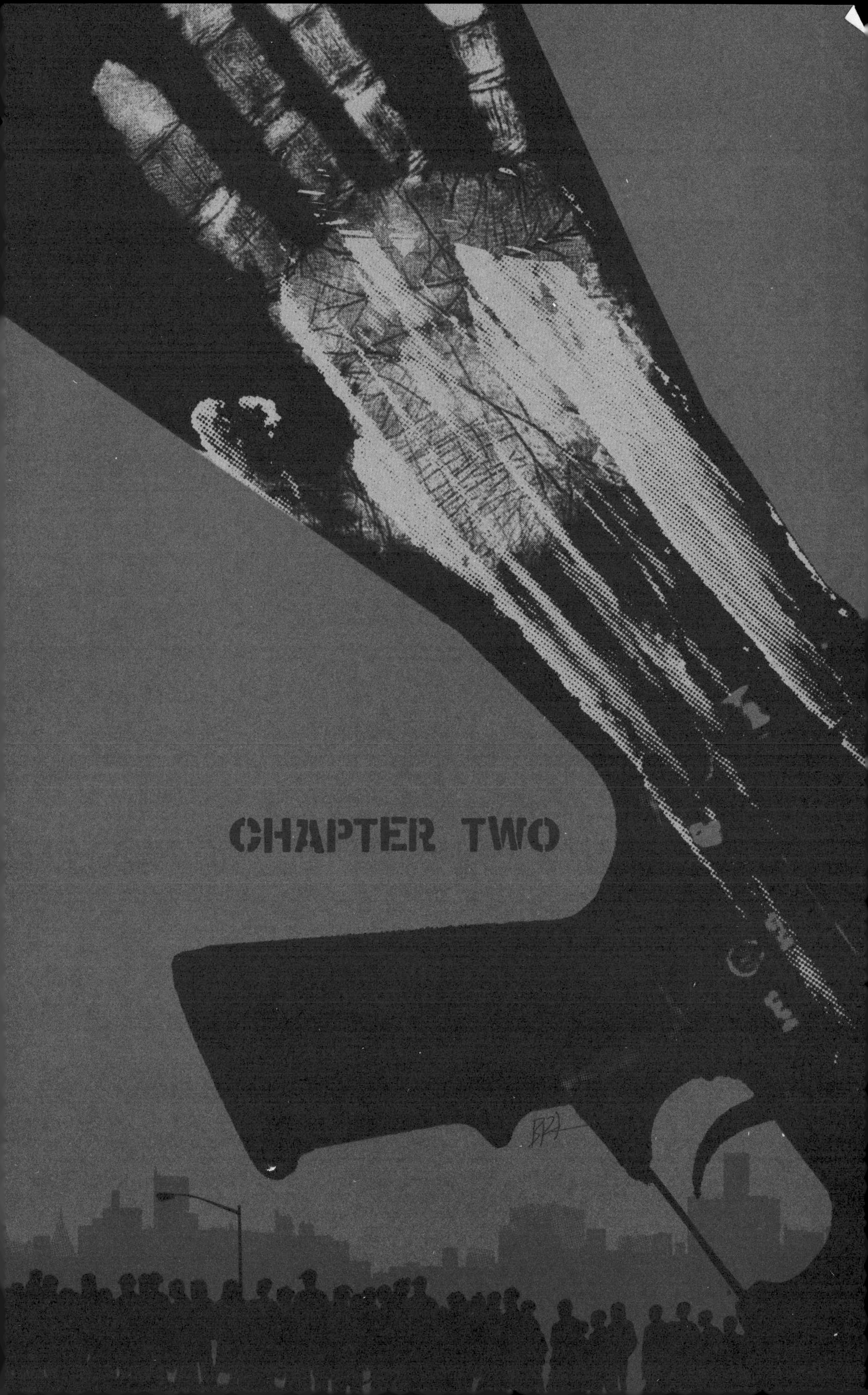
CHAPTER TWO

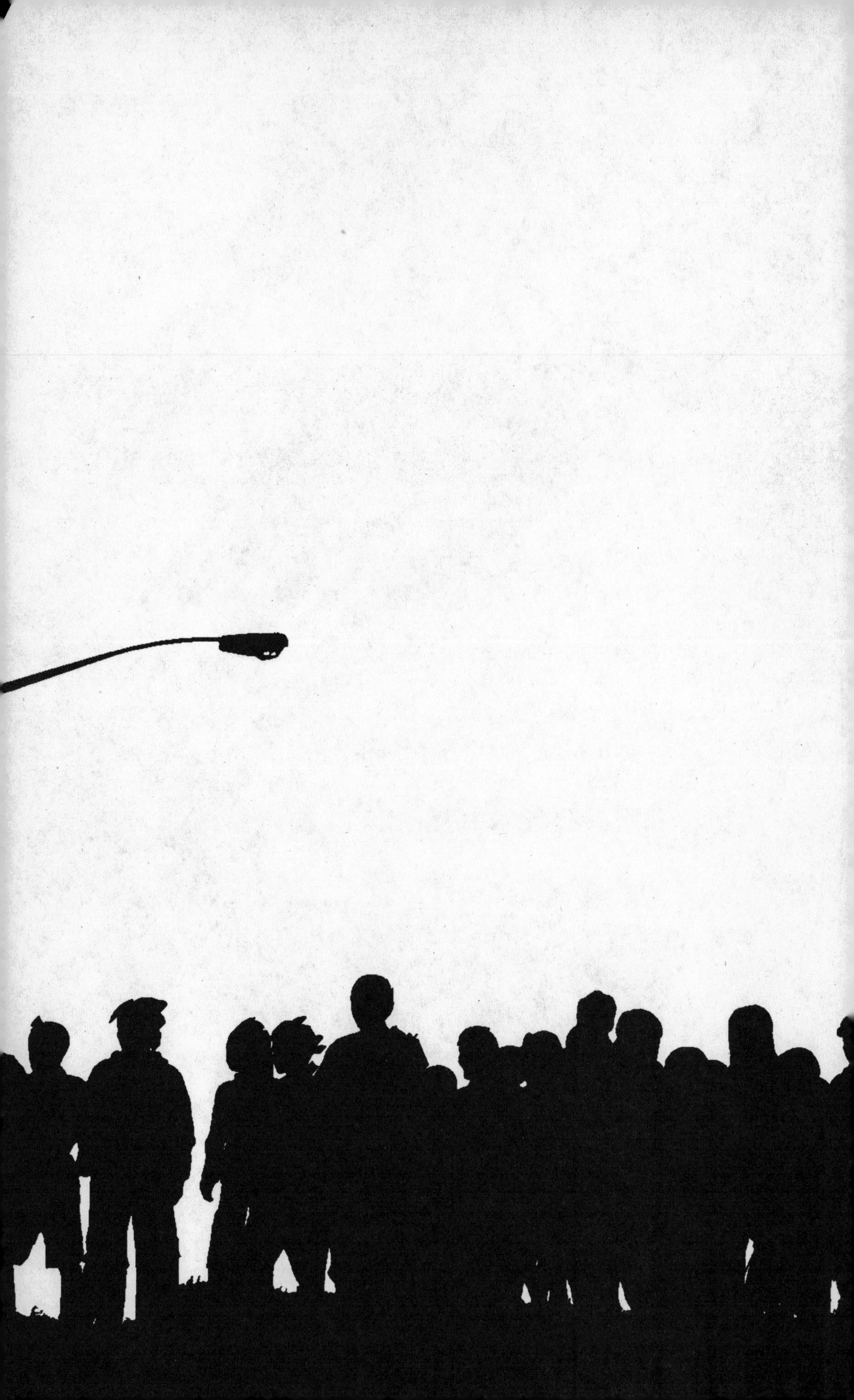

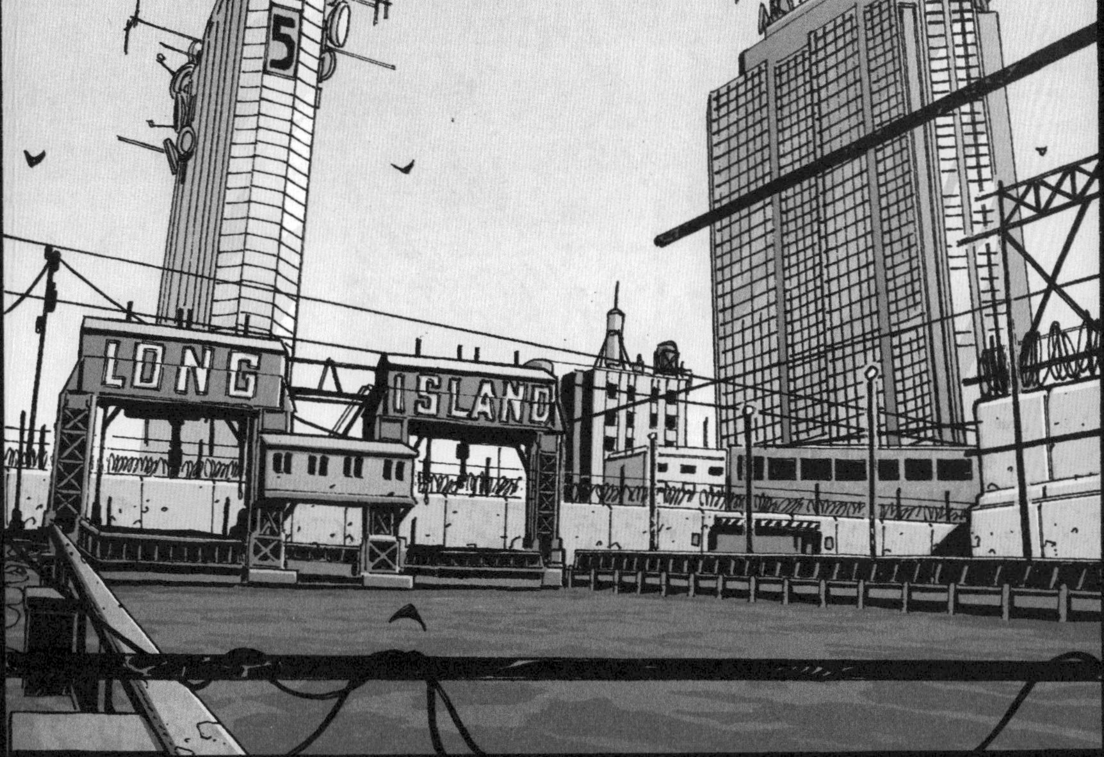
LONG
ISLAND
5

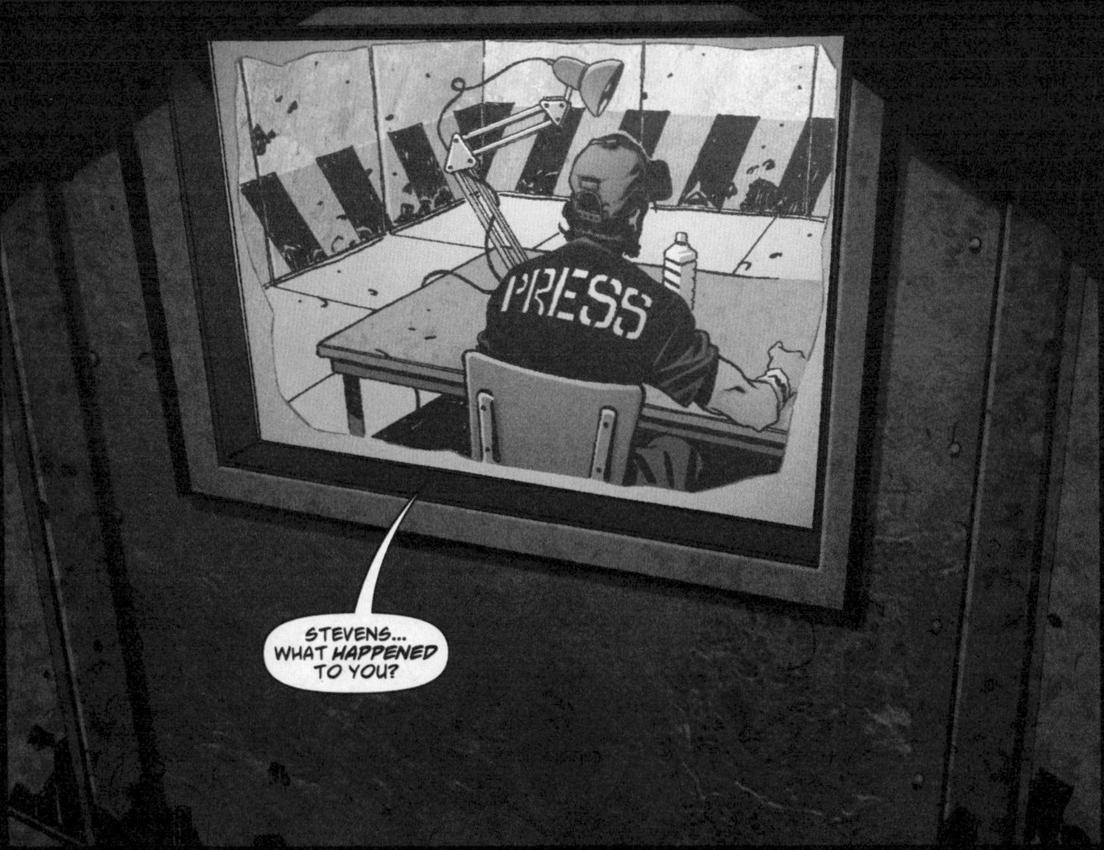
PRESS
STEVENS... WHAT HAPPENED TO YOU?

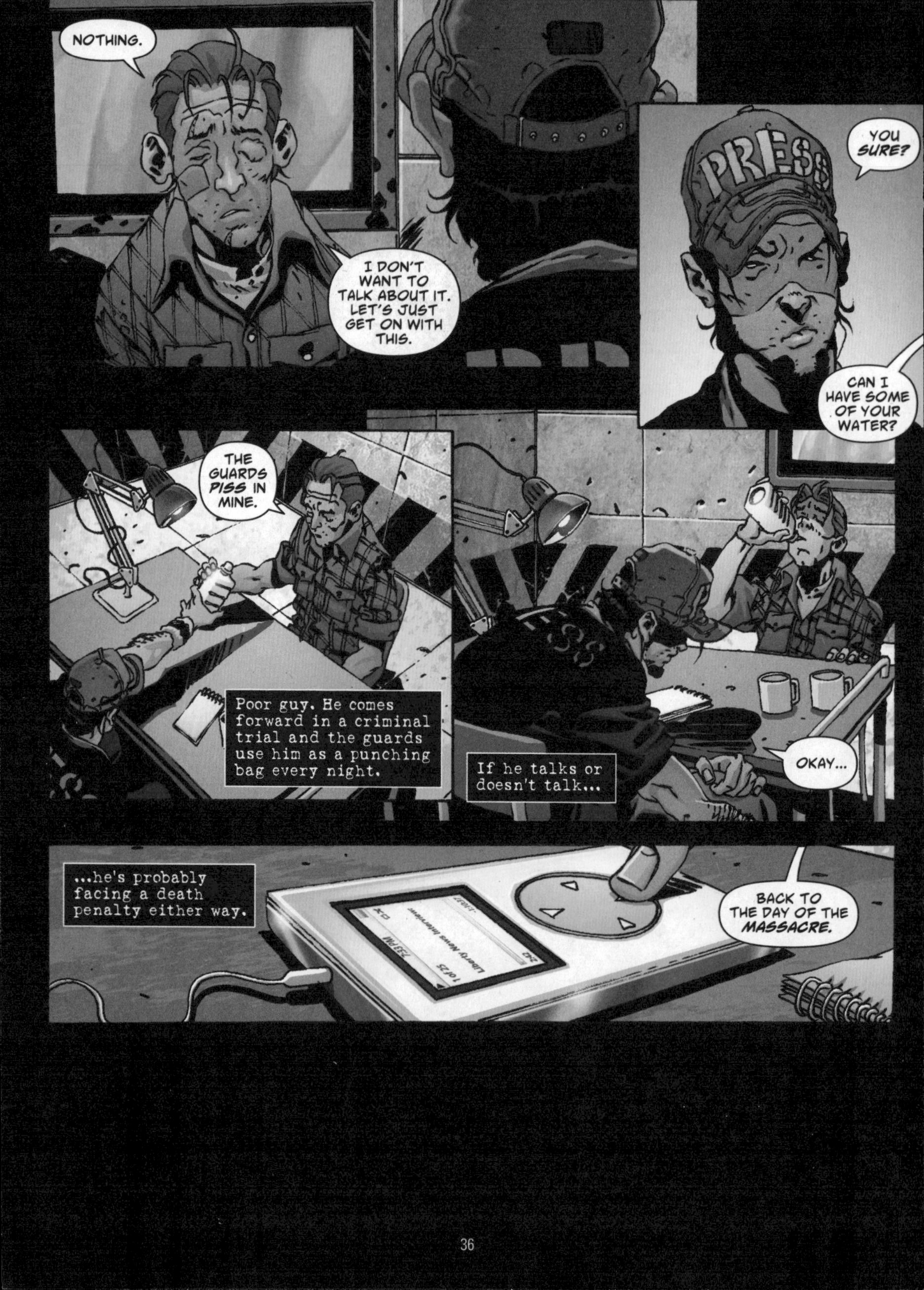
NOTHING.
I DON'T WANT TO TALK ABOUT IT. LET'S JUST GET ON WITH THIS.
YOU SURE?
CAN I HAVE SOME OF YOUR WATER?
THE GUARDS PISS IN MINE.
Poor guy. He comes forward in a criminal trial and the guards use him as a punching bag every night.
If he talks or doesn't talk...
OKAY...
...he's probably facing a death penalty either way.
BACK TO THE DAY OF THE MASSACRE.

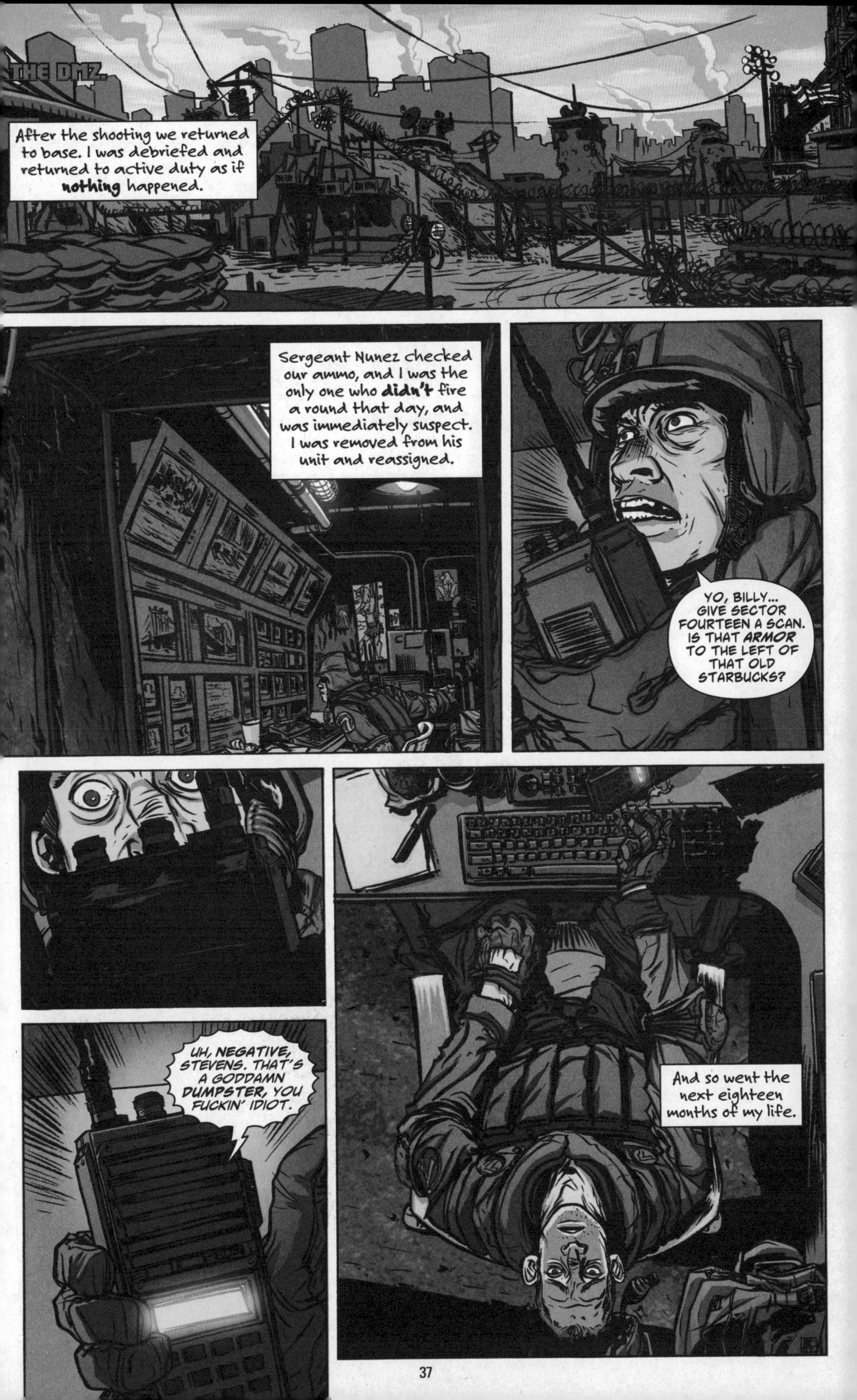
THE DMZ.
After the shooting we returned to base. I was debriefed and returned to active duty as if **nothing** happened.
Sergeant Nunez checked our ammo, and I was the only one who **didn't** fire a round that day, and was immediately suspect. I was removed from his unit and reassigned.
YO, BILLY... GIVE SECTOR FOURTEEN A SCAN. IS THAT *ARMOR* TO THE LEFT OF THAT OLD STARBUCKS?
UH, NEGATIVE, STEVENS. THAT'S A GODDAMN DUMPSTER, YOU FUCKIN' IDIOT.
And so went the next eighteen months of my life.

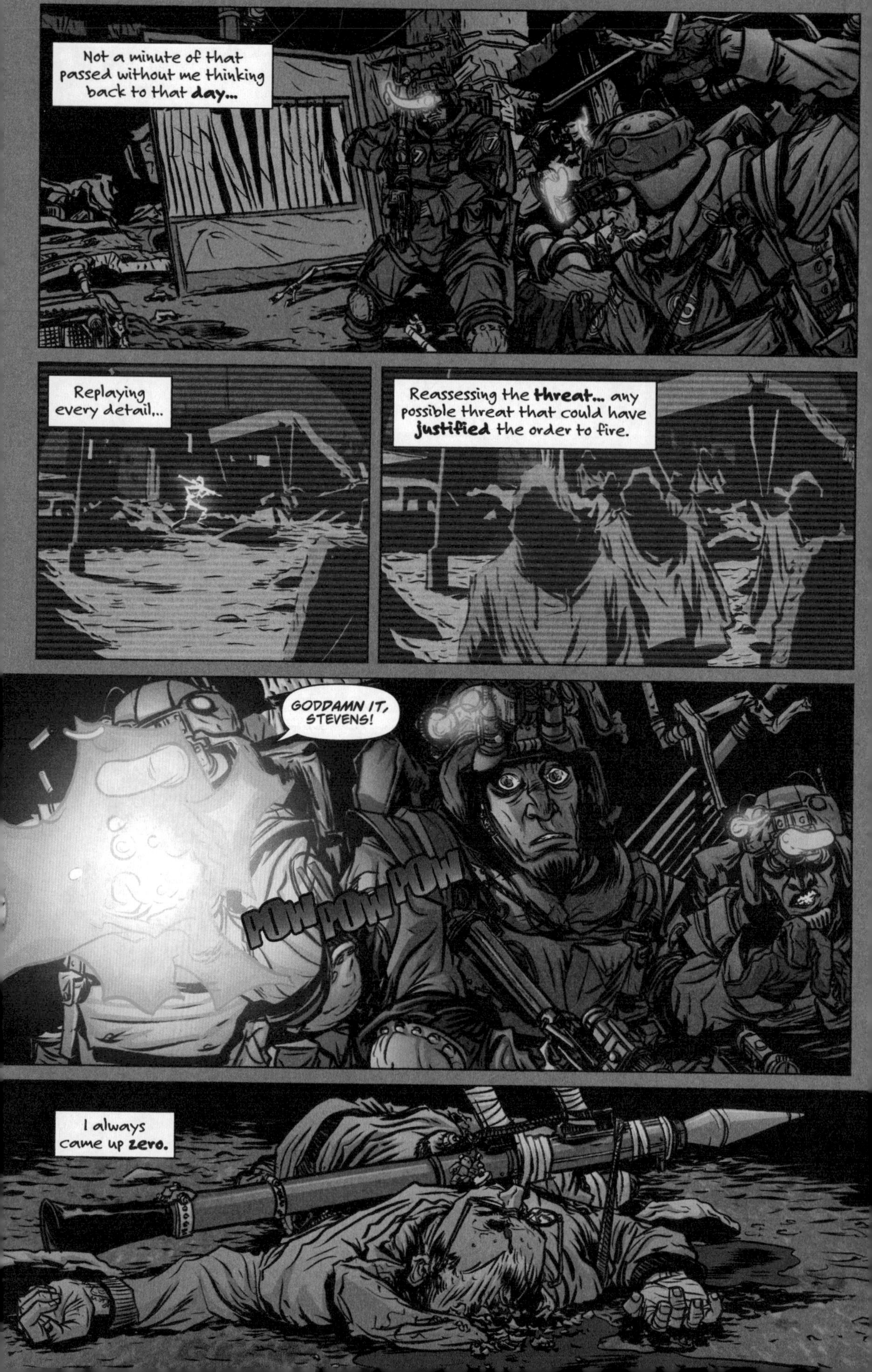
Not a minute of that passed without me thinking back to that **day...**
Replaying every detail...
Reassessing the **threat...** any possible threat that could have **justified** the order to fire.
GODDAMN IT, STEVENS!
POW POW POW
I always came up **zero.**

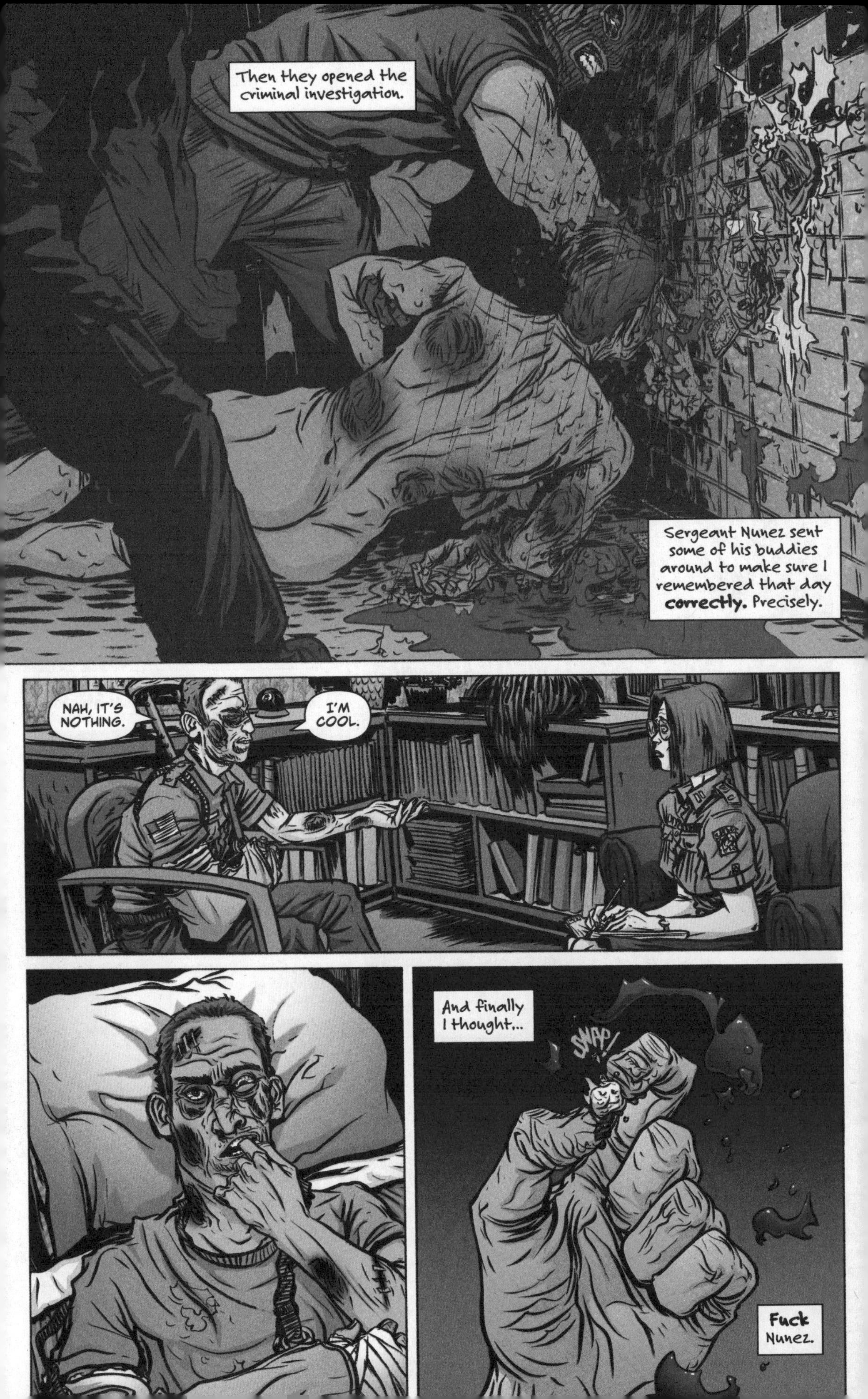
Then they opened the criminal investigation.
Sergeant Nunez sent some of his buddies around to make sure I remembered that day **correctly.** Precisely.
NAH, IT'S NOTHING.
I'M COOL.
And finally I thought...
SNAP!
Fuck Nunez.

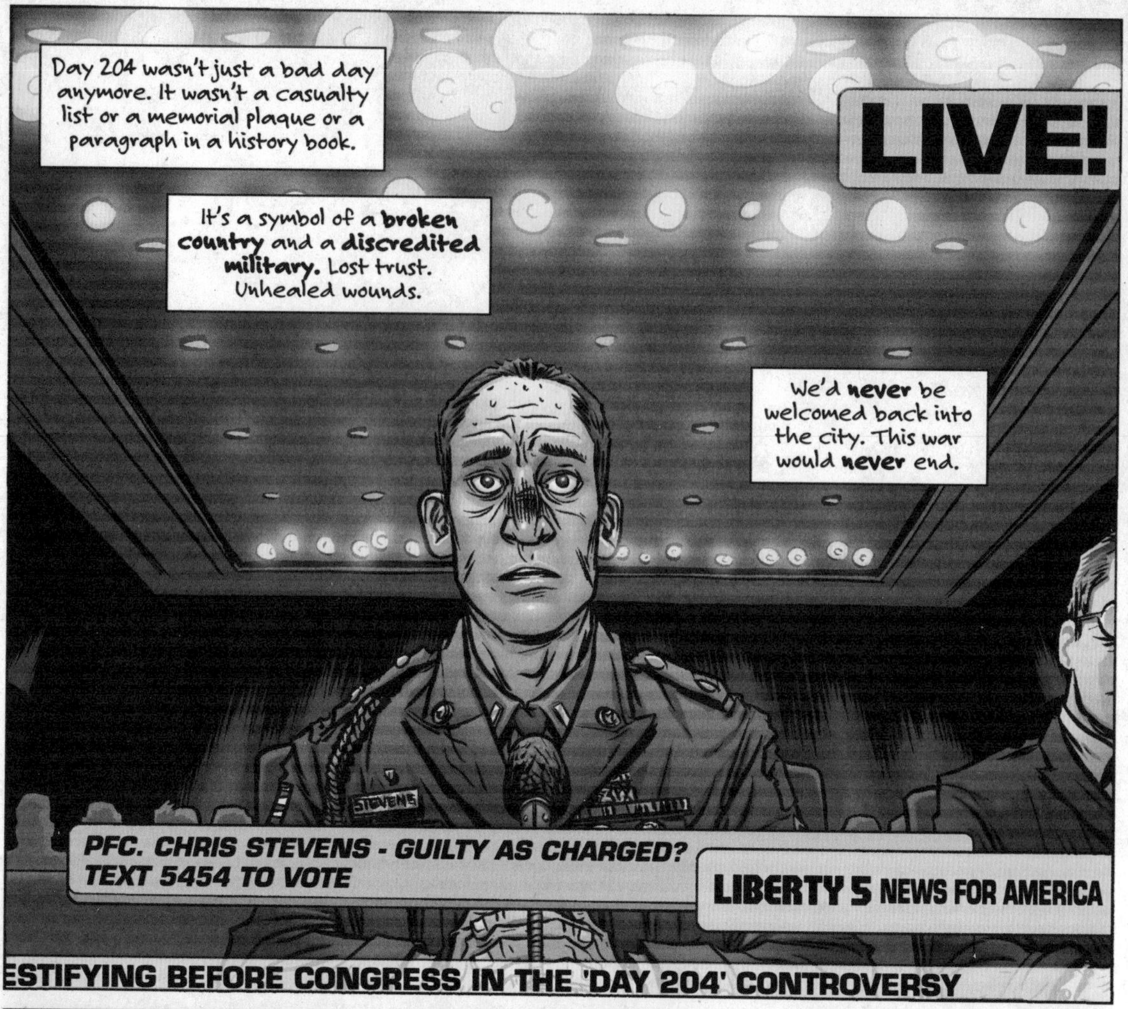
Day 204 wasn't just a bad day anymore. It wasn't a casualty list or a memorial plaque or a paragraph in a history book.
LIVE!
It's a symbol of a **broken country** and a **discredited military.** Lost trust. Unhealed wounds.
We'd **never** be welcomed back into the city. This war would **never** end.
STEVENS
PFC. CHRIS STEVENS - GUILTY AS CHARGED?
TEXT 5454 TO VOTE
LIBERTY 5 NEWS FOR AMERICA
ESTIFYING BEFORE CONGRESS IN THE 'DAY 204' CONTROVERSY

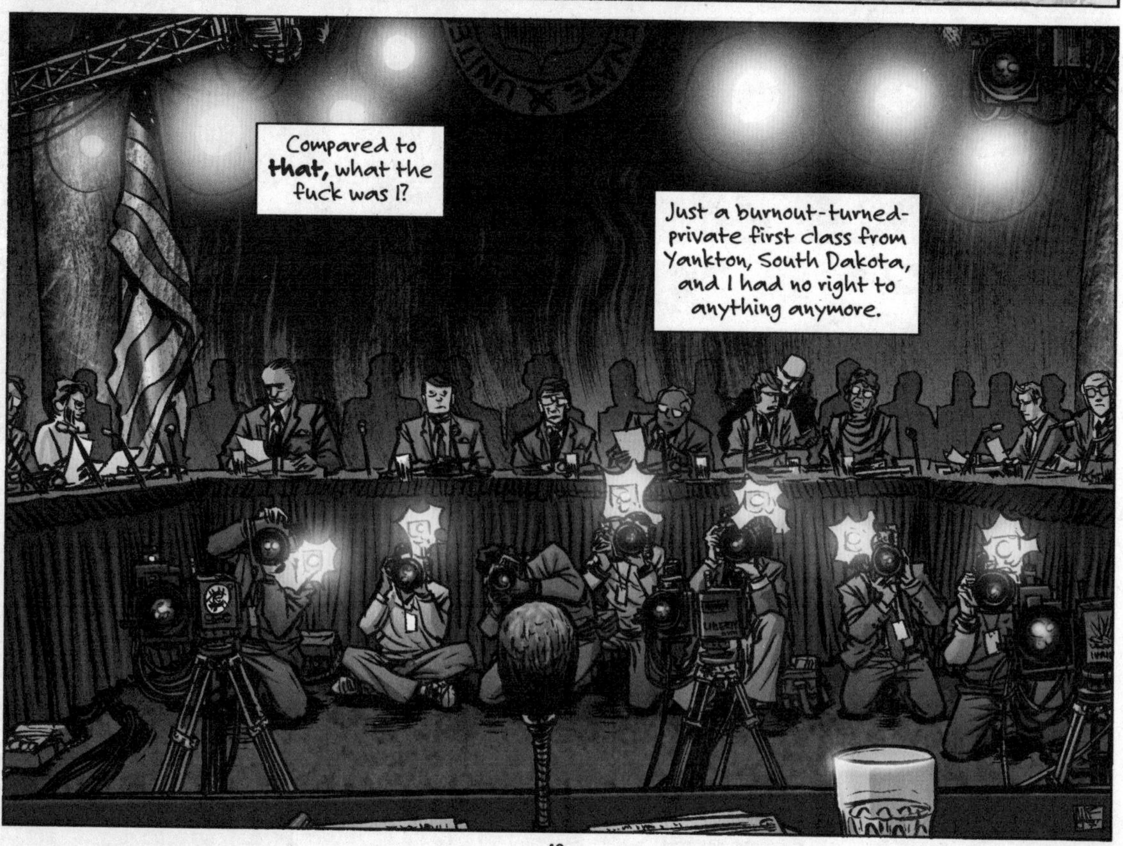
Compared to **that,** what the fuck was I?
Just a burnout-turned-private first class from Yankton, South Dakota, and I had no right to anything anymore.

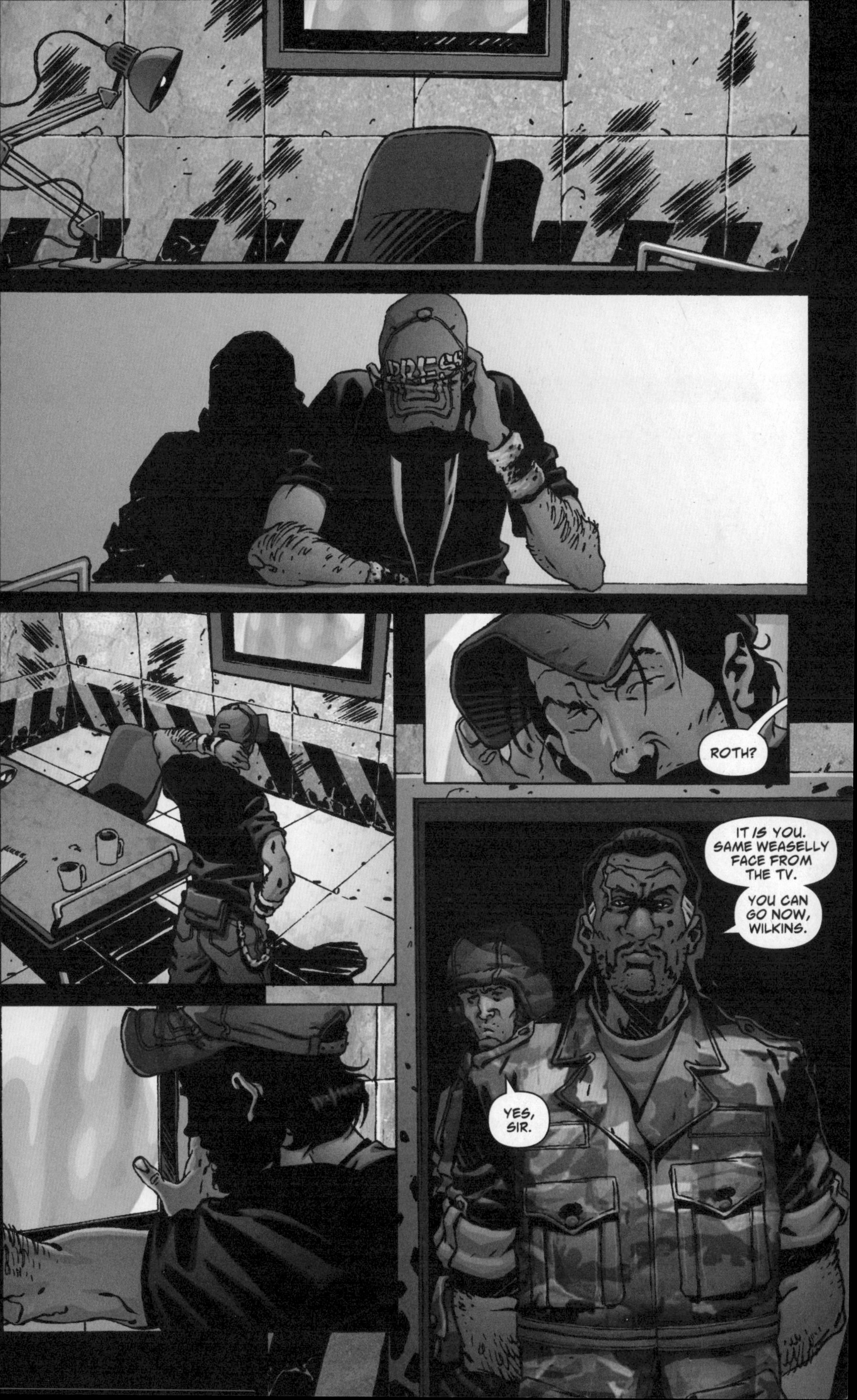
ROTH?
IT IS YOU. SAME WEASELLY FACE FROM THE TV.
YOU CAN GO NOW, WILKINS.
YES, SIR.

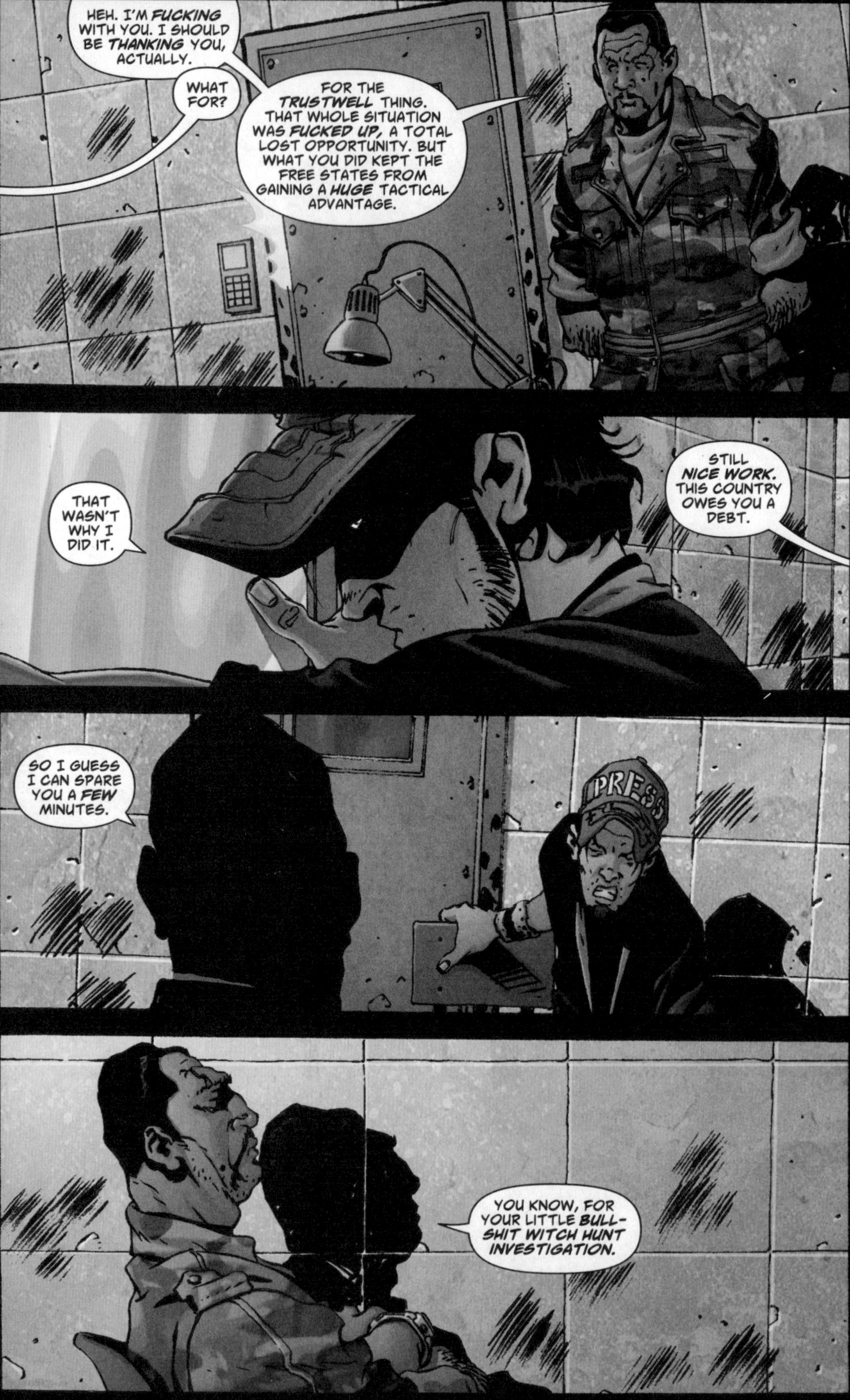

HEH. I'M *FUCKING* WITH YOU. I SHOULD BE *THANKING* YOU, ACTUALLY.
WHAT FOR?
FOR THE *TRUSTWELL* THING. THAT WHOLE SITUATION WAS *FUCKED UP,* A TOTAL LOST OPPORTUNITY. BUT WHAT YOU DID KEPT THE FREE STATES FROM GAINING A *HUGE* TACTICAL ADVANTAGE.
THAT WASN'T WHY I DID IT.
STILL *NICE WORK.* THIS COUNTRY OWES YOU A DEBT.
SO I GUESS I CAN SPARE YOU A *FEW* MINUTES.
PRESS
YOU KNOW, FOR YOUR LITTLE *BULL-SHIT WITCH HUNT INVESTIGATION.*

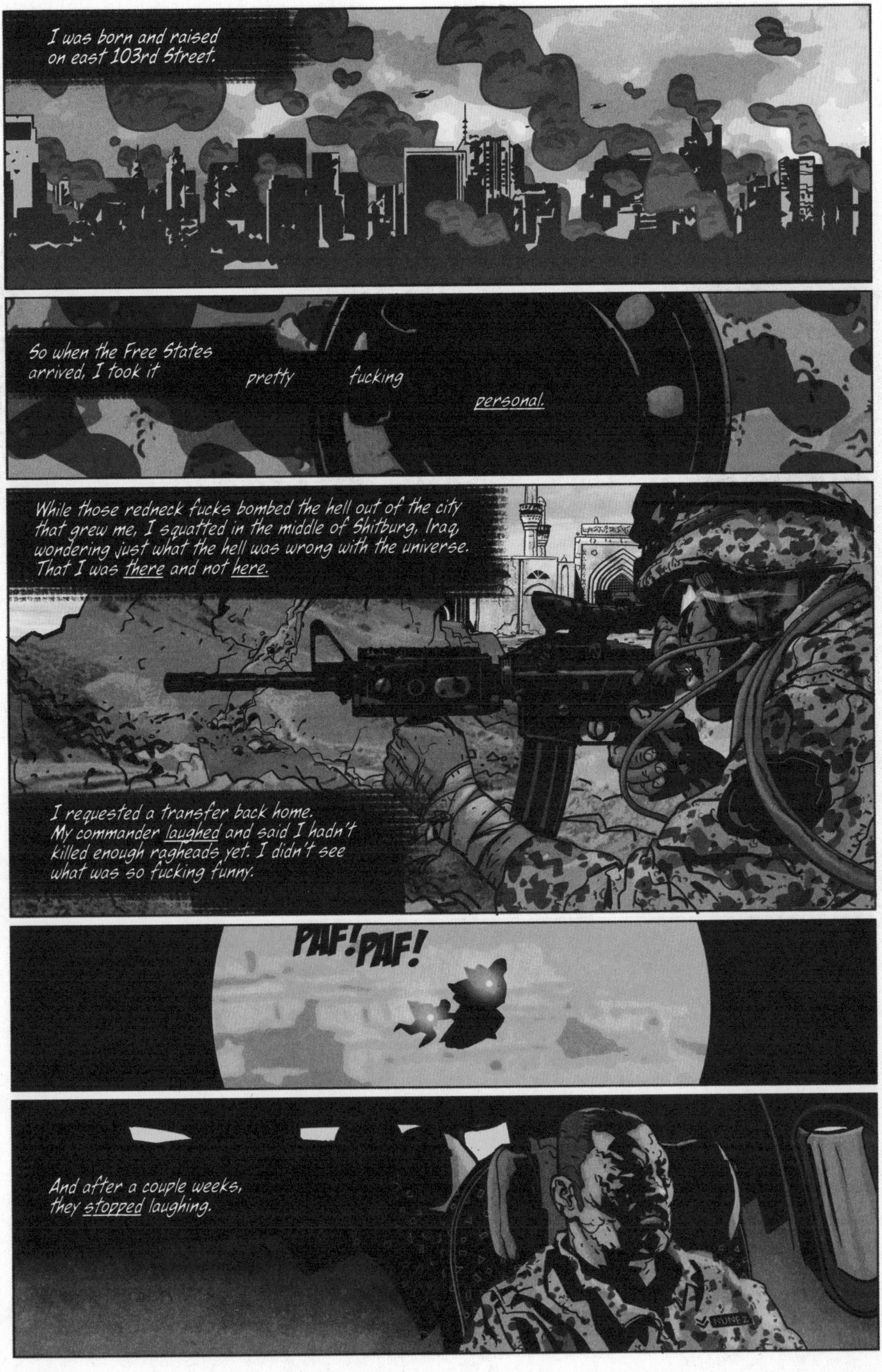
I was born and raised on east 103rd Street.
So when the Free States arrived, I took it
pretty
fucking
personal.
While those redneck fucks bombed the hell out of the city that grew me, I squatted in the middle of Shitburg, Iraq, wondering just what the hell was wrong with the universe. That I was there and not here.
I requested a transfer back home. My commander laughed and said I hadn't killed enough ragheads yet. I didn't see what was so fucking funny.
PAF! PAF!
And after a couple weeks, they stopped laughing.
NUNEZ

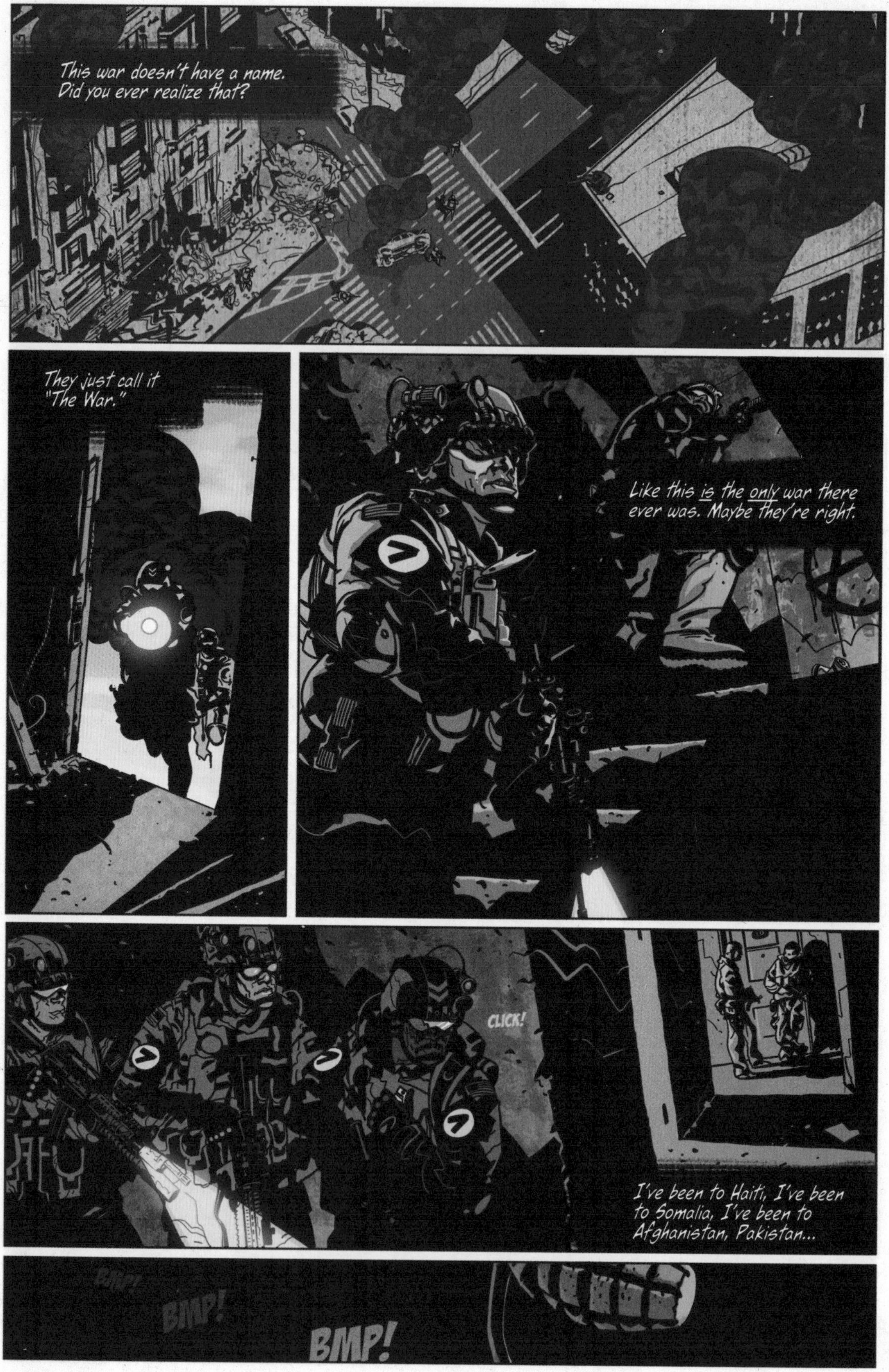
This war doesn't have a name.
Did you ever realize that?
They just call it
"The War."
Like this is the only war there
ever was. Maybe they're right.
CLICK!
I've been to Haiti, I've been
to Somalia, I've been to
Afghanistan, Pakistan...
BMP!
BMP!
BMP!

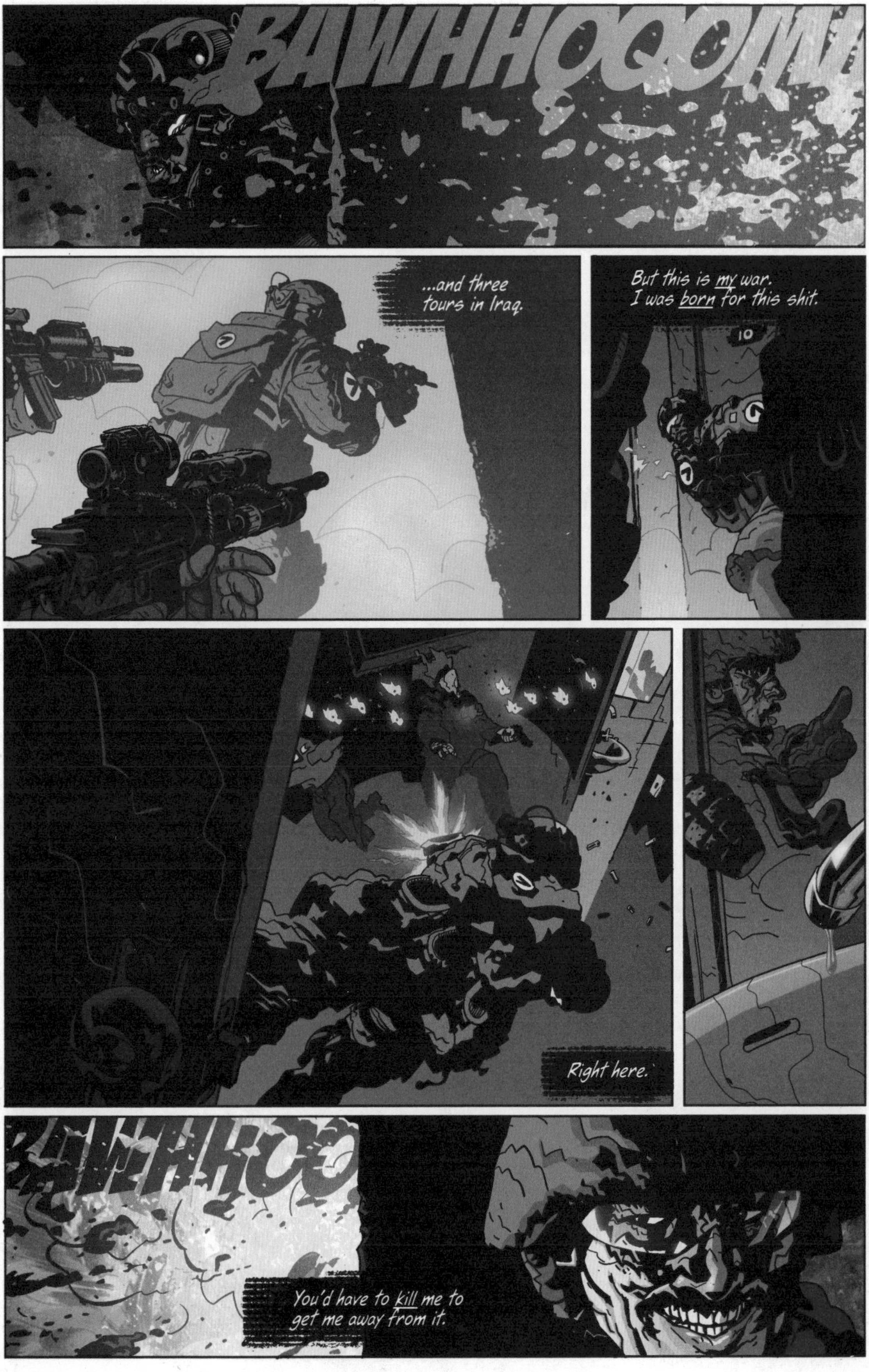
BAWHHOOOM
...and three tours in Iraq.
But this is my war. I was born for this shit.
Right here.
BAWHHOO
You'd have to kill me to get me away from it.

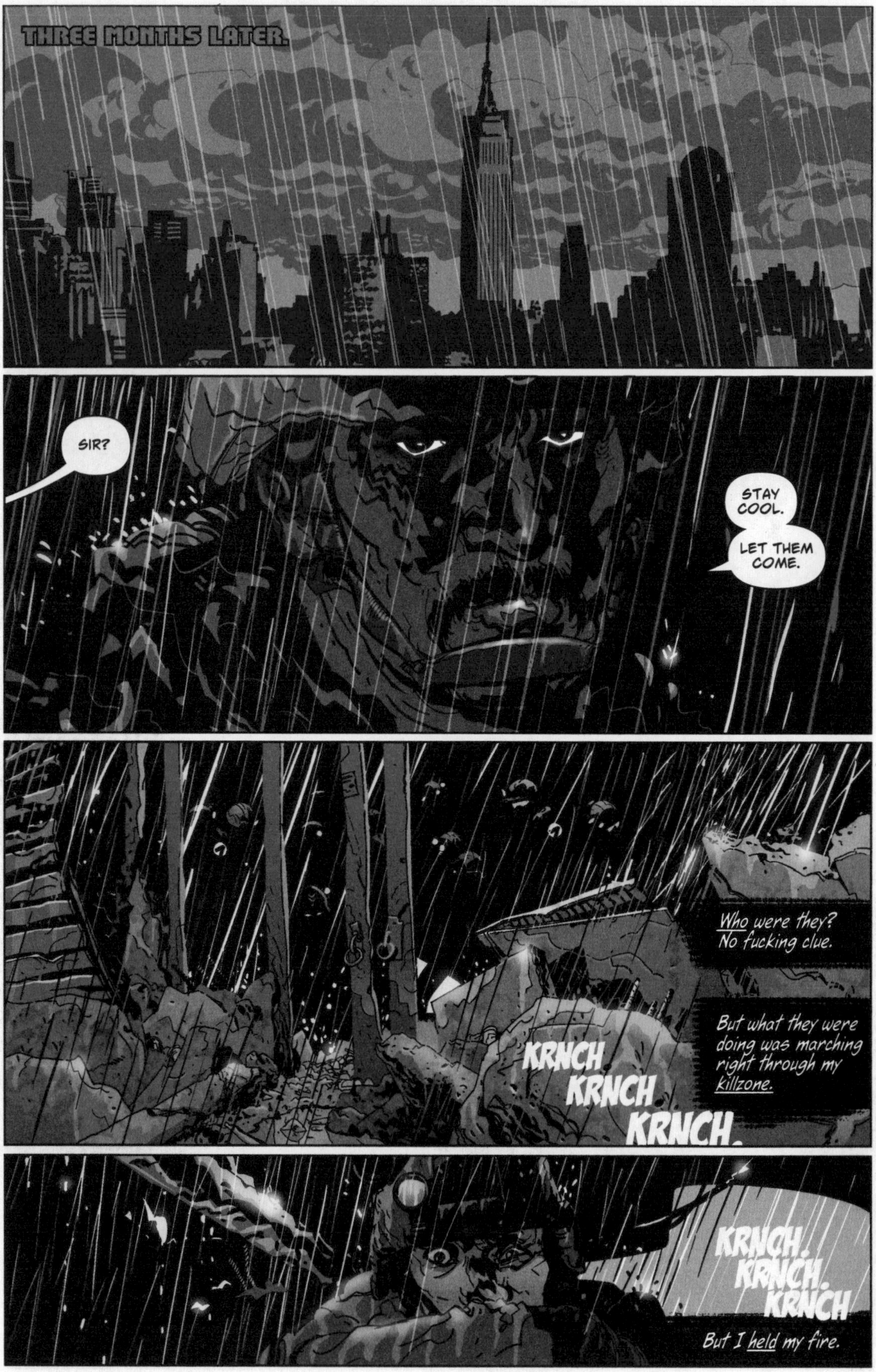
THREE MONTHS LATER.
SIR?
STAY COOL.
LET THEM COME.
Who were they? No fucking clue.
But what they were doing was marching right through my killzone.
KRNCH KRNCH KRNCH.
KRNCH. KRNCH. KRNCH
But I held my fire.

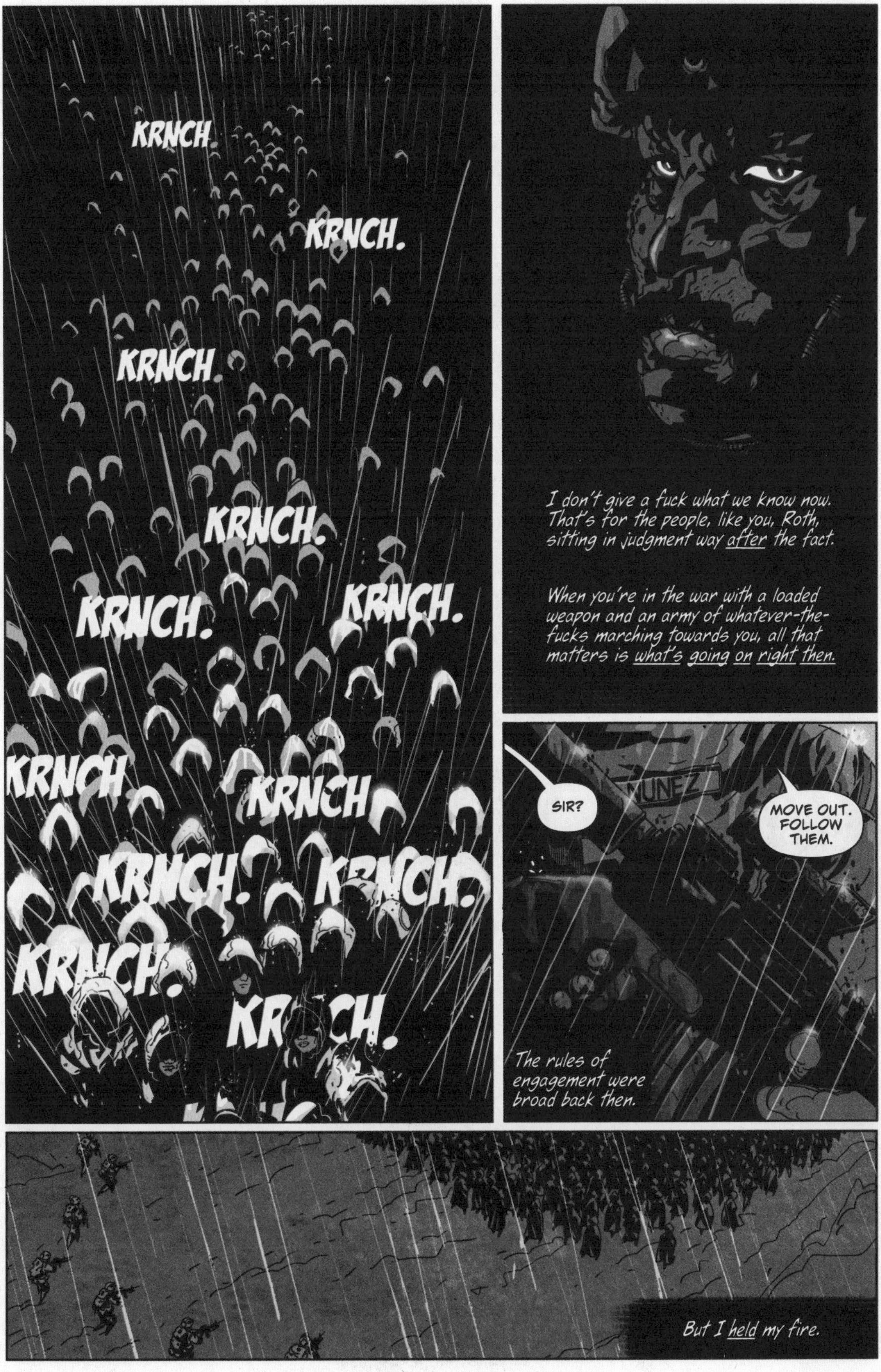
KRNCH.
KRNCH.
KRNCH.
KRNCH.
KRNCH.
KRNCH.
KRNCH
KRNCH
KRNCH.
KRNCH.
KRNCH.
KRNCH.
I don't give a fuck what we know now. That's for the people, like you, Roth, sitting in judgment way after the fact.
When you're in the war with a loaded weapon and an army of whatever-the-fucks marching towards you, all that matters is what's going on right then.
NUNEZ
SIR?
MOVE OUT. FOLLOW THEM.
The rules of engagement were broad back then.
But I held my fire.

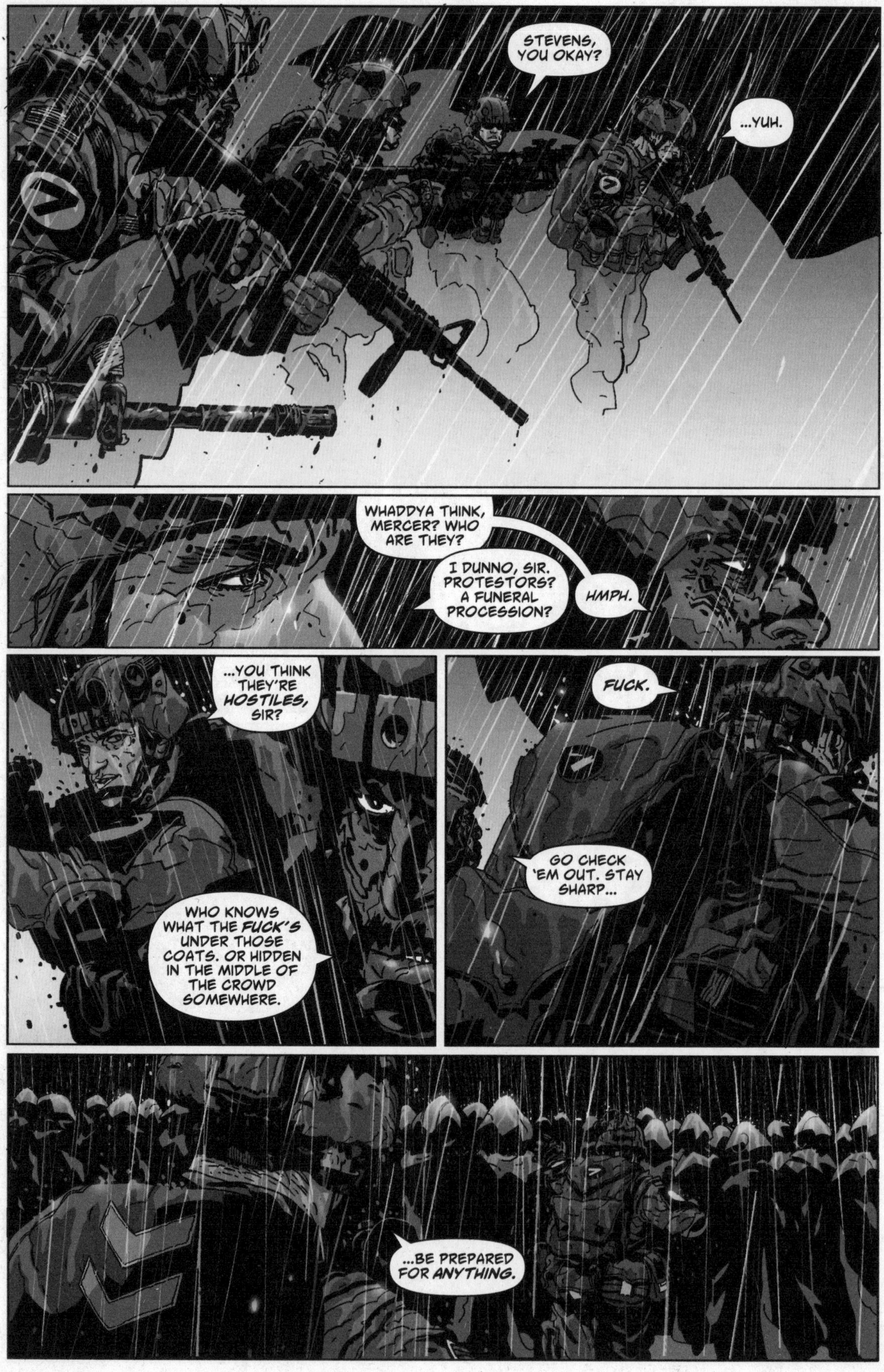
STEVENS, YOU OKAY?
...YUH.
WHADDYA THINK, MERCER? WHO ARE THEY?
I DUNNO, SIR. PROTESTORS? A FUNERAL PROCESSION?
HMPH.
...YOU THINK THEY'RE HOSTILES, SIR?
WHO KNOWS WHAT THE FUCK'S UNDER THOSE COATS. OR HIDDEN IN THE MIDDLE OF THE CROWD SOMEWHERE.
FUCK.
GO CHECK 'EM OUT. STAY SHARP...
...BE PREPARED FOR ANYTHING.

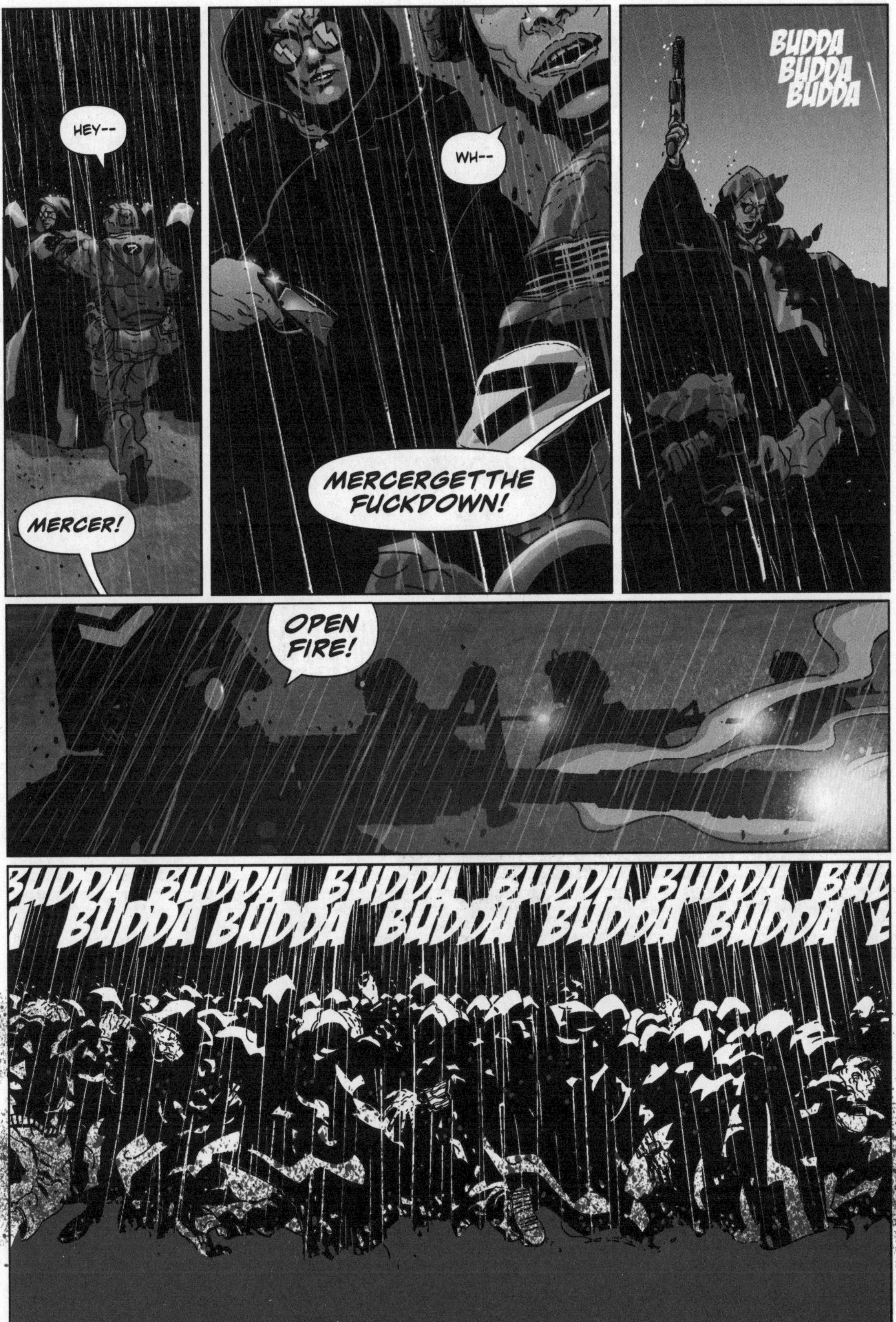
HEY--
MERCER!
WH--
MERCERGETTHE FUCKDOWN!
BUDDA BUDDA BUDDA
OPEN FIRE!
BUDDA BUDDA BUDDA BUDDA BUDDA BUDDA BUDDA BUDDA BUDDA BUDDA

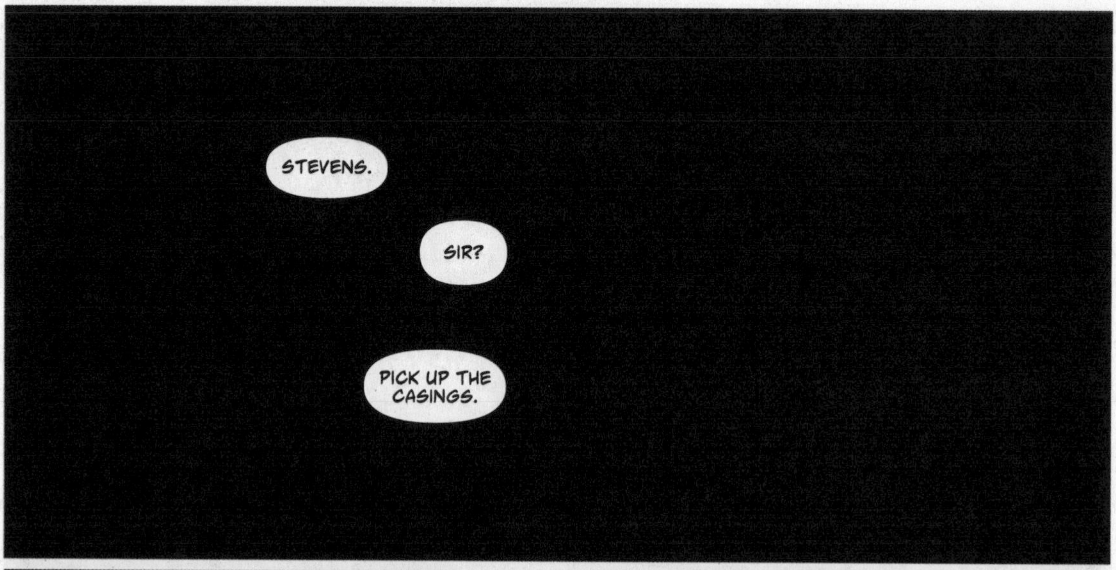
STEVENS.
SIR?
PICK UP THE CASINGS.

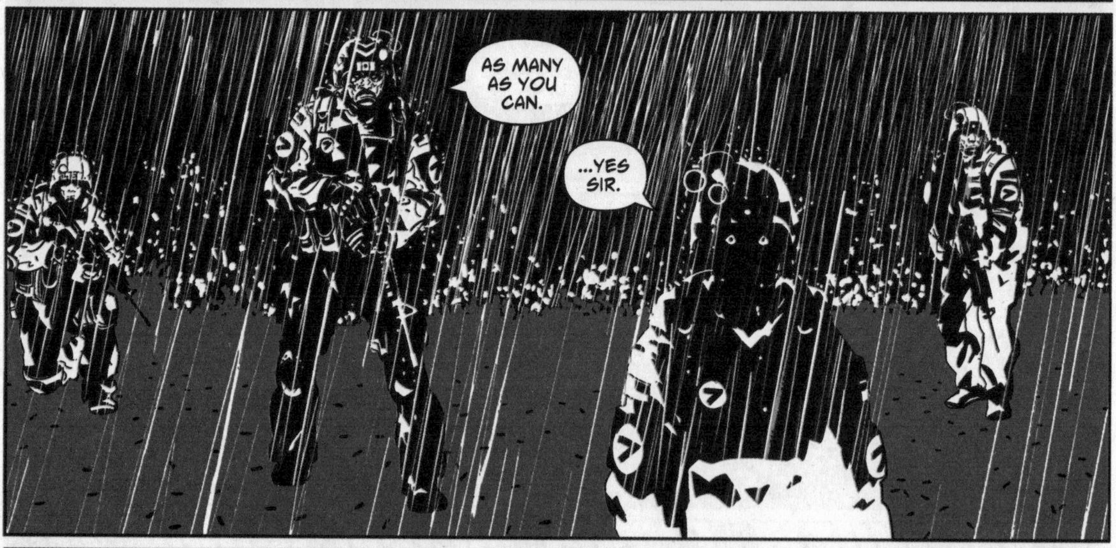
AS MANY AS YOU CAN.
...YES SIR.

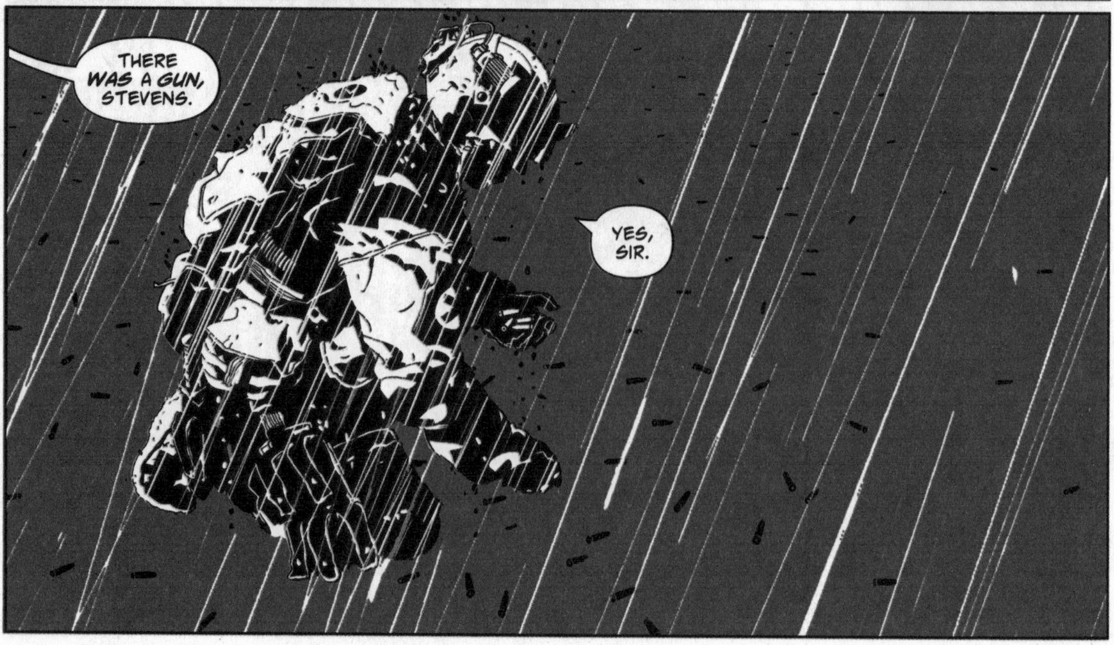
THERE WAS A GUN, STEVENS.
YES, SIR.

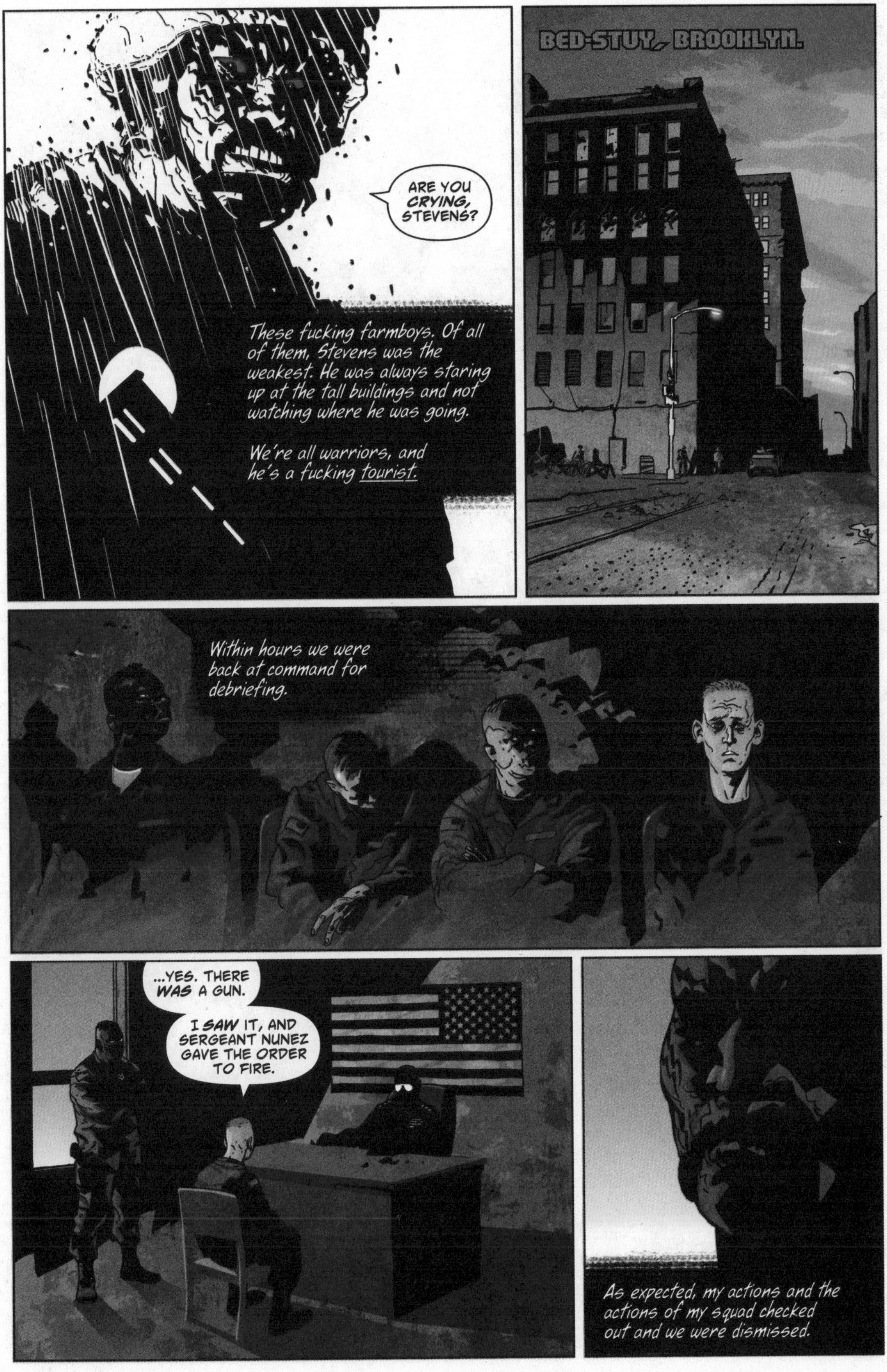
ARE YOU CRYING, STEVENS?
These fucking farmboys. Of all of them, Stevens was the weakest. He was always staring up at the tall buildings and not watching where he was going.
We're all warriors, and he's a fucking tourist.
BED-STUY, BROOKLYN.
Within hours we were back at command for debriefing.
...YES. THERE WAS A GUN.
I SAW IT, AND SERGEANT NUNEZ GAVE THE ORDER TO FIRE.
As expected, my actions and the actions of my squad checked out and we were dismissed.

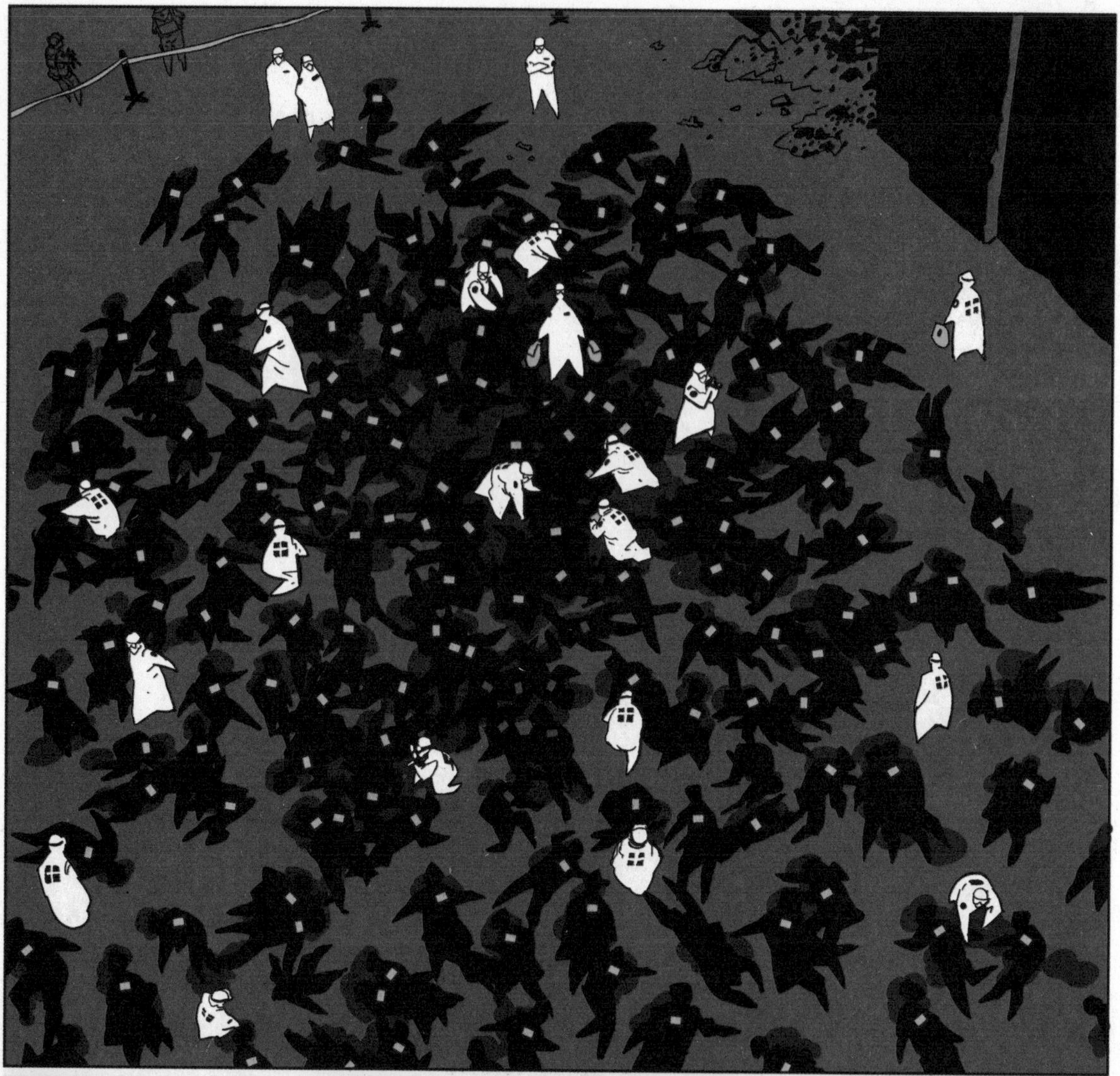

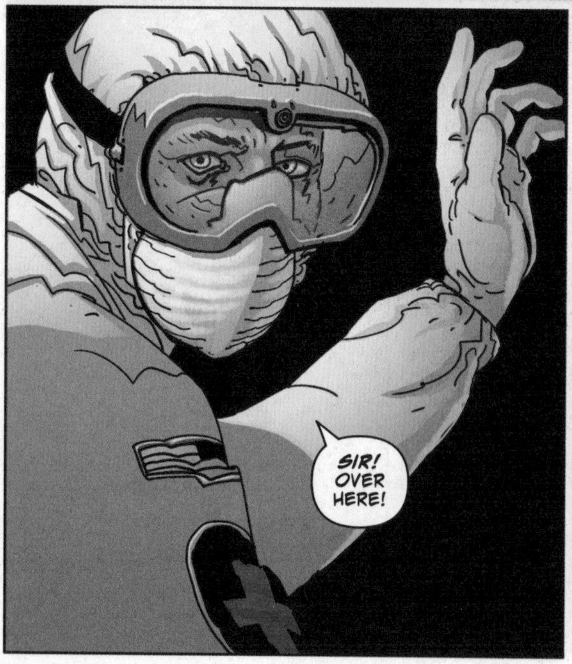
SIR! OVER HERE!

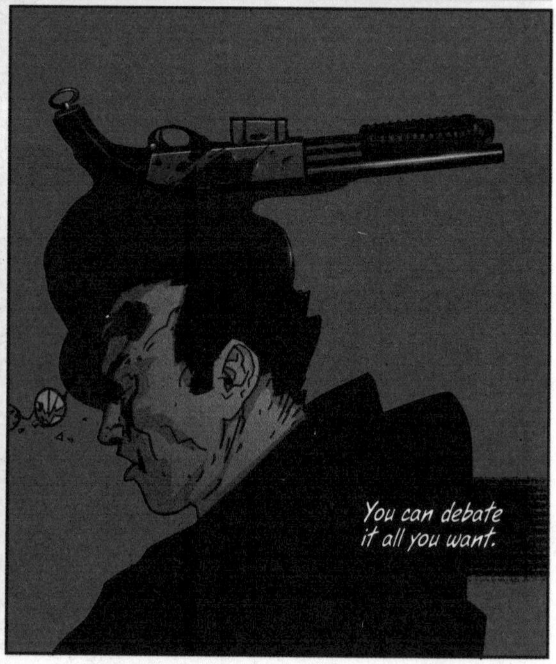
You can debate it all you want.

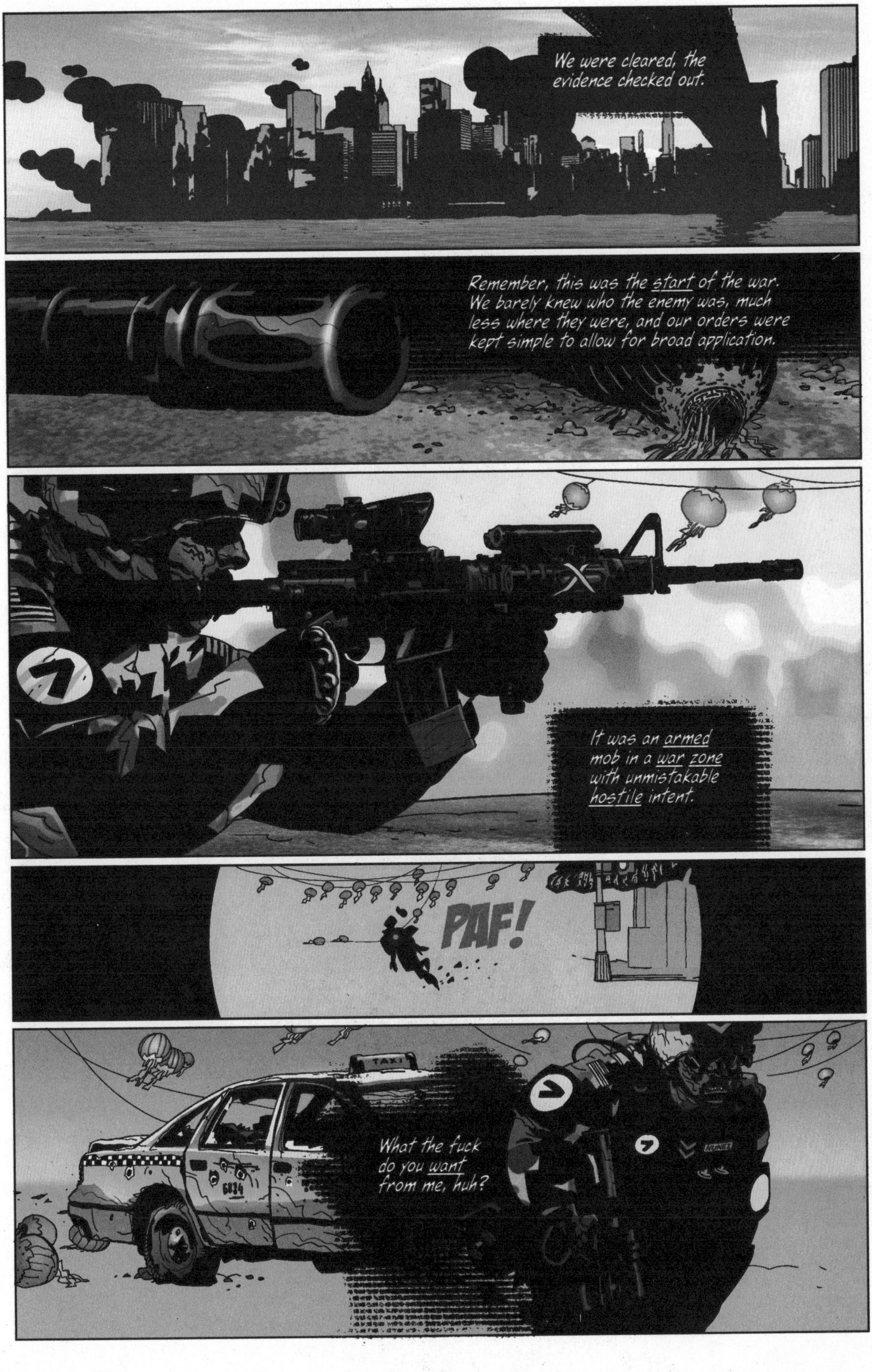
We were cleared, the evidence checked out.
Remember, this was the start of the war. We barely knew who the enemy was, much less where they were, and our orders were kept simple to allow for broad application.
It was an armed mob in a war zone with unmistakable hostile intent.
PAF!
TAXI
What the fuck do you want from me, huh?

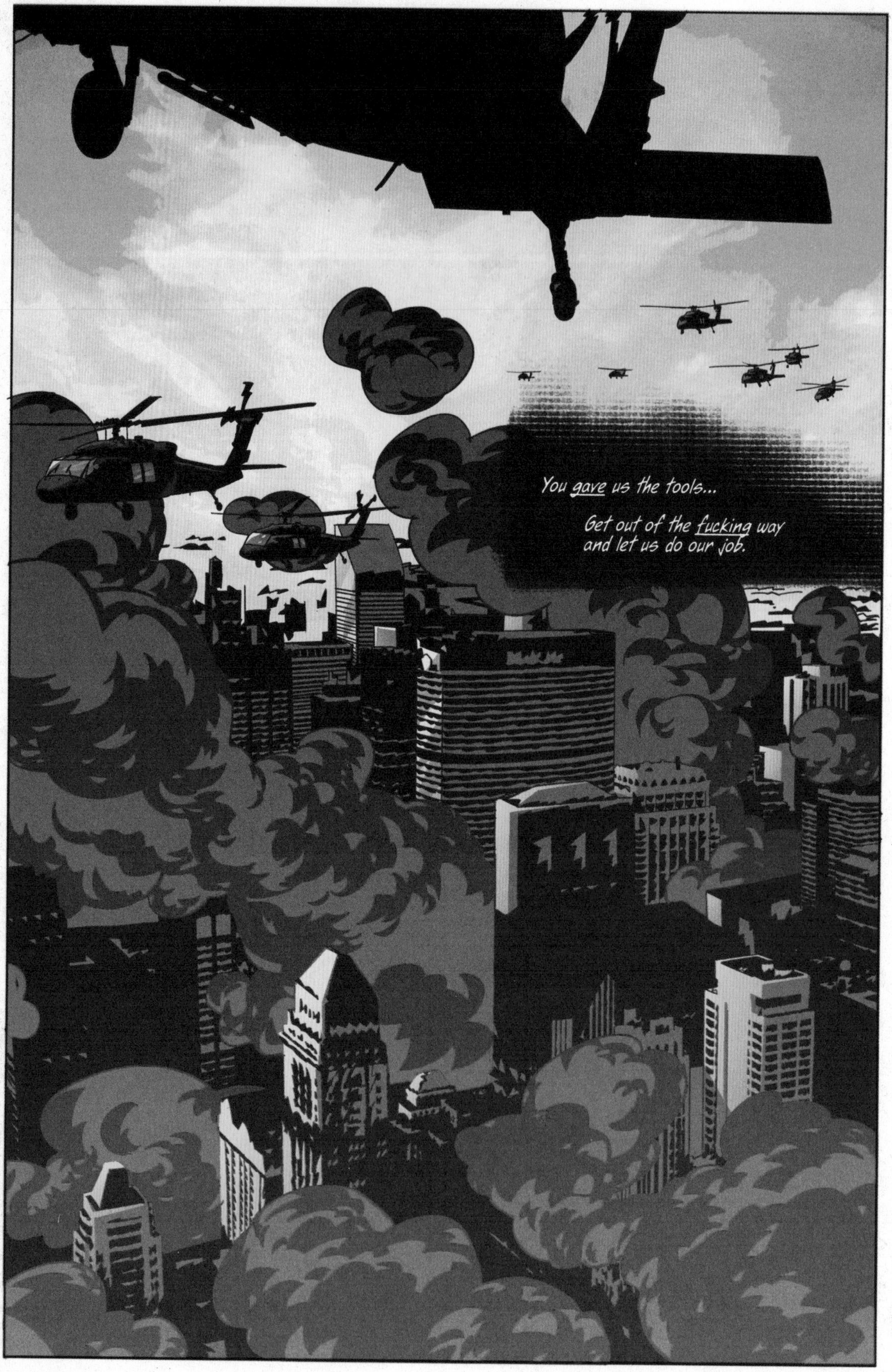
You gave us the tools...
Get out of the fucking way and let us do our job.

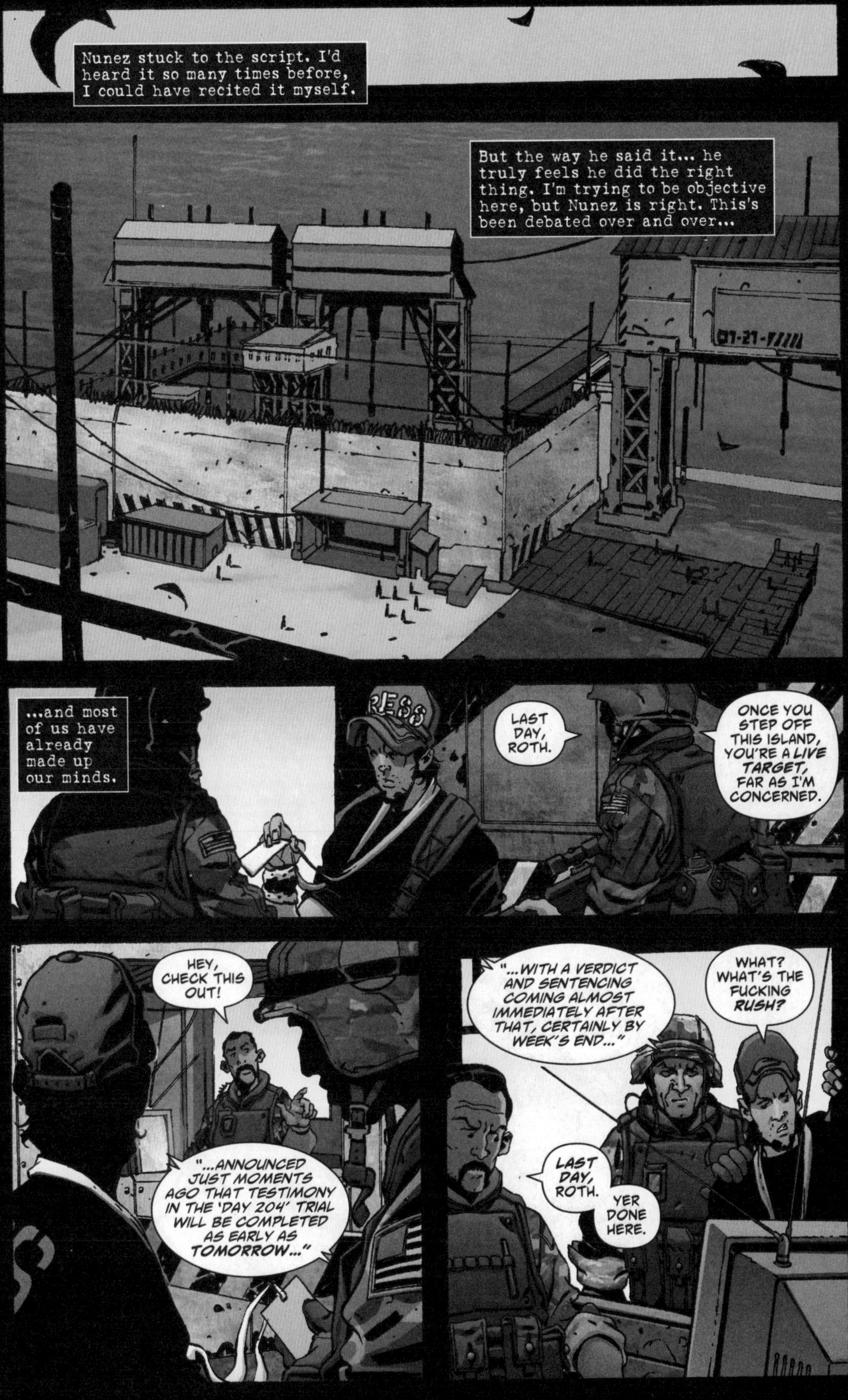

Nunez stuck to the script. I'd heard it so many times before, I could have recited it myself.
But the way he said it... he truly feels he did the right thing. I'm trying to be objective here, but Nunez is right. This's been debated over and over...
07-21-
...and most of us have already made up our minds.
LAST DAY, ROTH.
ONCE YOU STEP OFF THIS ISLAND, YOU'RE A *LIVE TARGET,* FAR AS I'M CONCERNED.
HEY, CHECK THIS OUT!
"...ANNOUNCED JUST MOMENTS AGO THAT TESTIMONY IN THE 'DAY 204' TRIAL WILL BE COMPLETED AS EARLY AS **TOMORROW...**"
"...WITH A VERDICT AND SENTENCING COMING ALMOST IMMEDIATELY AFTER THAT, CERTAINLY BY WEEK'S END..."
WHAT? WHAT'S THE FUCKING *RUSH?*
LAST DAY, ROTH.
YER DONE HERE.

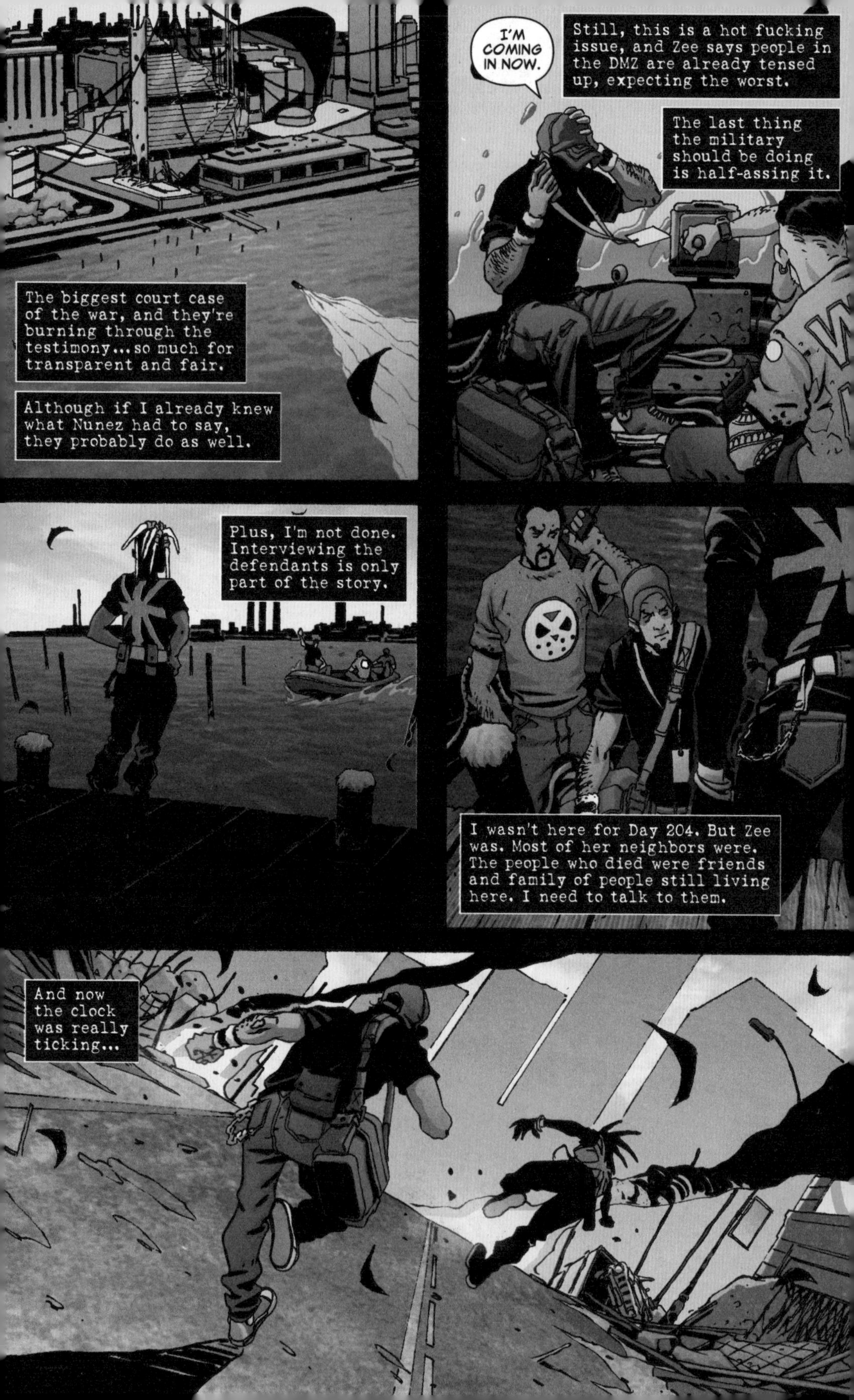
The biggest court case of the war, and they're burning through the testimony...so much for transparent and fair.
Although if I already knew what Nunez had to say, they probably do as well.
I'M COMING IN NOW.
Still, this is a hot fucking issue, and Zee says people in the DMZ are already tensed up, expecting the worst.
The last thing the military should be doing is half-assing it.
Plus, I'm not done. Interviewing the defendants is only part of the story.
I wasn't here for Day 204. But Zee was. Most of her neighbors were. The people who died were friends and family of people still living here. I need to talk to them.
And now the clock was really ticking...

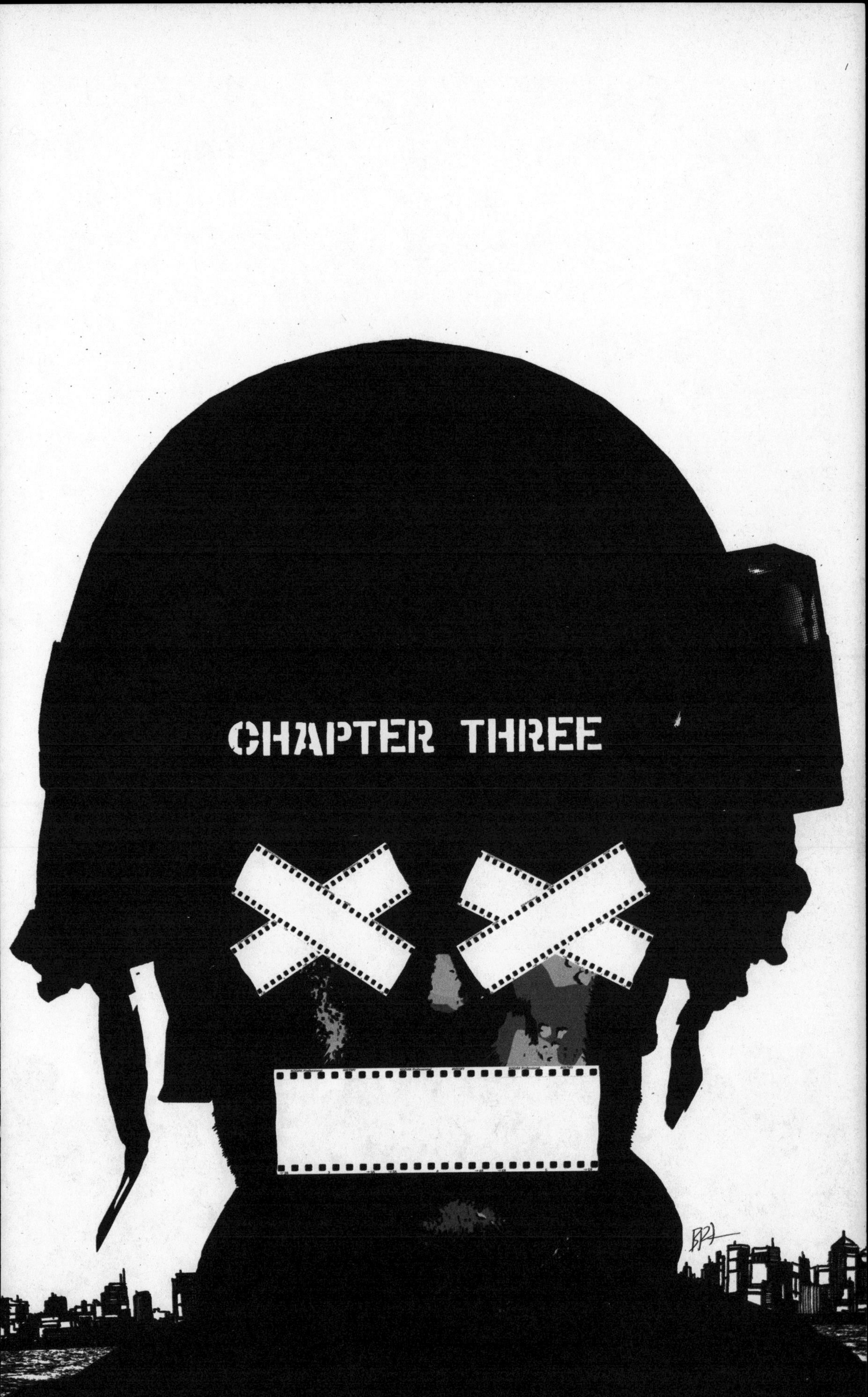
CHAPTER THREE

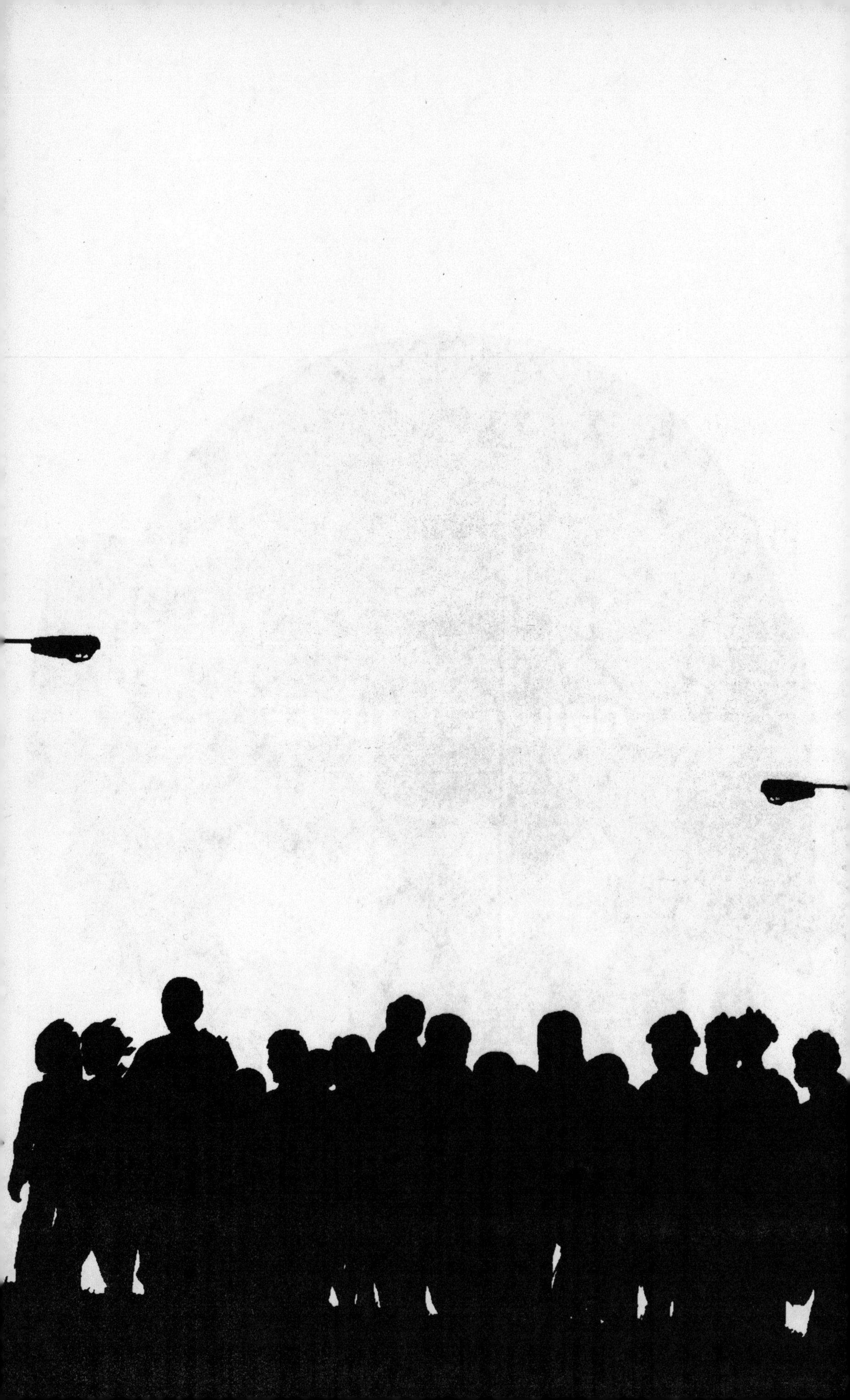

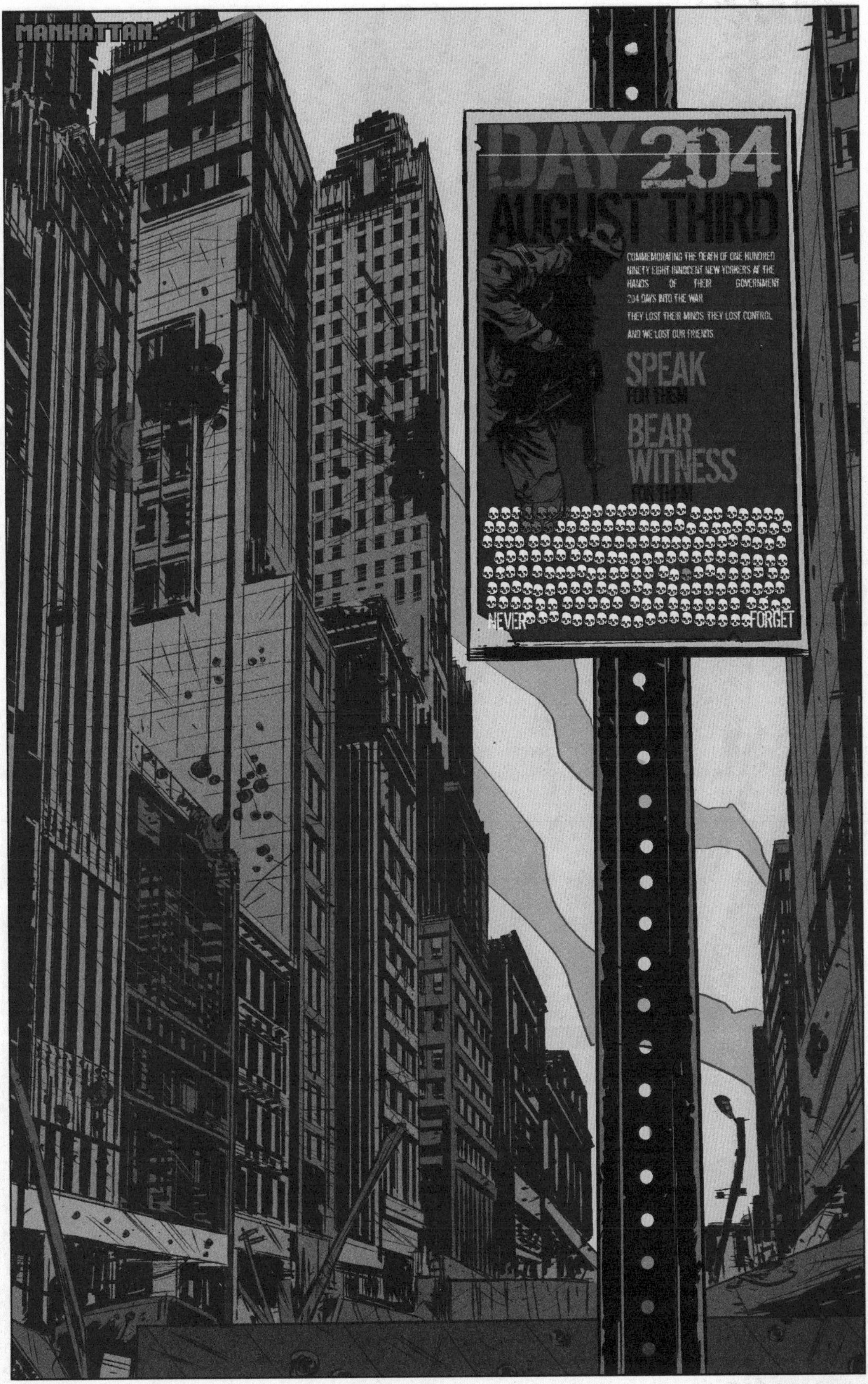
MANHATTAN.
DAY 204
AUGUST THIRD
COMMEMORATING THE DEATH OF ONE HUNDRED NINETY EIGHT INNOCENT NEW YORKERS AT THE HANDS OF THEIR GOVERNMENT 204 DAYS INTO THE WAR.
THEY LOST THEIR MINDS. THEY LOST CONTROL.
AND WE LOST OUR FRIENDS.
SPEAK
FOR THEM
BEAR WITNESS
FOR THEM
NEVER FORGET

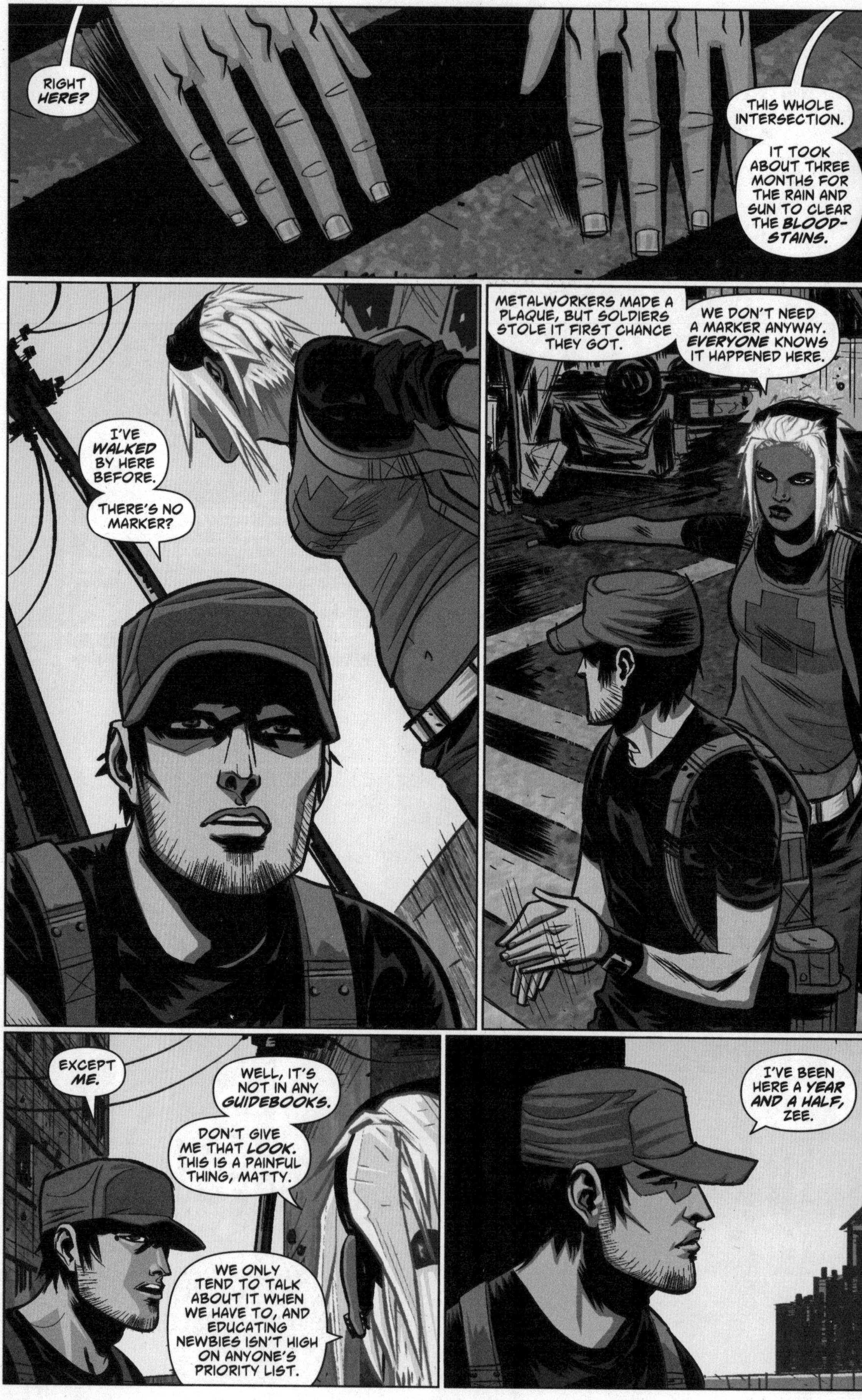
RIGHT HERE?
THIS WHOLE INTERSECTION.
IT TOOK ABOUT THREE MONTHS FOR THE RAIN AND SUN TO CLEAR THE BLOOD-STAINS.
I'VE WALKED BY HERE BEFORE.
THERE'S NO MARKER?
METALWORKERS MADE A PLAQUE, BUT SOLDIERS STOLE IT FIRST CHANCE THEY GOT.
WE DON'T NEED A MARKER ANYWAY. EVERYONE KNOWS IT HAPPENED HERE.
EXCEPT ME.
WELL, IT'S NOT IN ANY GUIDEBOOKS.
DON'T GIVE ME THAT LOOK. THIS IS A PAINFUL THING, MATTY.
WE ONLY TEND TO TALK ABOUT IT WHEN WE HAVE TO, AND EDUCATING NEWBIES ISN'T HIGH ON ANYONE'S PRIORITY LIST.
I'VE BEEN HERE A YEAR AND A HALF, ZEE.

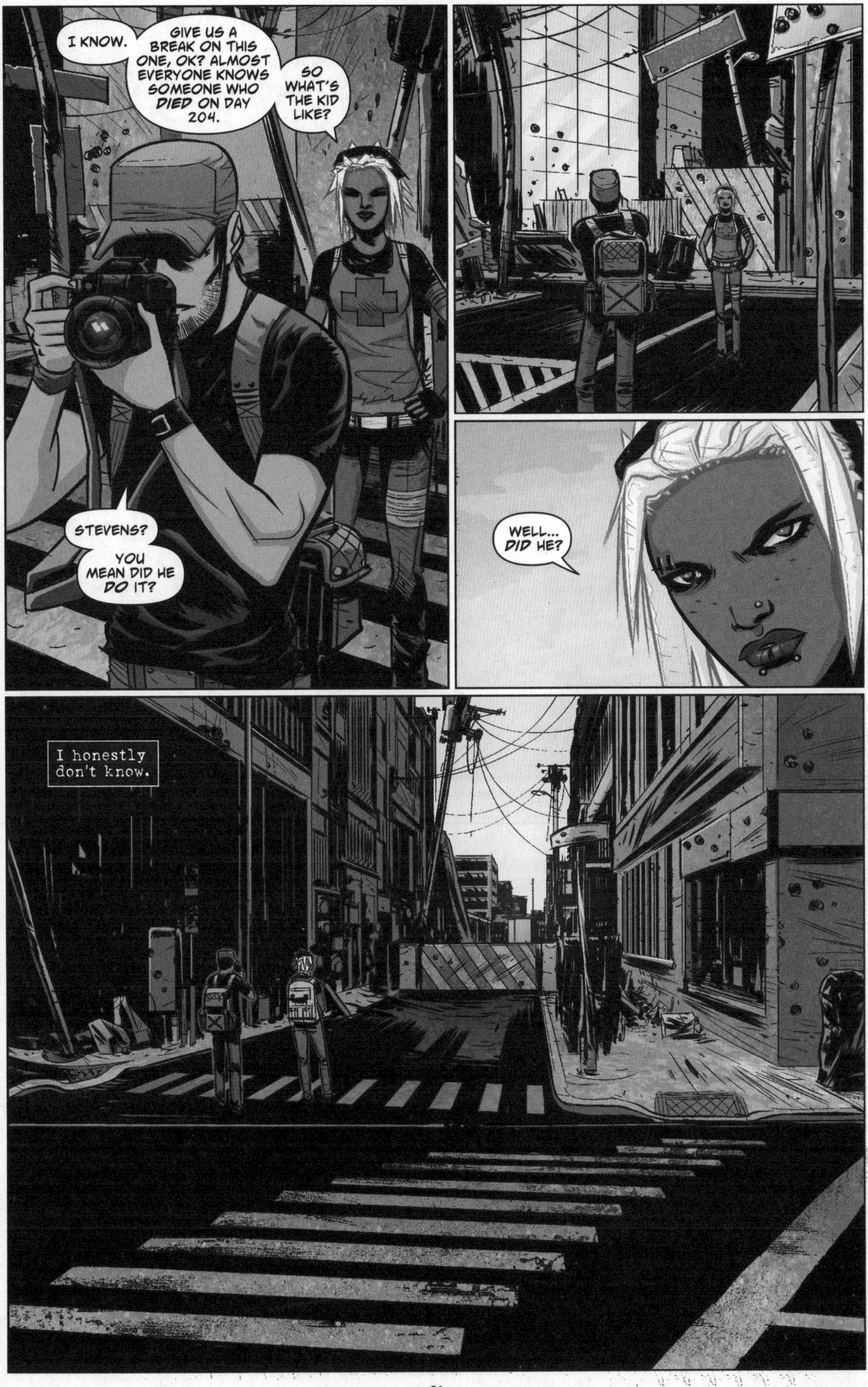
I KNOW.
GIVE US A BREAK ON THIS ONE, OK? ALMOST EVERYONE KNOWS SOMEONE WHO DIED ON DAY 204.
SO WHAT'S THE KID LIKE?
STEVENS?
YOU MEAN DID HE DO IT?
WELL... DID HE?
I honestly don't know.

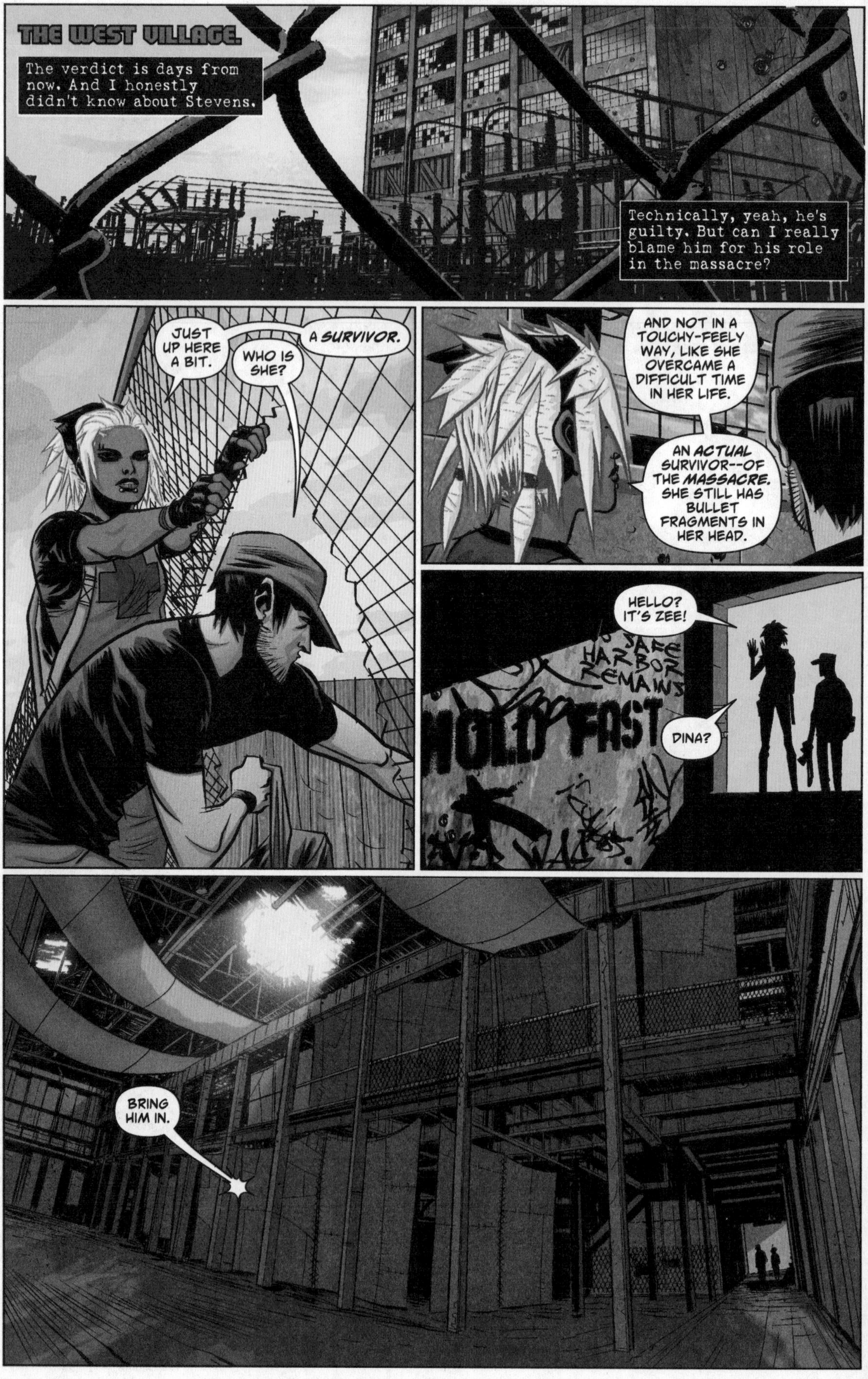
THE WEST VILLAGE.
The verdict is days from now. And I honestly didn't know about Stevens.
Technically, yeah, he's guilty. But can I really blame him for his role in the massacre?
JUST UP HERE A BIT.
WHO IS SHE?
A SURVIVOR.
AND NOT IN A TOUCHY-FEELY WAY, LIKE SHE OVERCAME A DIFFICULT TIME IN HER LIFE.
AN ACTUAL SURVIVOR--OF THE MASSACRE. SHE STILL HAS BULLET FRAGMENTS IN HER HEAD.
HELLO? IT'S ZEE!
SAFE HARBOR REMAINS
HOLD FAST
DINA?
BRING HIM IN.

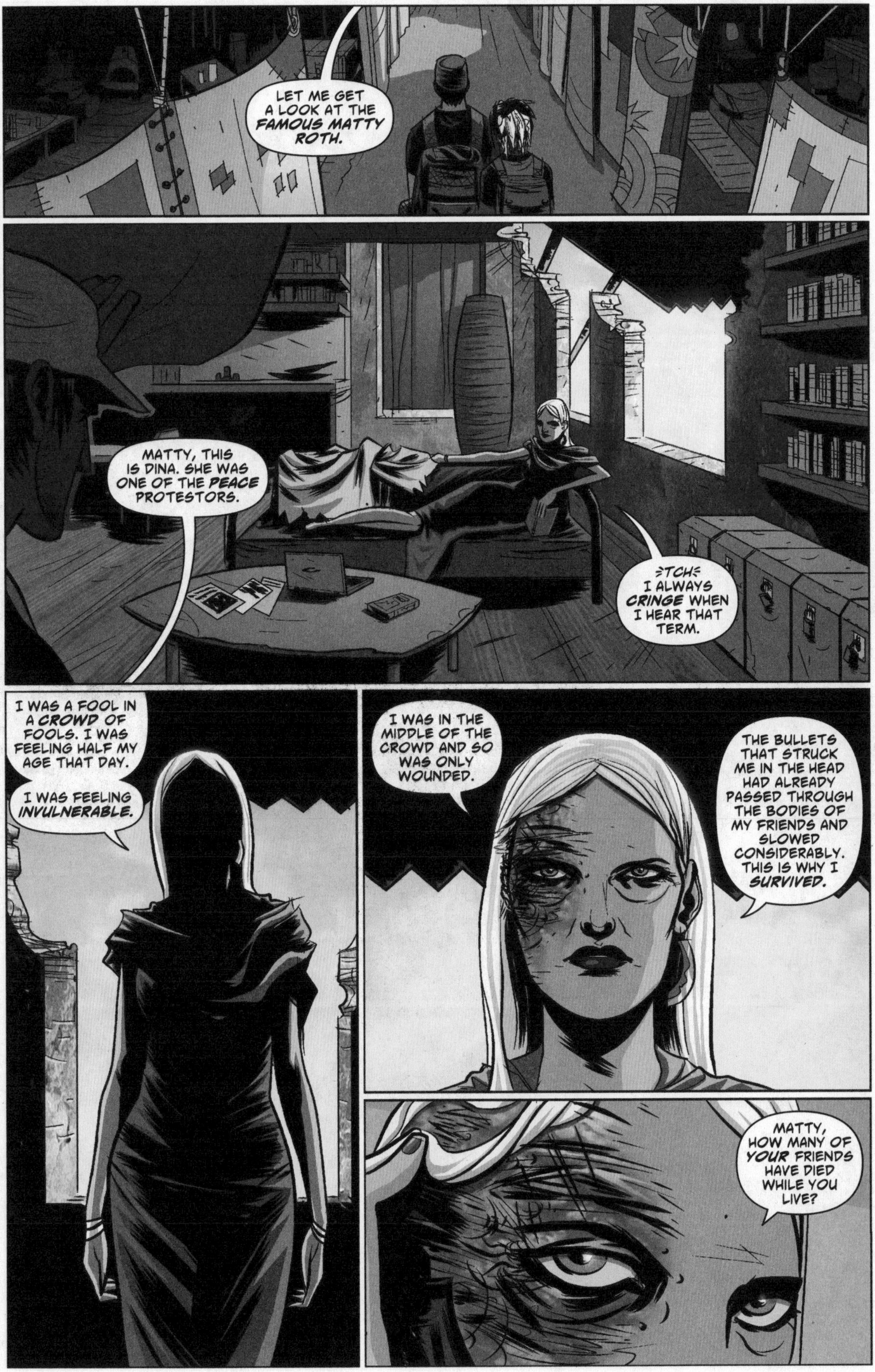
LET ME GET A LOOK AT THE FAMOUS MATTY ROTH.
MATTY, THIS IS DINA. SHE WAS ONE OF THE PEACE PROTESTORS.
TCH I ALWAYS CRINGE WHEN I HEAR THAT TERM.
I WAS A FOOL IN A CROWD OF FOOLS. I WAS FEELING HALF MY AGE THAT DAY.
I WAS FEELING INVULNERABLE.
I WAS IN THE MIDDLE OF THE CROWD AND SO WAS ONLY WOUNDED.
THE BULLETS THAT STRUCK ME IN THE HEAD HAD ALREADY PASSED THROUGH THE BODIES OF MY FRIENDS AND SLOWED CONSIDERABLY. THIS IS WHY I SURVIVED.
MATTY, HOW MANY OF YOUR FRIENDS HAVE DIED WHILE YOU LIVE?

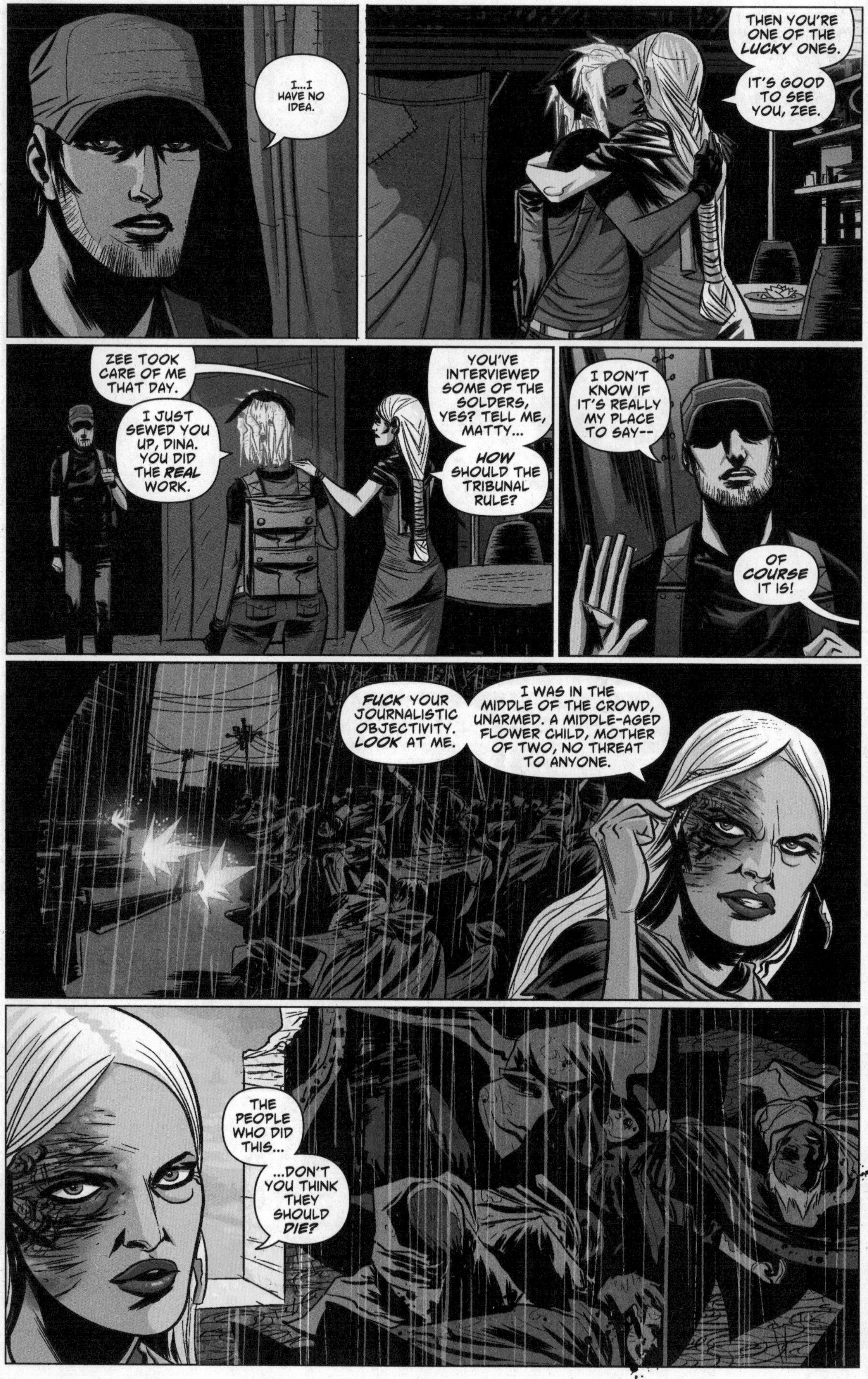
I...I HAVE NO IDEA.
THEN YOU'RE ONE OF THE LUCKY ONES.
IT'S GOOD TO SEE YOU, ZEE.
ZEE TOOK CARE OF ME THAT DAY.
I JUST SEWED YOU UP, DINA. YOU DID THE REAL WORK.
YOU'VE INTERVIEWED SOME OF THE SOLDERS, YES? TELL ME, MATTY...
HOW SHOULD THE TRIBUNAL RULE?
I DON'T KNOW IF IT'S REALLY MY PLACE TO SAY--
OF COURSE IT IS!
FUCK YOUR JOURNALISTIC OBJECTIVITY. LOOK AT ME.
I WAS IN THE MIDDLE OF THE CROWD, UNARMED. A MIDDLE-AGED FLOWER CHILD, MOTHER OF TWO, NO THREAT TO ANYONE.
THE PEOPLE WHO DID THIS...
...DON'T YOU THINK THEY SHOULD DIE?

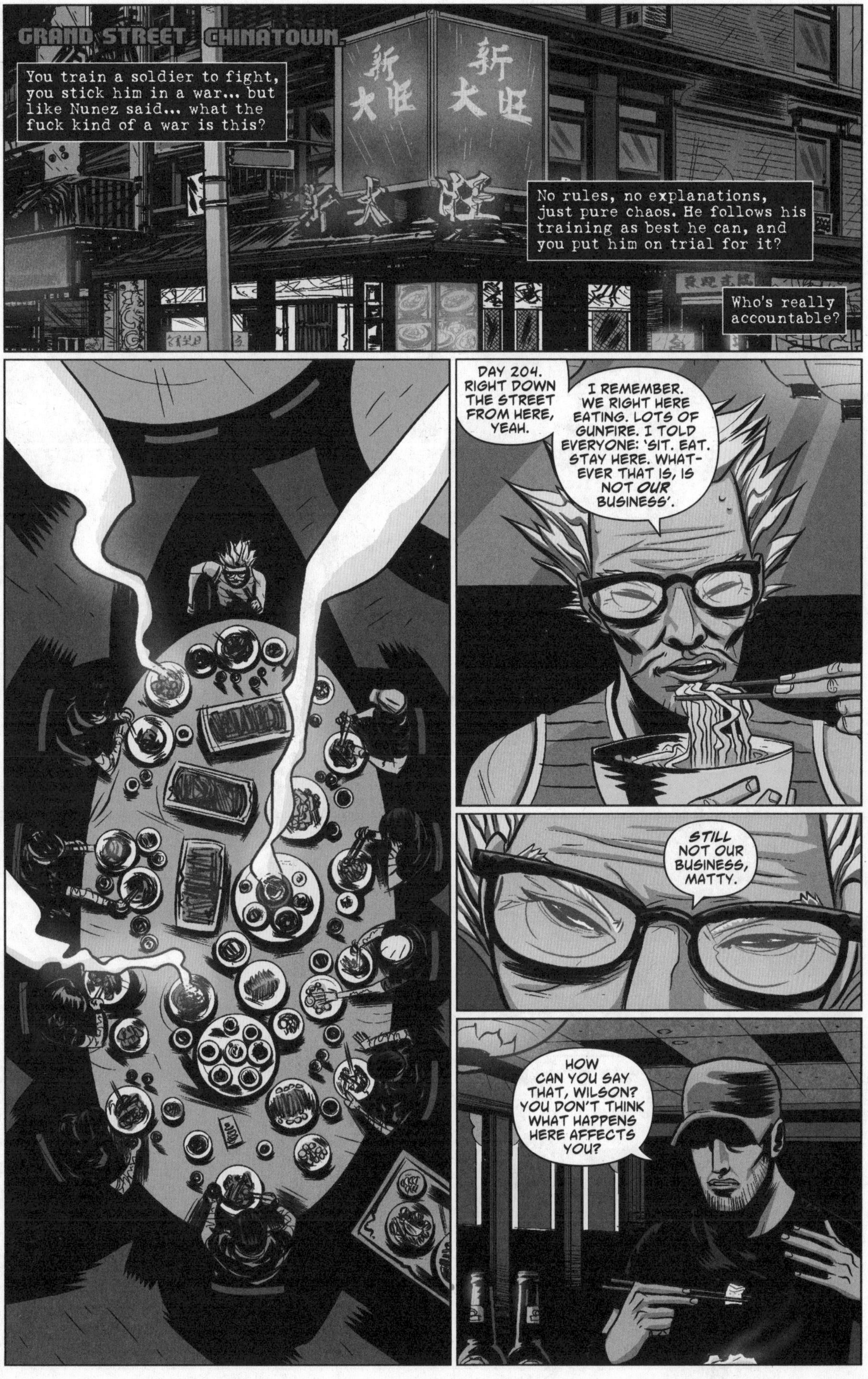
GRAND STREET CHINATOWN.
You train a soldier to fight, you stick him in a war... but like Nunez said... what the fuck kind of a war is this?
No rules, no explanations, just pure chaos. He follows his training as best he can, and you put him on trial for it?
Who's really accountable?
DAY 204. RIGHT DOWN THE STREET FROM HERE, YEAH.
I REMEMBER. WE RIGHT HERE EATING. LOTS OF GUNFIRE. I TOLD EVERYONE: 'SIT. EAT. STAY HERE. WHATEVER THAT IS, IS NOT OUR BUSINESS'.
STILL NOT OUR BUSINESS, MATTY.
HOW CAN YOU SAY THAT, WILSON? YOU DON'T THINK WHAT HAPPENS HERE AFFECTS YOU?

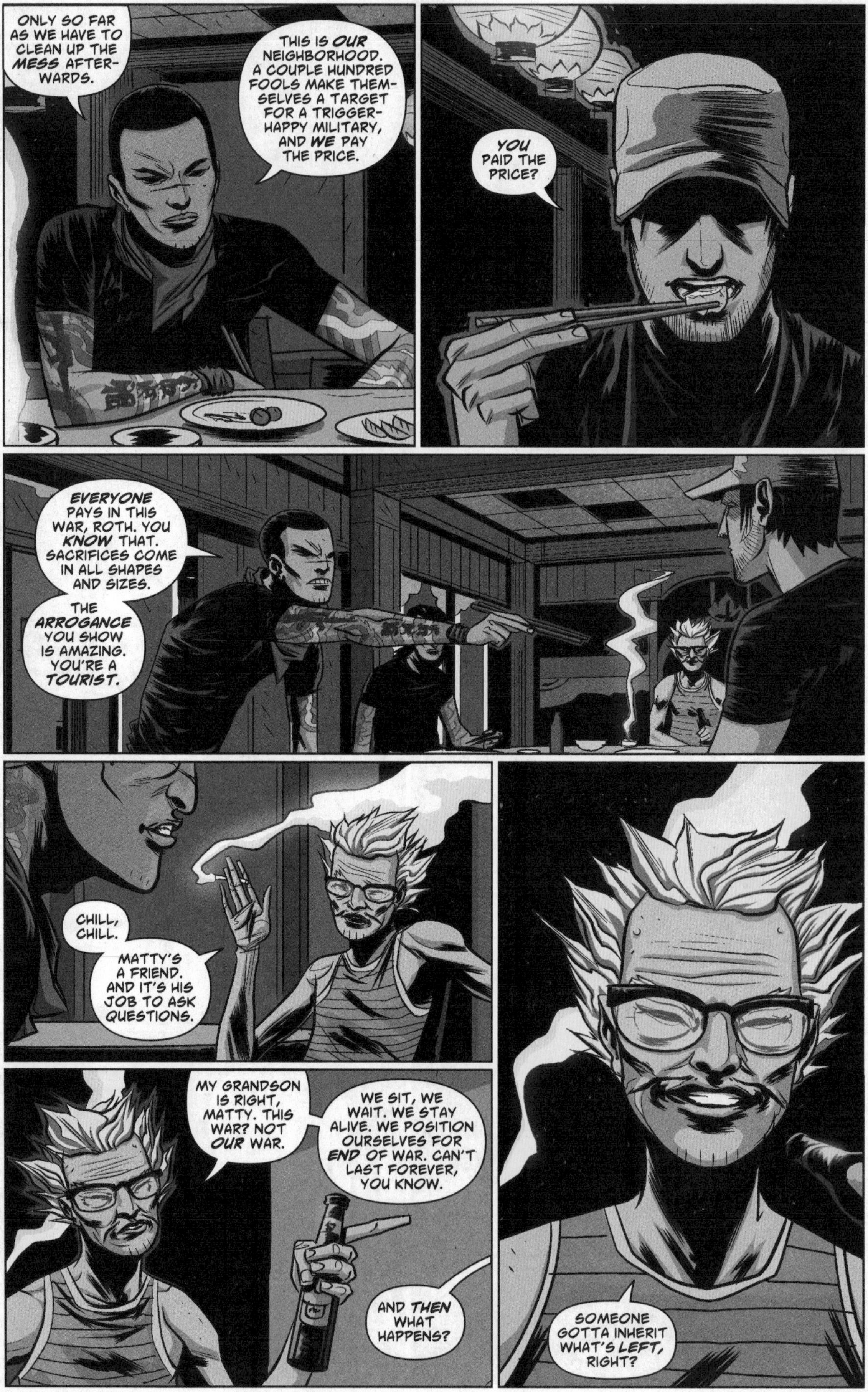

ONLY SO FAR AS WE HAVE TO CLEAN UP THE MESS AFTER-WARDS.
THIS IS OUR NEIGHBORHOOD. A COUPLE HUNDRED FOOLS MAKE THEM-SELVES A TARGET FOR A TRIGGER-HAPPY MILITARY, AND WE PAY THE PRICE.
YOU PAID THE PRICE?
EVERYONE PAYS IN THIS WAR, ROTH. YOU KNOW THAT. SACRIFICES COME IN ALL SHAPES AND SIZES.
THE ARROGANCE YOU SHOW IS AMAZING. YOU'RE A TOURIST.
CHILL, CHILL.
MATTY'S A FRIEND. AND IT'S HIS JOB TO ASK QUESTIONS.
MY GRANDSON IS RIGHT, MATTY. THIS WAR? NOT OUR WAR.
WE SIT, WE WAIT. WE STAY ALIVE. WE POSITION OURSELVES FOR END OF WAR. CAN'T LAST FOREVER, YOU KNOW.
AND THEN WHAT HAPPENS?
SOMEONE GOTTA INHERIT WHAT'S LEFT, RIGHT?

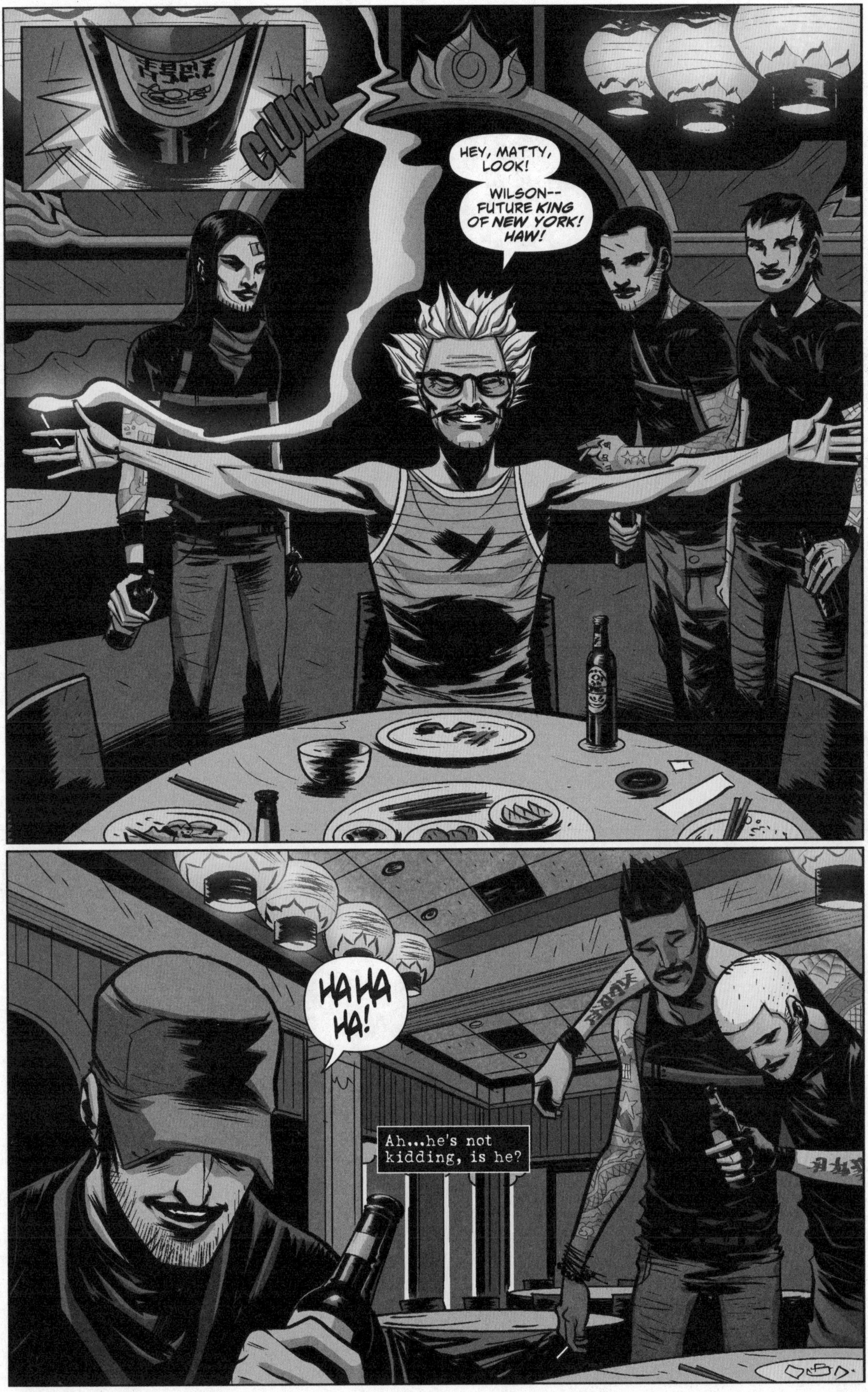
CLUNK
HEY, MATTY, LOOK!
WILSON-- FUTURE KING OF NEW YORK! HAW!
HA HA HA!
Ah...he's not kidding, is he?

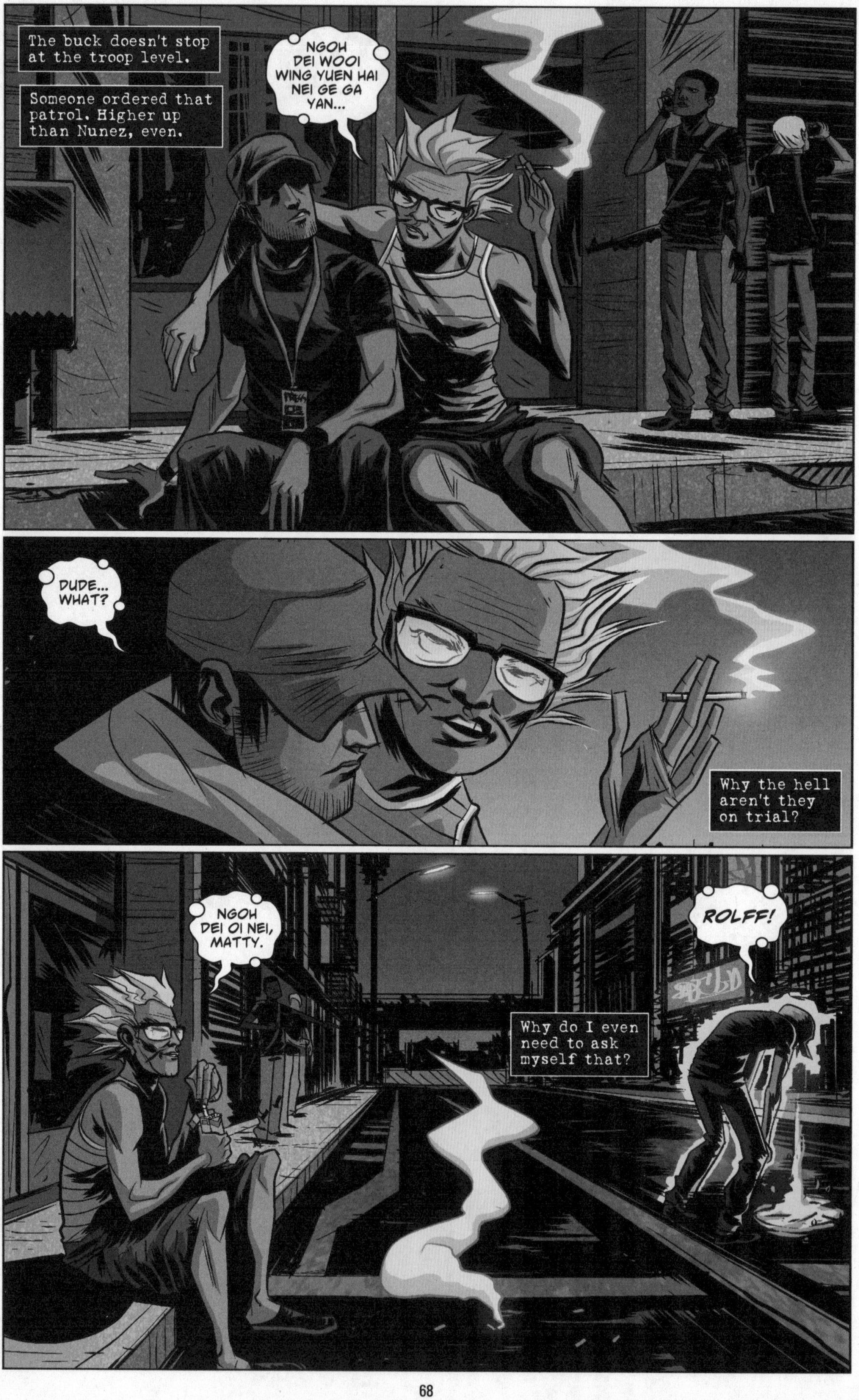

The buck doesn't stop at the troop level.
Someone ordered that patrol. Higher up than Nunez, even.
NGOH DEI WOOI WING YUEN HAI NEI GE GA YAN...
DUDE... WHAT?
Why the hell aren't they on trial?
NGOH DEI OI NEI, MATTY.
Why do I even need to ask myself that?
ROLFF!

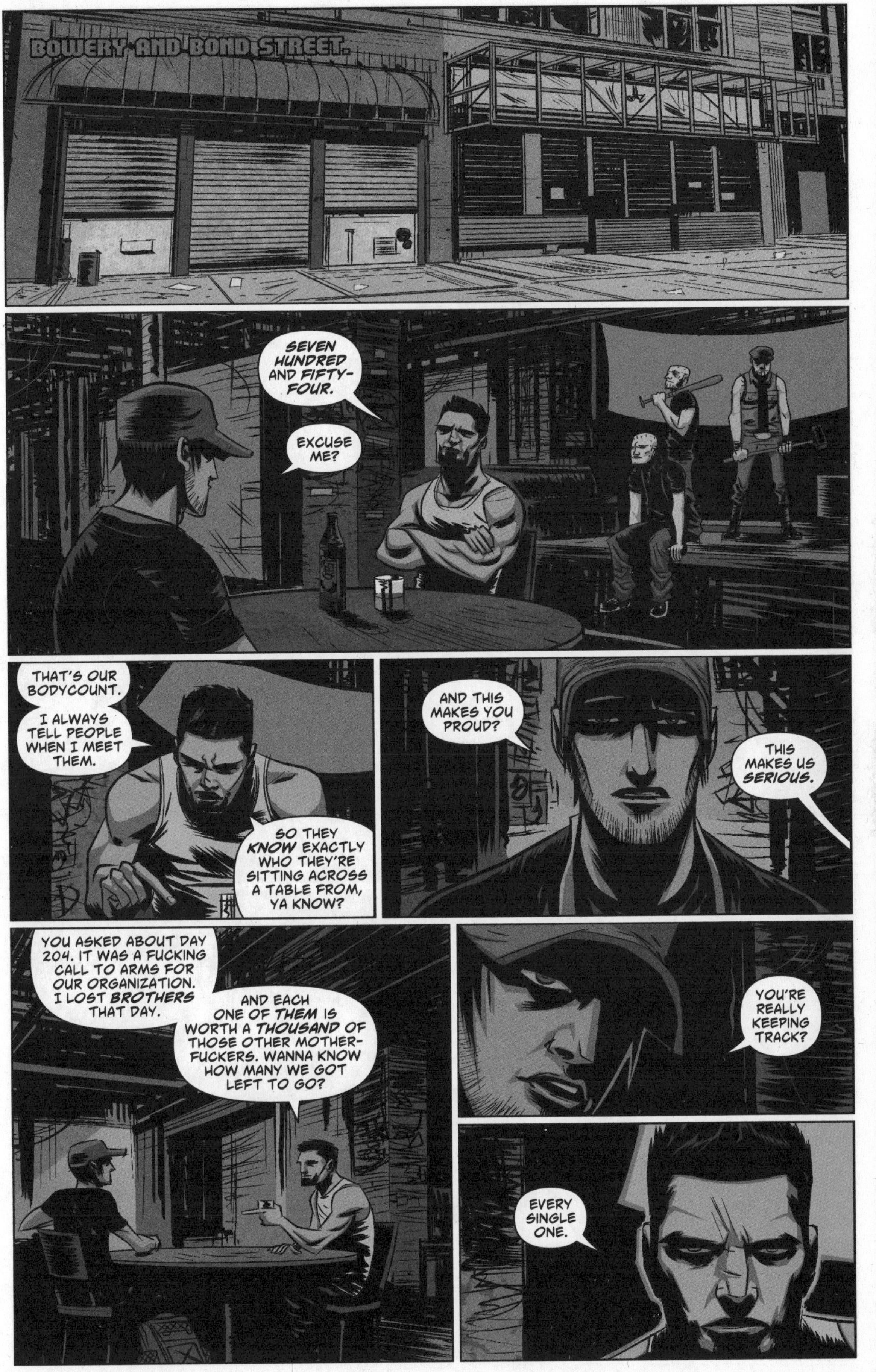
BOWERY AND BOND STREET.
SEVEN HUNDRED AND FIFTY-FOUR.
EXCUSE ME?
THAT'S OUR BODYCOUNT.
I ALWAYS TELL PEOPLE WHEN I MEET THEM.
SO THEY KNOW EXACTLY WHO THEY'RE SITTING ACROSS A TABLE FROM, YA KNOW?
AND THIS MAKES YOU PROUD?
THIS MAKES US SERIOUS.
YOU ASKED ABOUT DAY 204. IT WAS A FUCKING CALL TO ARMS FOR OUR ORGANIZATION. I LOST BROTHERS THAT DAY.
AND EACH ONE OF THEM IS WORTH A THOUSAND OF THOSE OTHER MOTHER-FUCKERS. WANNA KNOW HOW MANY WE GOT LEFT TO GO?
YOU'RE REALLY KEEPING TRACK?
EVERY SINGLE ONE.

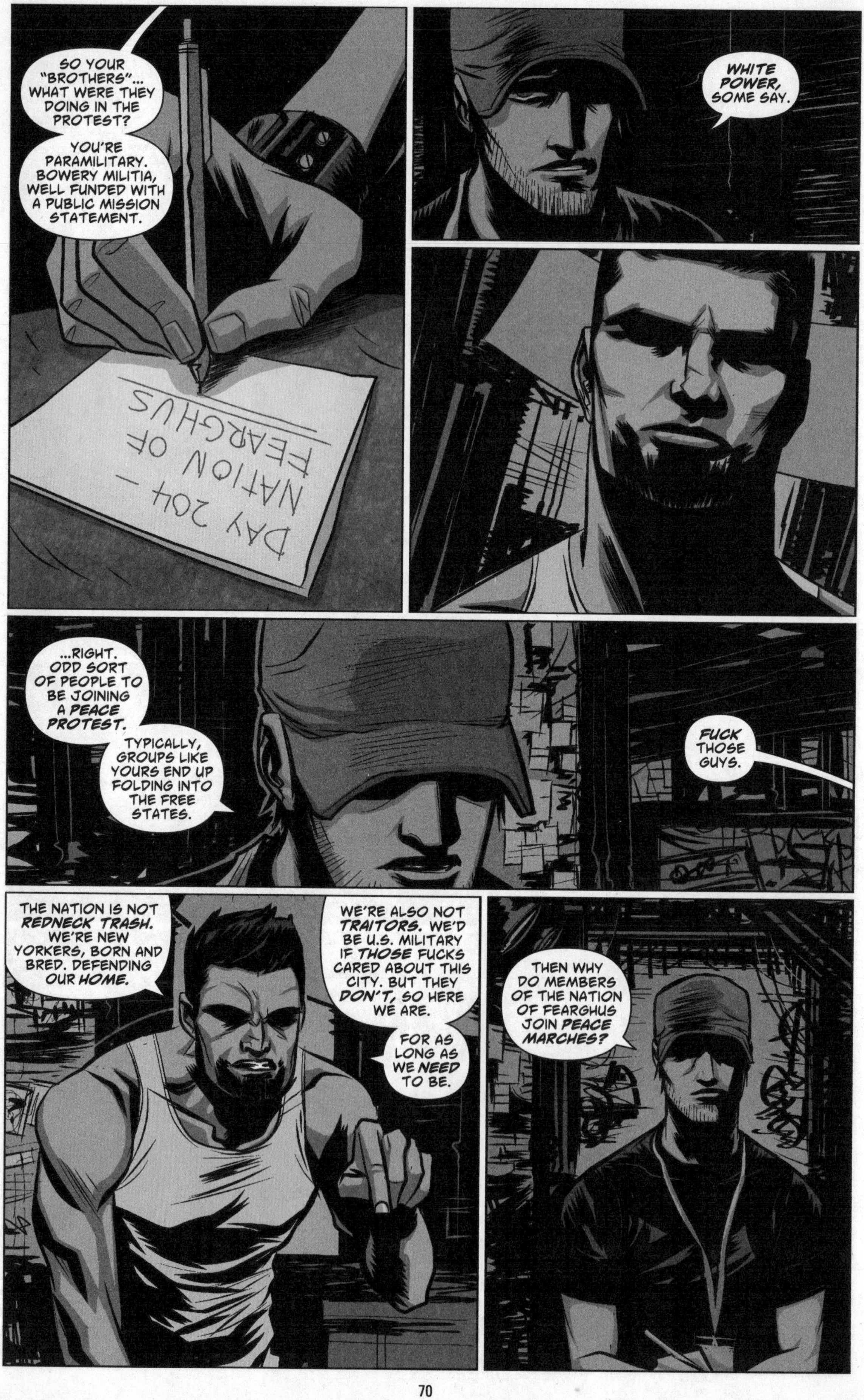
SO YOUR "BROTHERS"... WHAT WERE THEY DOING IN THE PROTEST?
YOU'RE PARAMILITARY. BOWERY MILITIA, WELL FUNDED WITH A PUBLIC MISSION STATEMENT.
DAY 204 — NATION OF FEARGHUS
WHITE POWER, SOME SAY.
...RIGHT. ODD SORT OF PEOPLE TO BE JOINING A PEACE PROTEST.
TYPICALLY, GROUPS LIKE YOURS END UP FOLDING INTO THE FREE STATES.
FUCK THOSE GUYS.
THE NATION IS NOT REDNECK TRASH. WE'RE NEW YORKERS, BORN AND BRED. DEFENDING OUR HOME.
WE'RE ALSO NOT TRAITORS. WE'D BE U.S. MILITARY IF THOSE FUCKS CARED ABOUT THIS CITY. BUT THEY DON'T, SO HERE WE ARE.
FOR AS LONG AS WE NEED TO BE.
THEN WHY DO MEMBERS OF THE NATION OF FEARGHUS JOIN PEACE MARCHES?

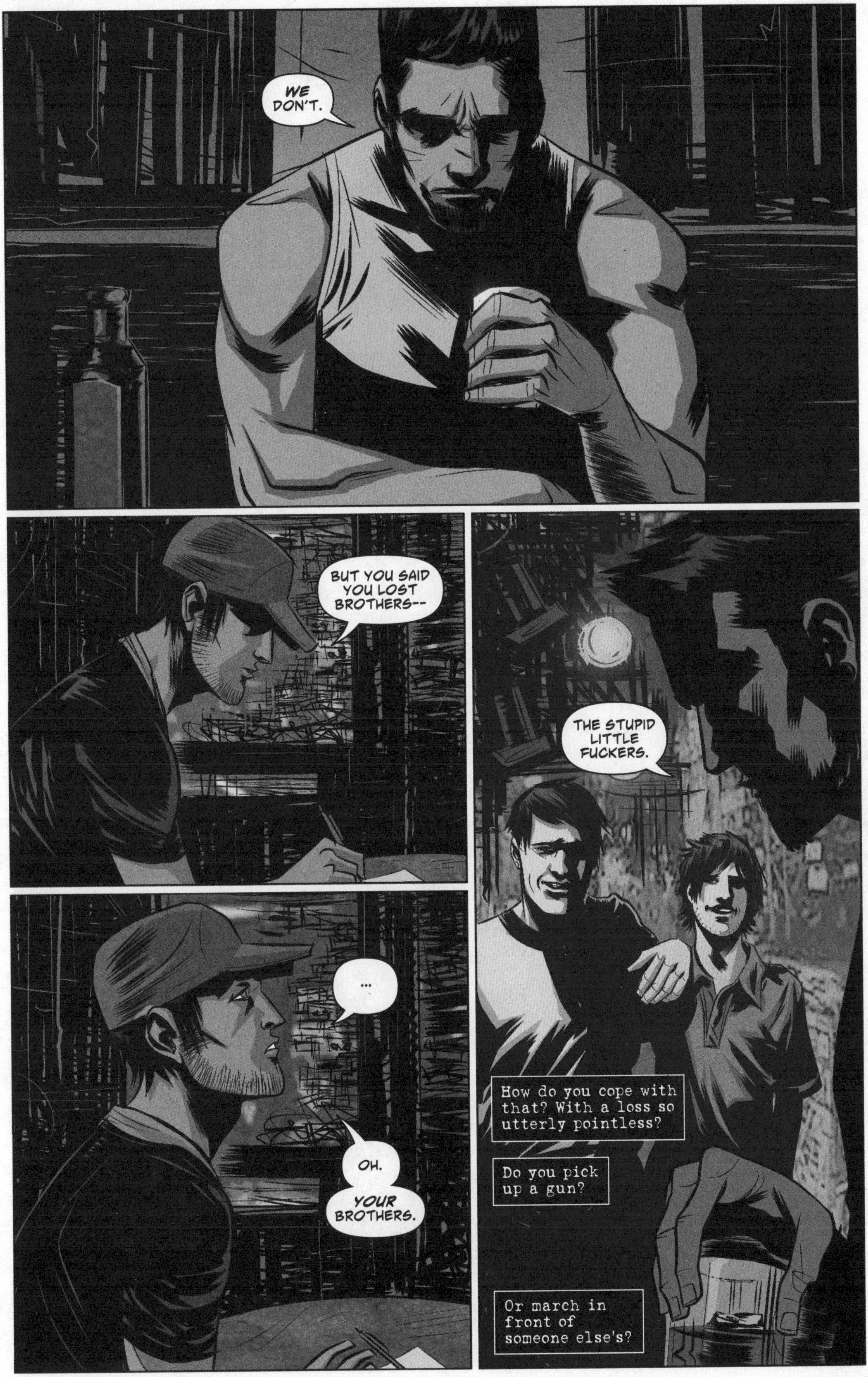
WE DON'T.
BUT YOU SAID YOU LOST BROTHERS--
THE STUPID LITTLE FUCKERS.
...
OH.
YOUR BROTHERS.
How do you cope with that? With a loss so utterly pointless?
Do you pick up a gun?
Or march in front of someone else's?

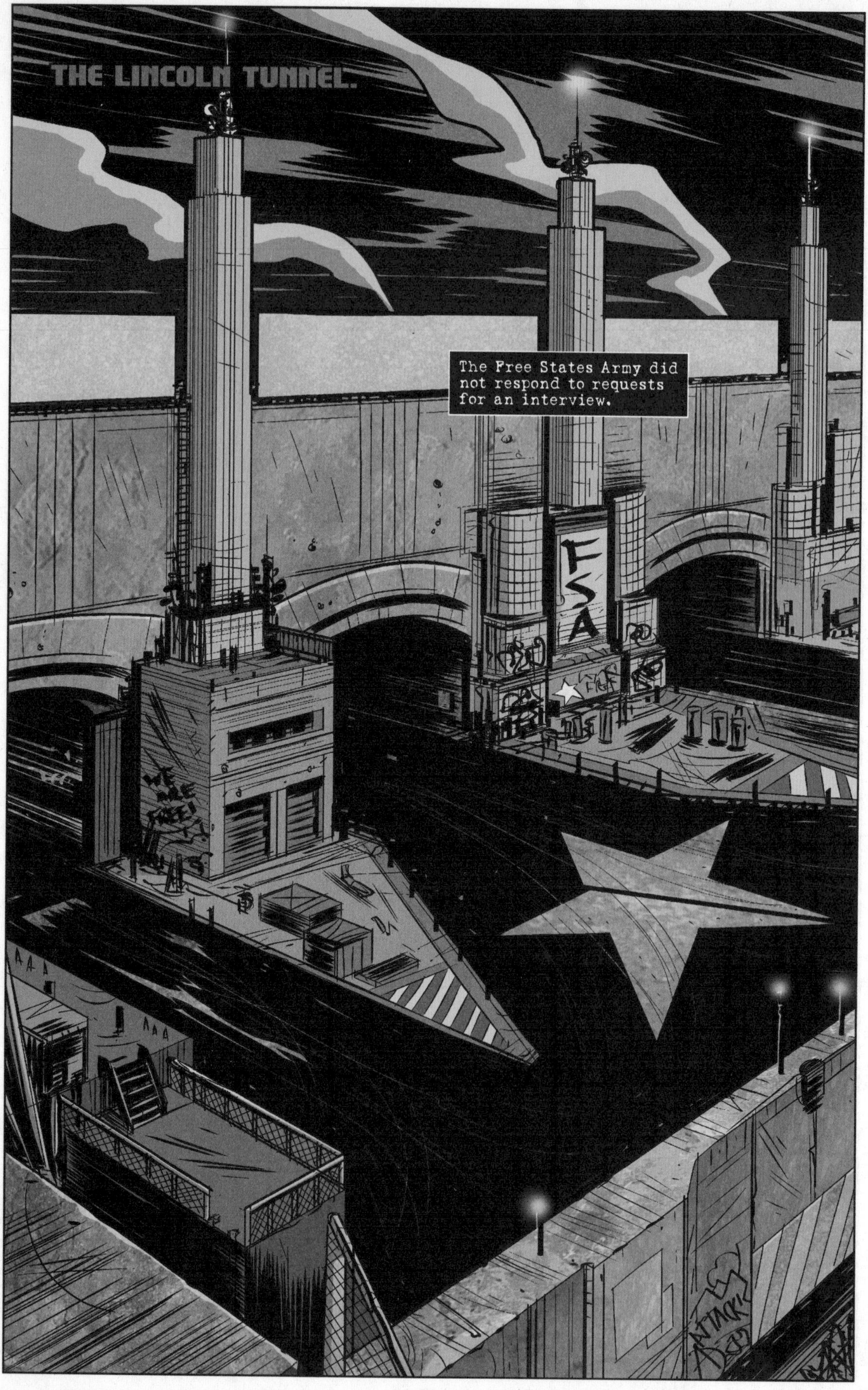
THE LINCOLN TUNNEL.
The Free States Army did not respond to requests for an interview.
FSA

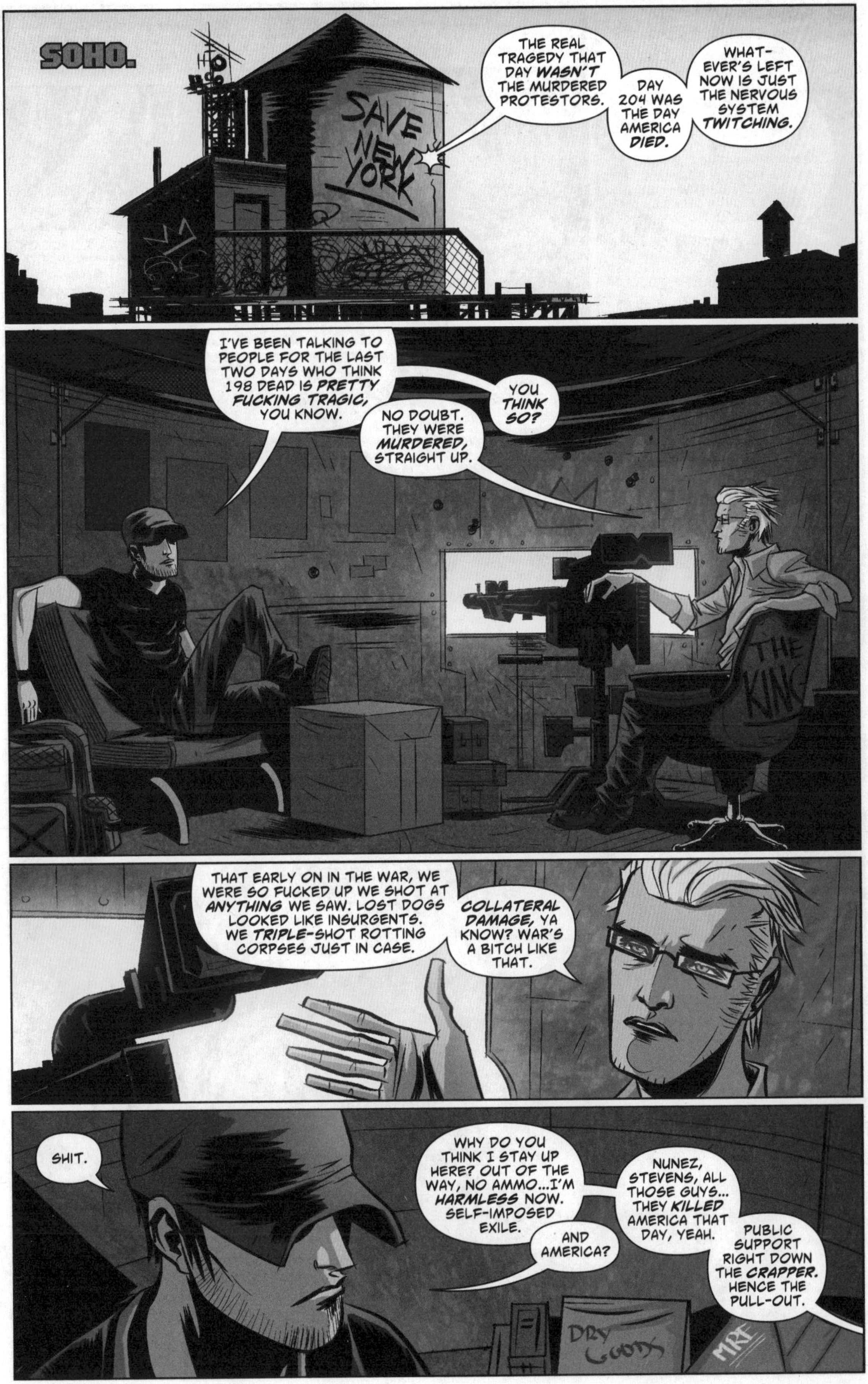
SOHO.
SAVE NEW YORK
THE REAL TRAGEDY THAT DAY WASN'T THE MURDERED PROTESTORS.
DAY 204 WAS THE DAY AMERICA DIED.
WHAT-EVER'S LEFT NOW IS JUST THE NERVOUS SYSTEM TWITCHING.
I'VE BEEN TALKING TO PEOPLE FOR THE LAST TWO DAYS WHO THINK 198 DEAD IS PRETTY FUCKING TRAGIC, YOU KNOW.
YOU THINK SO?
NO DOUBT. THEY WERE MURDERED, STRAIGHT UP.
THE KING
THAT EARLY ON IN THE WAR, WE WERE SO FUCKED UP WE SHOT AT ANYTHING WE SAW. LOST DOGS LOOKED LIKE INSURGENTS. WE TRIPLE-SHOT ROTTING CORPSES JUST IN CASE.
COLLATERAL DAMAGE, YA KNOW? WAR'S A BITCH LIKE THAT.
SHIT.
WHY DO YOU THINK I STAY UP HERE? OUT OF THE WAY, NO AMMO...I'M HARMLESS NOW. SELF-IMPOSED EXILE.
AND AMERICA?
NUNEZ, STEVENS, ALL THOSE GUYS... THEY KILLED AMERICA THAT DAY, YEAH.
PUBLIC SUPPORT RIGHT DOWN THE CRAPPER. HENCE THE PULL-OUT.
DRY GOODS
MRF

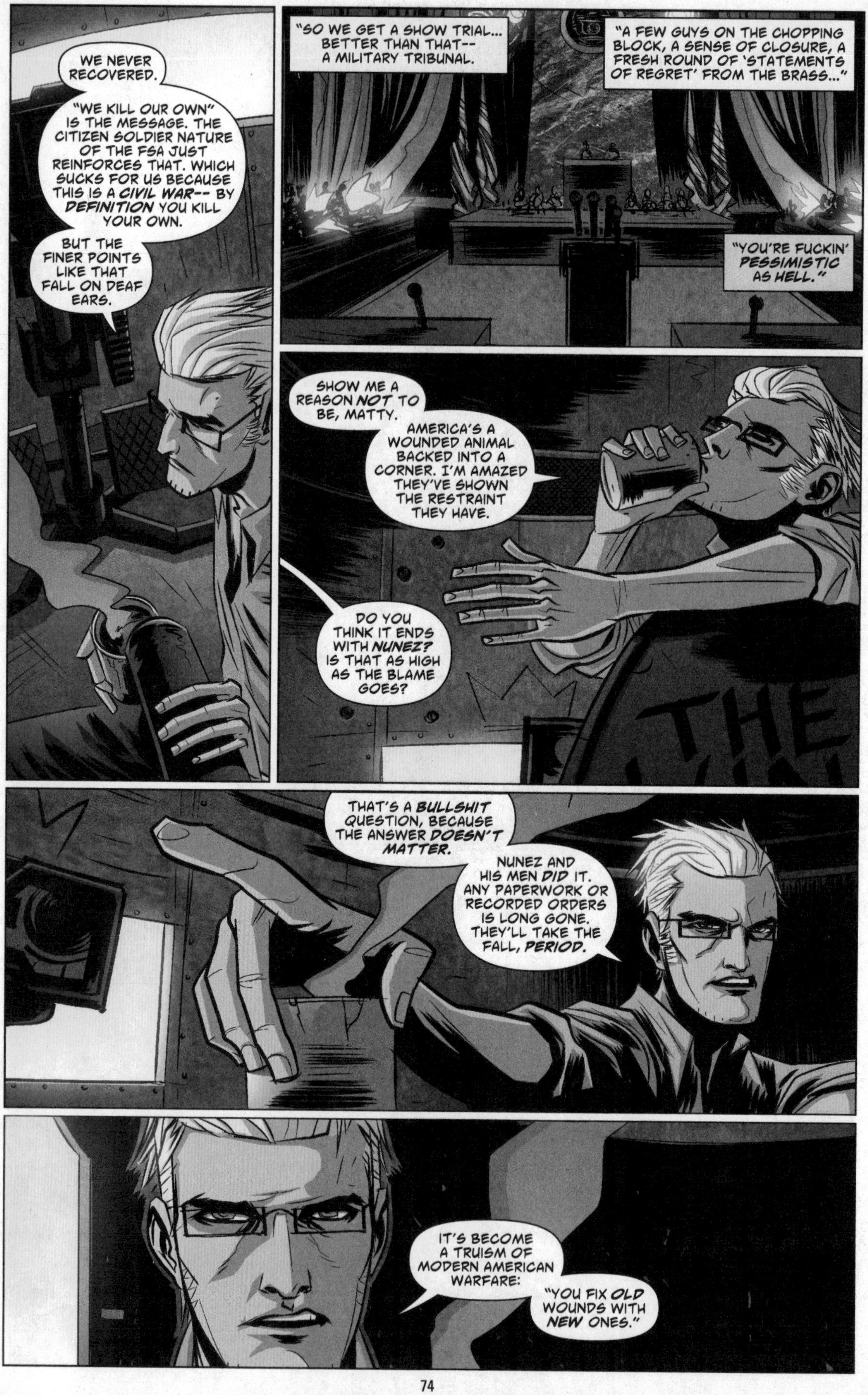
WE NEVER RECOVERED.
"WE KILL OUR OWN" IS THE MESSAGE. THE CITIZEN SOLDIER NATURE OF THE FSA JUST REINFORCES THAT. WHICH SUCKS FOR US BECAUSE THIS IS A CIVIL WAR-- BY DEFINITION YOU KILL YOUR OWN.
BUT THE FINER POINTS LIKE THAT FALL ON DEAF EARS.
"SO WE GET A SHOW TRIAL... BETTER THAN THAT-- A MILITARY TRIBUNAL.
"A FEW GUYS ON THE CHOPPING BLOCK, A SENSE OF CLOSURE, A FRESH ROUND OF 'STATEMENTS OF REGRET' FROM THE BRASS..."
"YOU'RE FUCKIN' PESSIMISTIC AS HELL."
SHOW ME A REASON NOT TO BE, MATTY.
AMERICA'S A WOUNDED ANIMAL BACKED INTO A CORNER. I'M AMAZED THEY'VE SHOWN THE RESTRAINT THEY HAVE.
DO YOU THINK IT ENDS WITH NUNEZ? IS THAT AS HIGH AS THE BLAME GOES?
THAT'S A BULLSHIT QUESTION, BECAUSE THE ANSWER DOESN'T MATTER.
NUNEZ AND HIS MEN DID IT. ANY PAPERWORK OR RECORDED ORDERS IS LONG GONE. THEY'LL TAKE THE FALL, PERIOD.
IT'S BECOME A TRUISM OF MODERN AMERICAN WARFARE:
"YOU FIX OLD WOUNDS WITH NEW ONES."

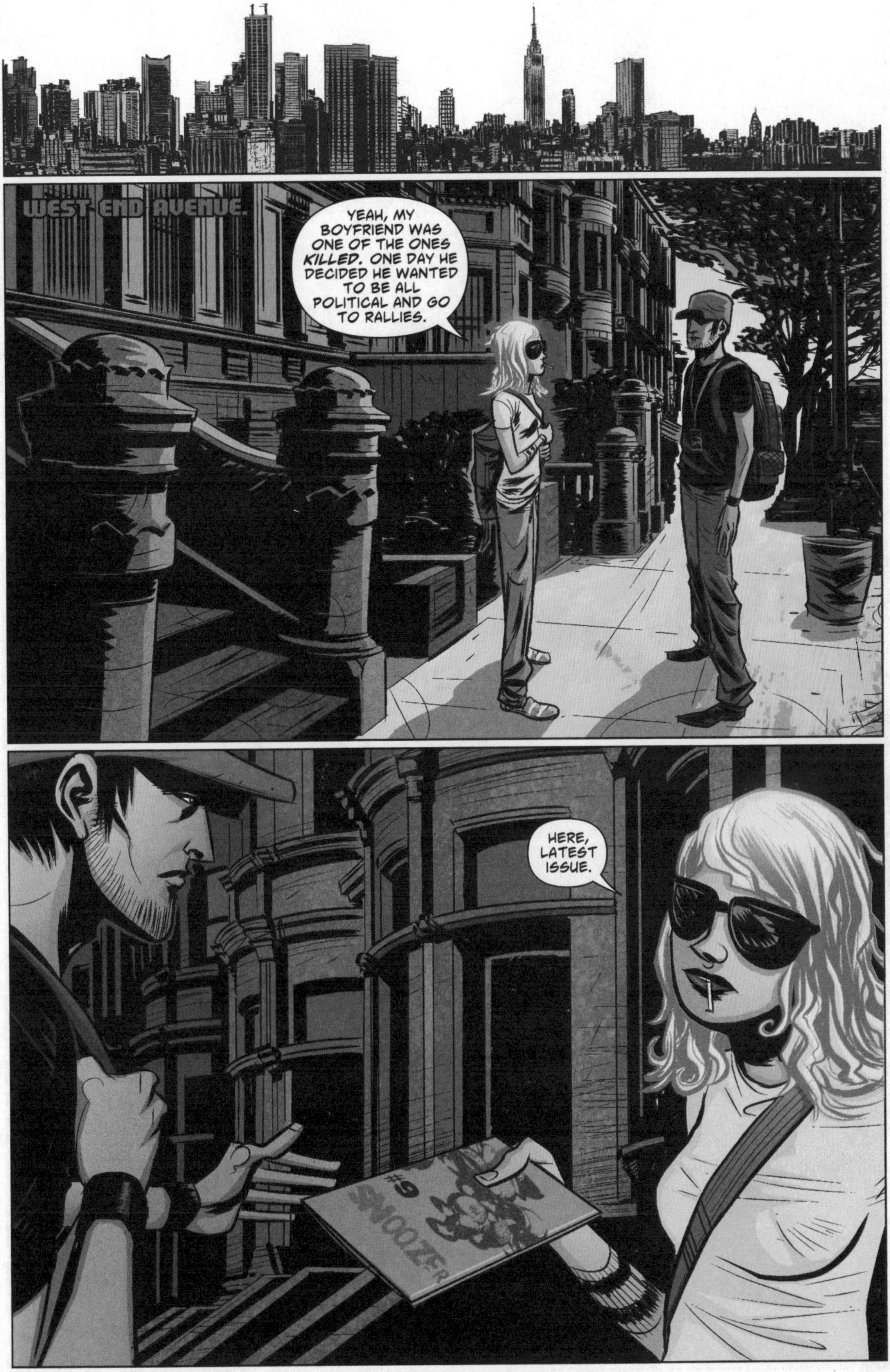
WEST END AVENUE.
YEAH, MY BOYFRIEND WAS ONE OF THE ONES KILLED. ONE DAY HE DECIDED HE WANTED TO BE ALL POLITICAL AND GO TO RALLIES.
HERE, LATEST ISSUE.
#9
SNOOZER

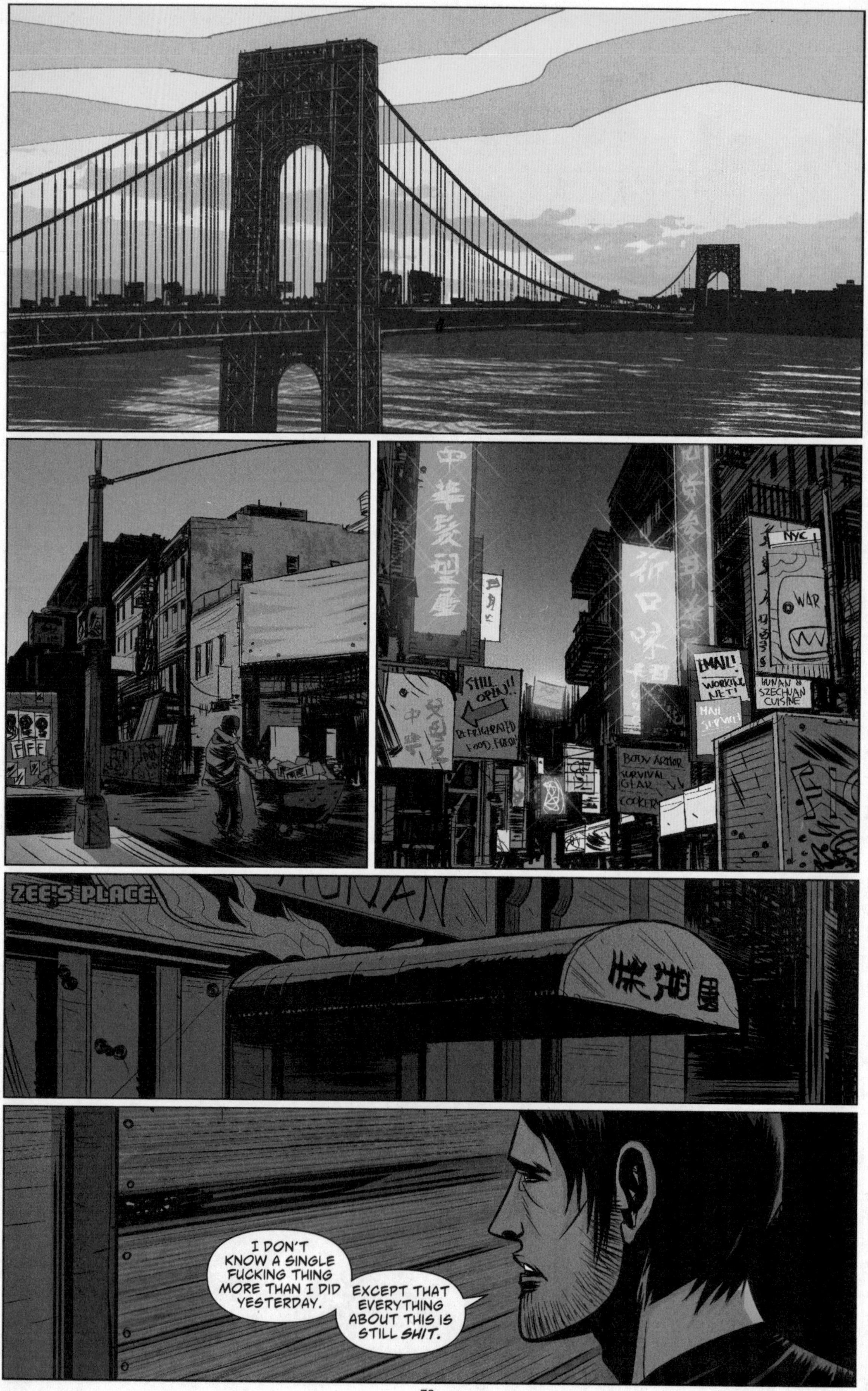
NYC
WAR
EMAIL!
HUNAN & SZECHUAN CUISINE
STILL OPEN!!
BODY ARMOR
SURVIVAL GEAR
ZEE'S PLACE.
I DON'T KNOW A SINGLE FUCKING THING MORE THAN I DID YESTERDAY.
EXCEPT THAT EVERYTHING ABOUT THIS IS STILL *SHIT*.

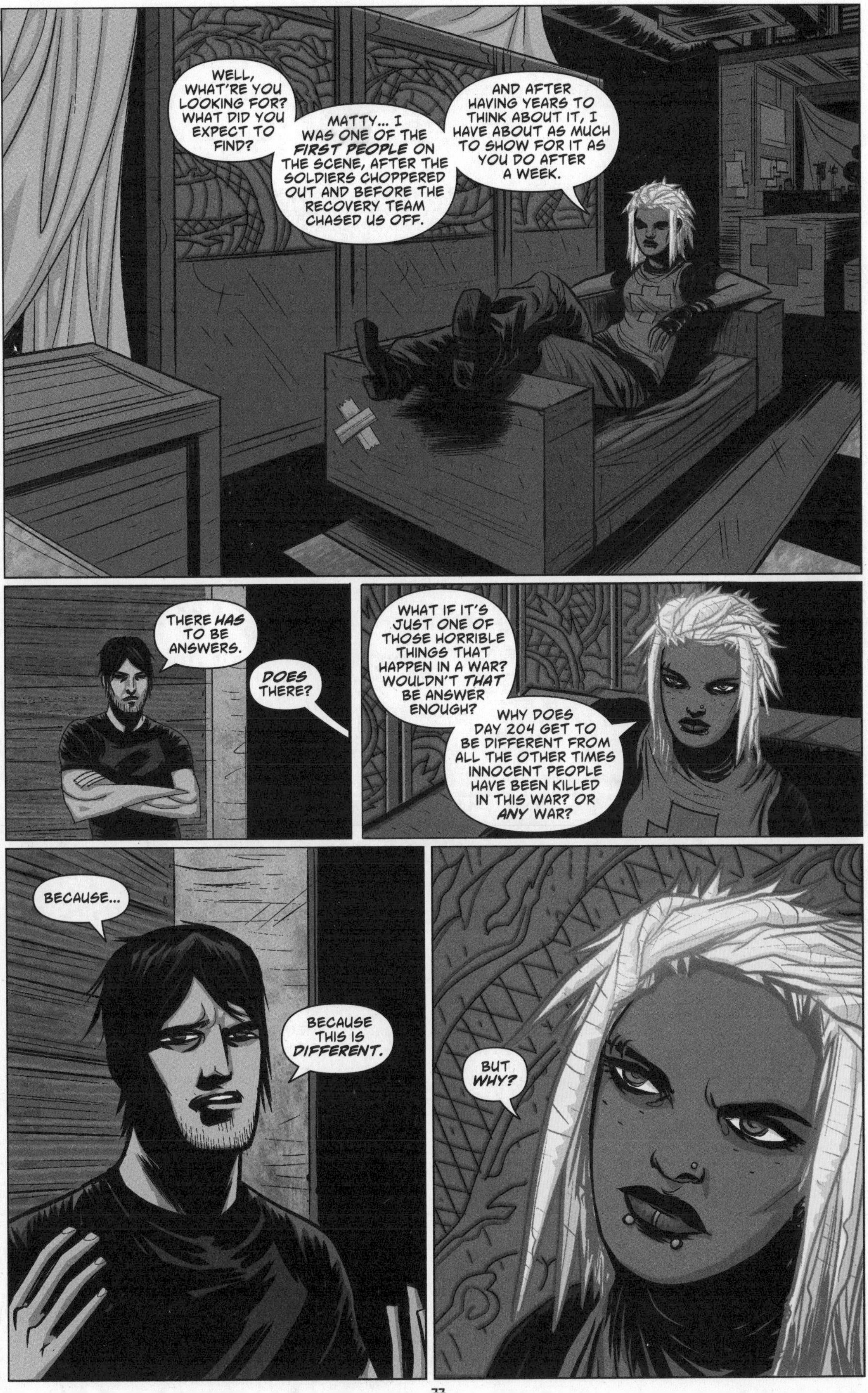
WELL, WHAT'RE YOU LOOKING FOR? WHAT DID YOU EXPECT TO FIND?
MATTY... I WAS ONE OF THE FIRST PEOPLE ON THE SCENE, AFTER THE SOLDIERS CHOPPERED OUT AND BEFORE THE RECOVERY TEAM CHASED US OFF.
AND AFTER HAVING YEARS TO THINK ABOUT IT, I HAVE ABOUT AS MUCH TO SHOW FOR IT AS YOU DO AFTER A WEEK.
THERE HAS TO BE ANSWERS.
DOES THERE?
WHAT IF IT'S JUST ONE OF THOSE HORRIBLE THINGS THAT HAPPEN IN A WAR? WOULDN'T THAT BE ANSWER ENOUGH?
WHY DOES DAY 204 GET TO BE DIFFERENT FROM ALL THE OTHER TIMES INNOCENT PEOPLE HAVE BEEN KILLED IN THIS WAR? OR ANY WAR?
BECAUSE...
BECAUSE THIS IS DIFFERENT.
BUT WHY?

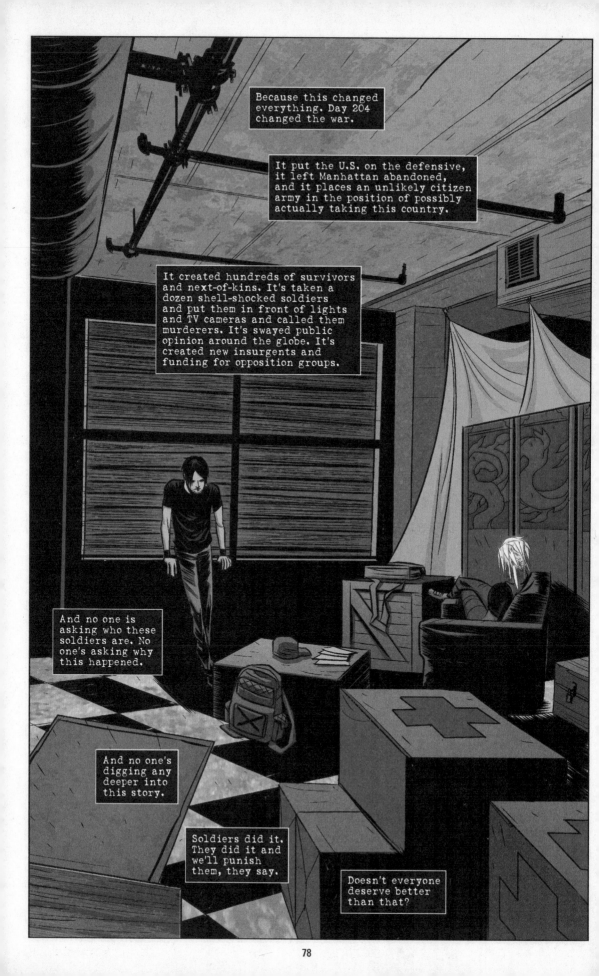

Because this changed everything. Day 204 changed the war.

It put the U.S. on the defensive, it left Manhattan abandoned, and it places an unlikely citizen army in the position of possibly actually taking this country.

It created hundreds of survivors and next-of-kins. It's taken a dozen shell-shocked soldiers and put them in front of lights and TV cameras and called them murderers. It's swayed public opinion around the globe. It's created new insurgents and funding for opposition groups.

And no one is asking who these soldiers are. No one's asking why this happened.

And no one's digging any deeper into this story.

Soldiers did it. They did it and we'll punish them, they say.

Doesn't everyone deserve better than that?

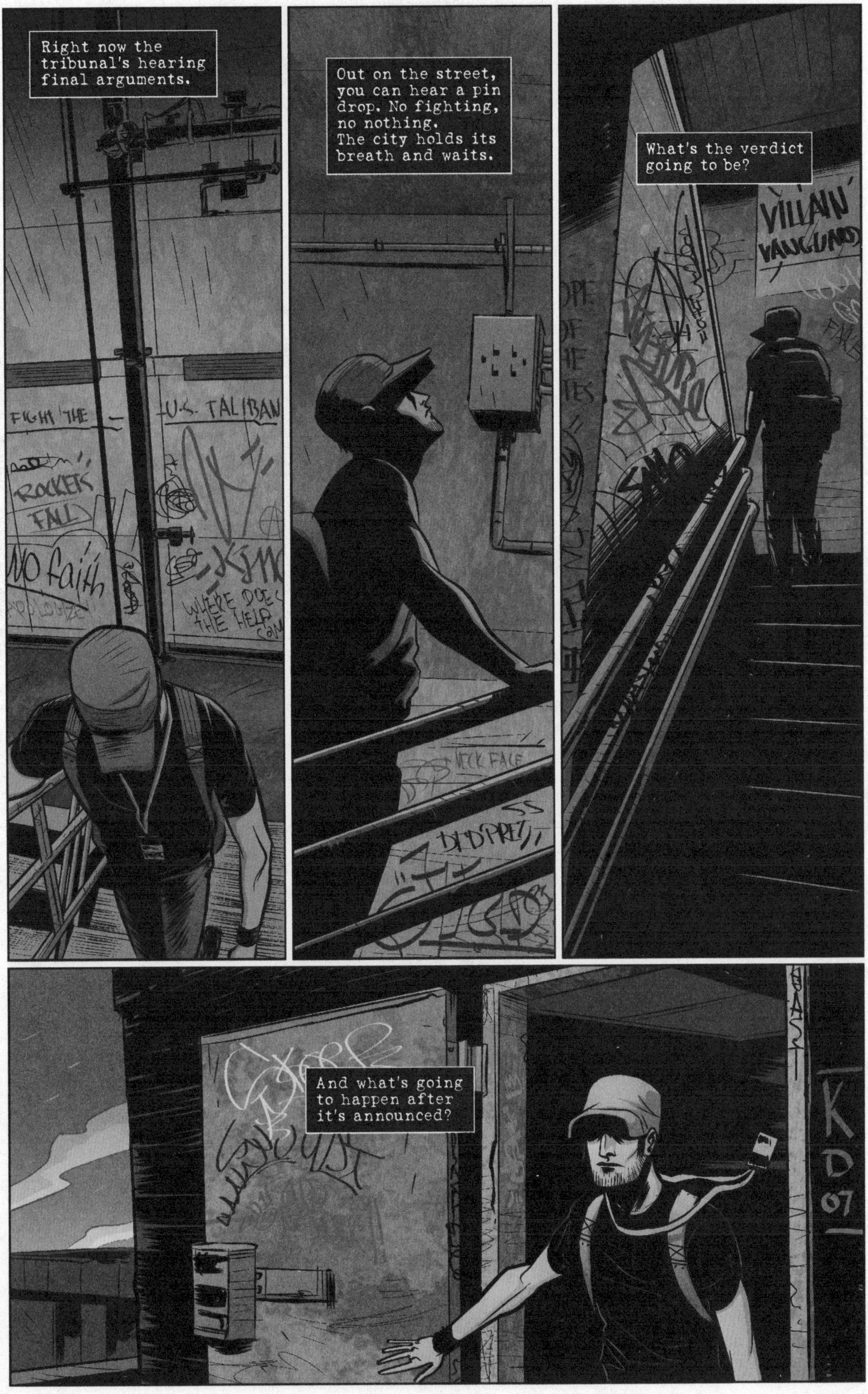
Right now the tribunal's hearing final arguments.
FIGHT THE
U.S. TALIBAN
ROCKETS FALL
NO faith
WHERE DOES THE HELP
Out on the street, you can hear a pin drop. No fighting, no nothing. The city holds its breath and waits.
NECK FACE
What's the verdict going to be?
VILLAIN VANGUARD
And what's going to happen after it's announced?
KD 07

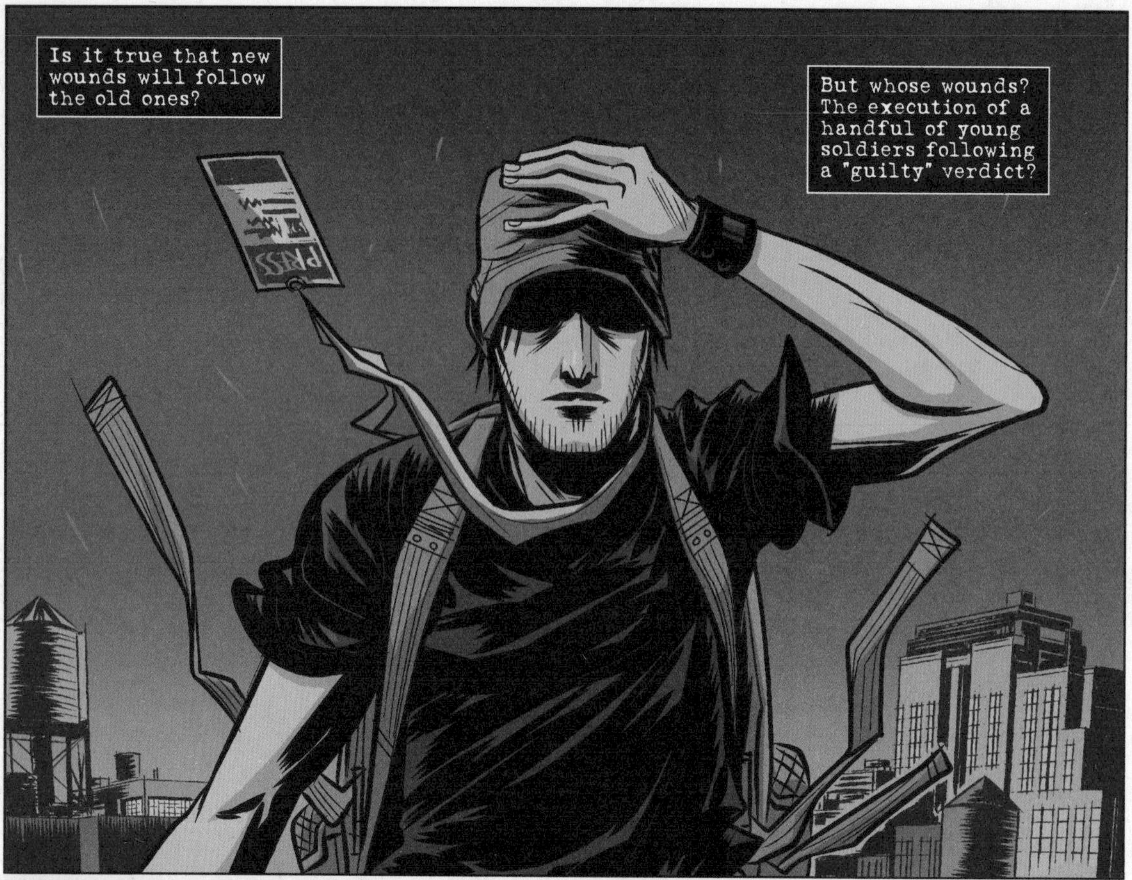
Is it true that new wounds will follow the old ones?
But whose wounds? The execution of a handful of young soldiers following a "guilty" verdict?

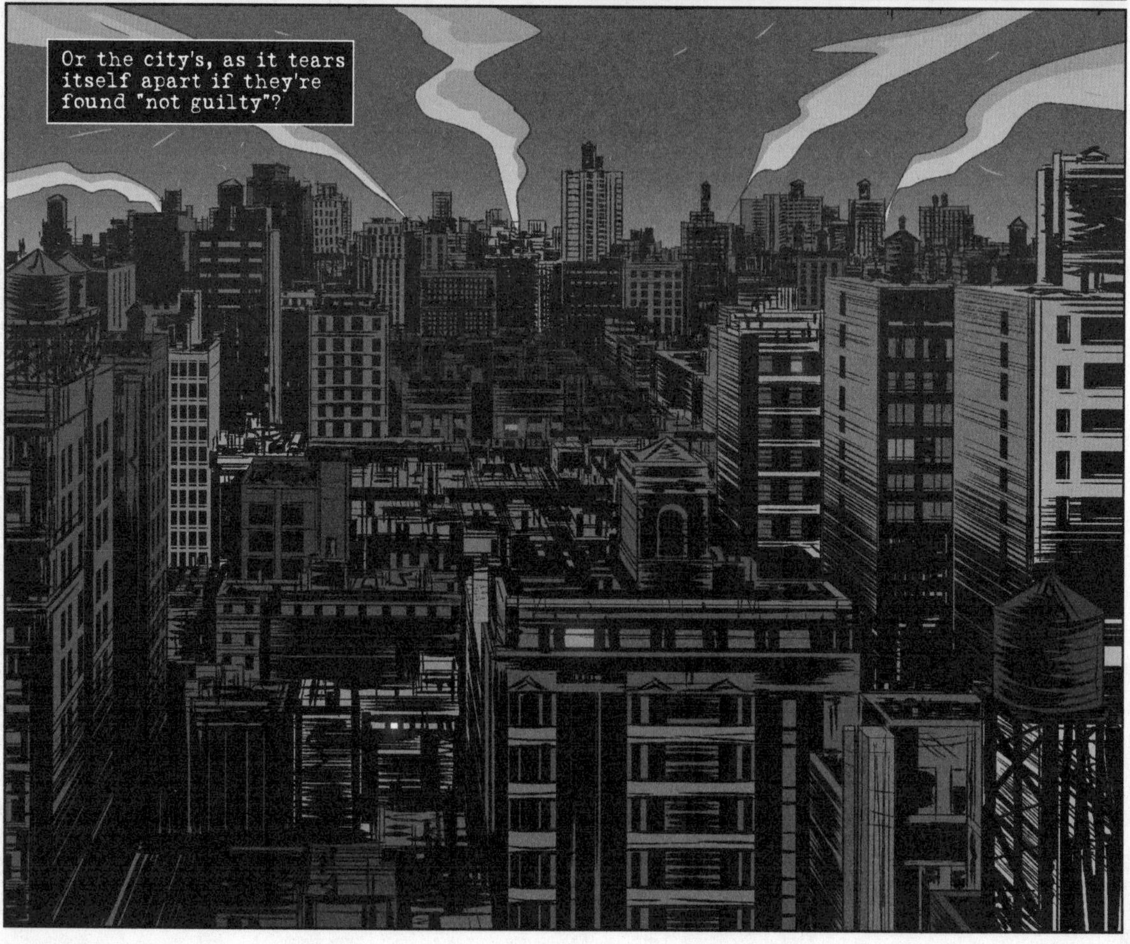
Or the city's, as it tears itself apart if they're found "not guilty"?

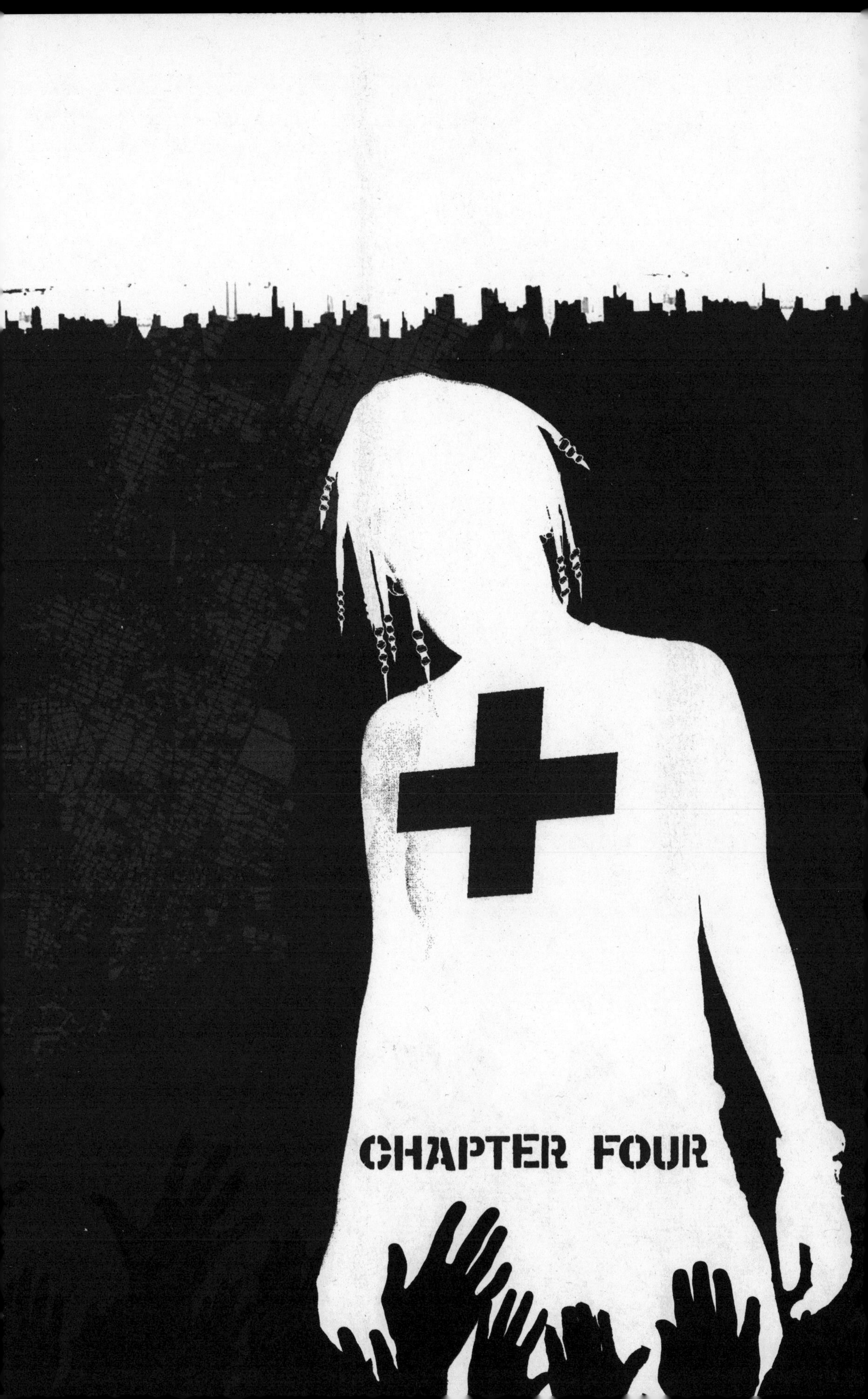
CHAPTER FOUR

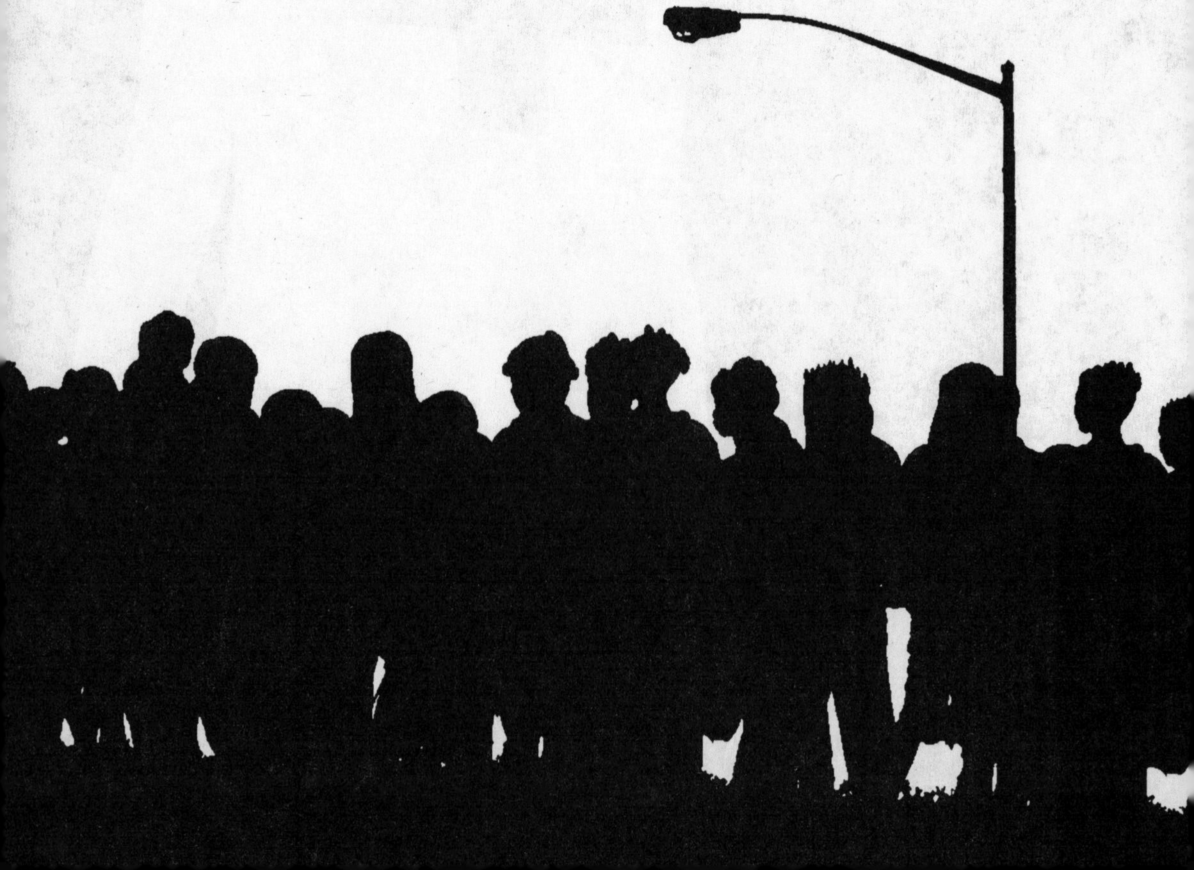

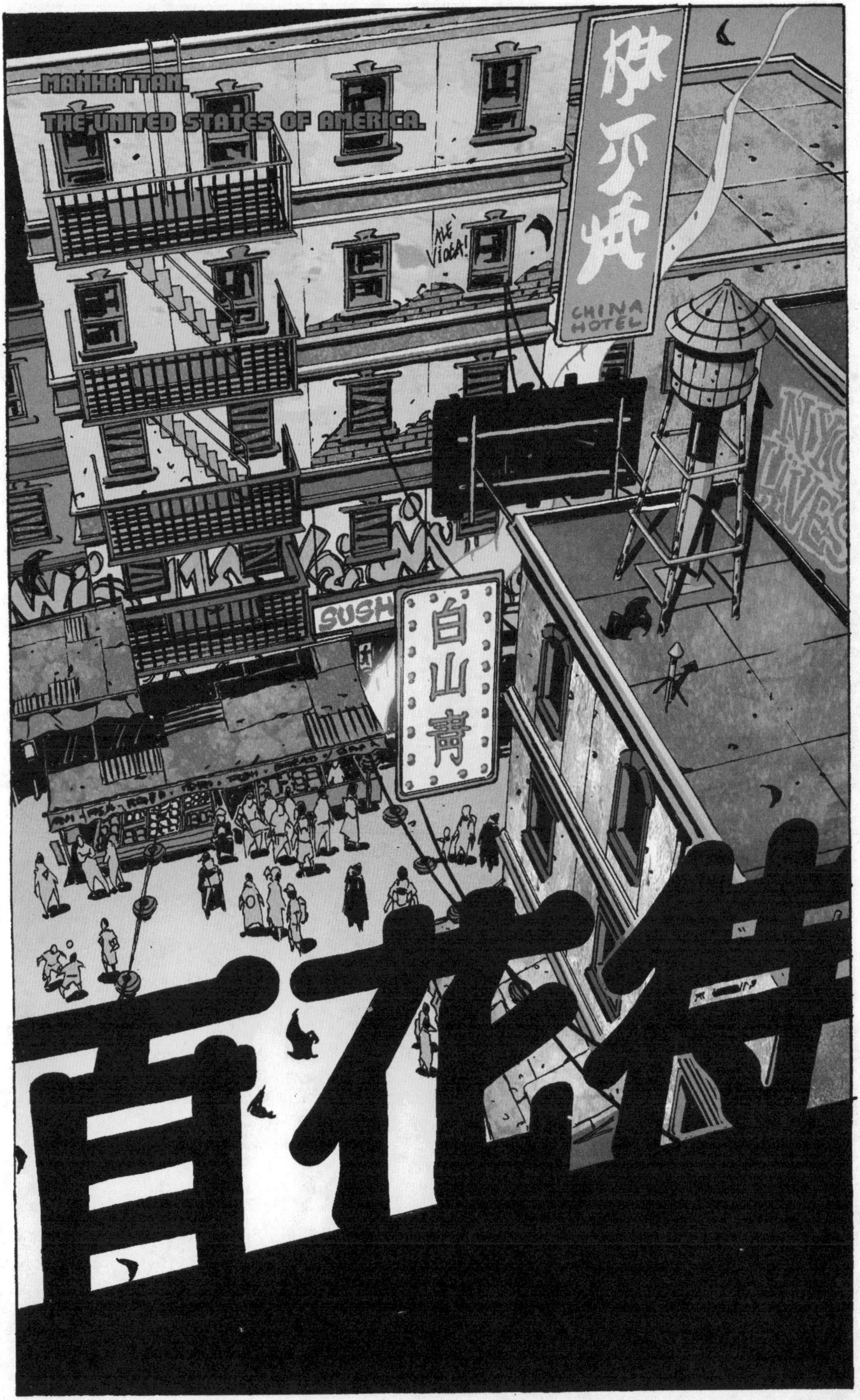
MANHATTAN.
THE UNITED STATES OF AMERICA.
CHINA HOTEL

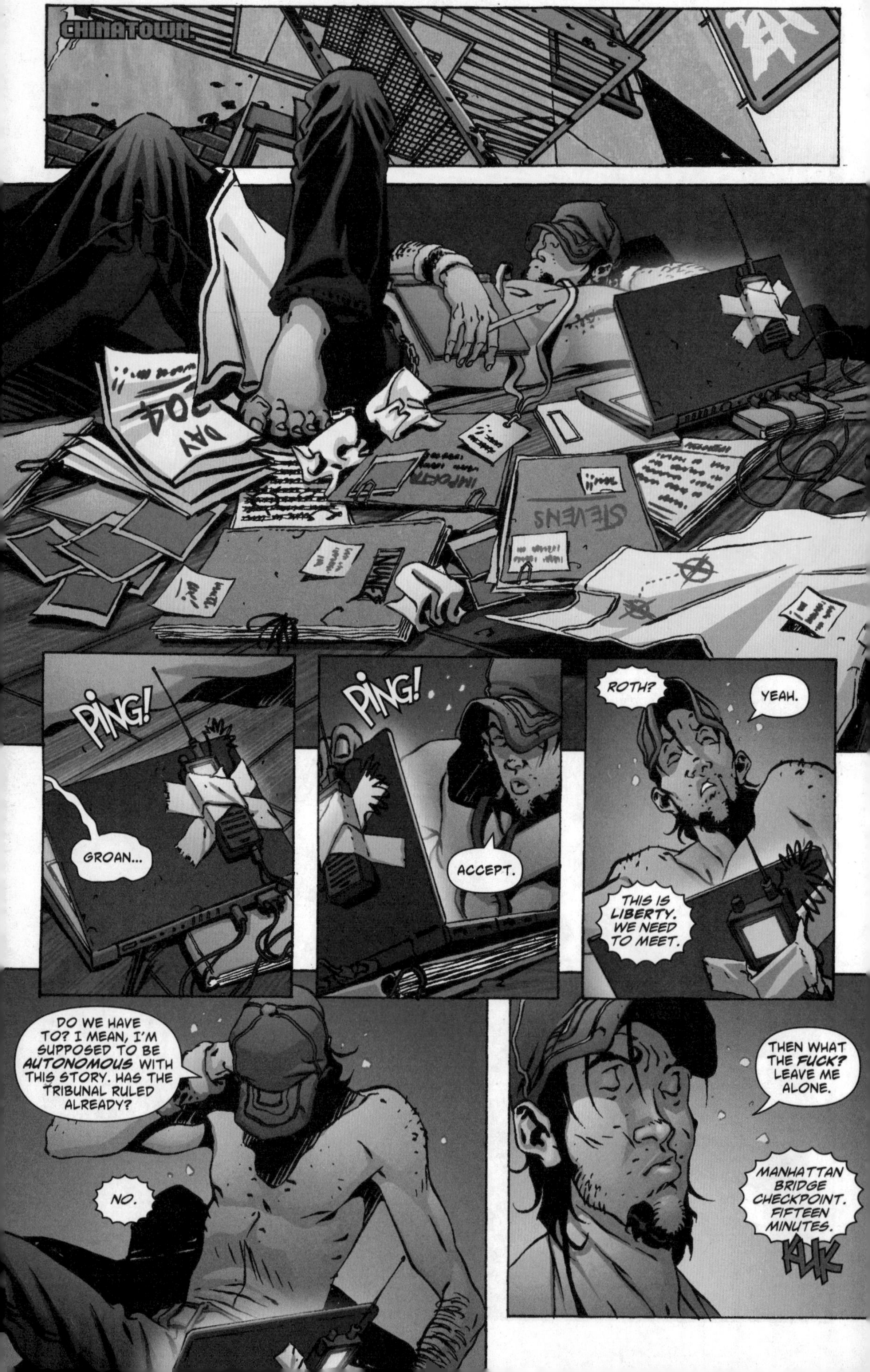
CHINATOWN.
DAY 204
IMPORTA
STEVENS
PING!
GROAN...
PING!
ACCEPT.
ROTH?
YEAH.
THIS IS LIBERTY. WE NEED TO MEET.
DO WE HAVE TO? I MEAN, I'M SUPPOSED TO BE AUTONOMOUS WITH THIS STORY. HAS THE TRIBUNAL RULED ALREADY?
NO.
THEN WHAT THE FUCK? LEAVE ME ALONE.
MANHATTAN BRIDGE CHECKPOINT. FIFTEEN MINUTES.
KLIK

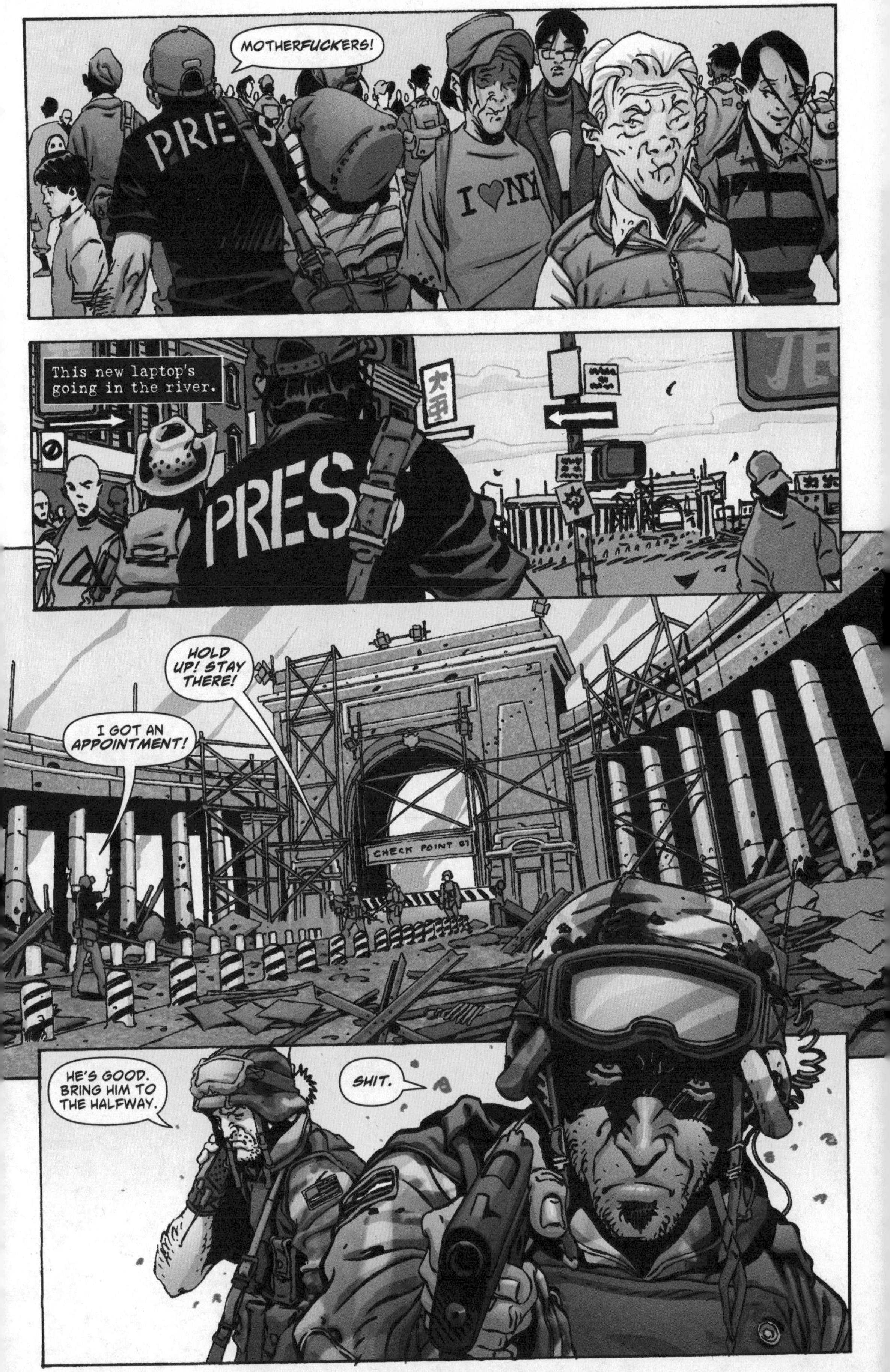
MOTHERFUCKERS!
PRES
I ♥ NY
This new laptop's going in the river.
PRES
HOLD UP! STAY THERE!
I GOT AN APPOINTMENT!
CHECK POINT 67
HE'S GOOD. BRING HIM TO THE HALFWAY.
SHIT.

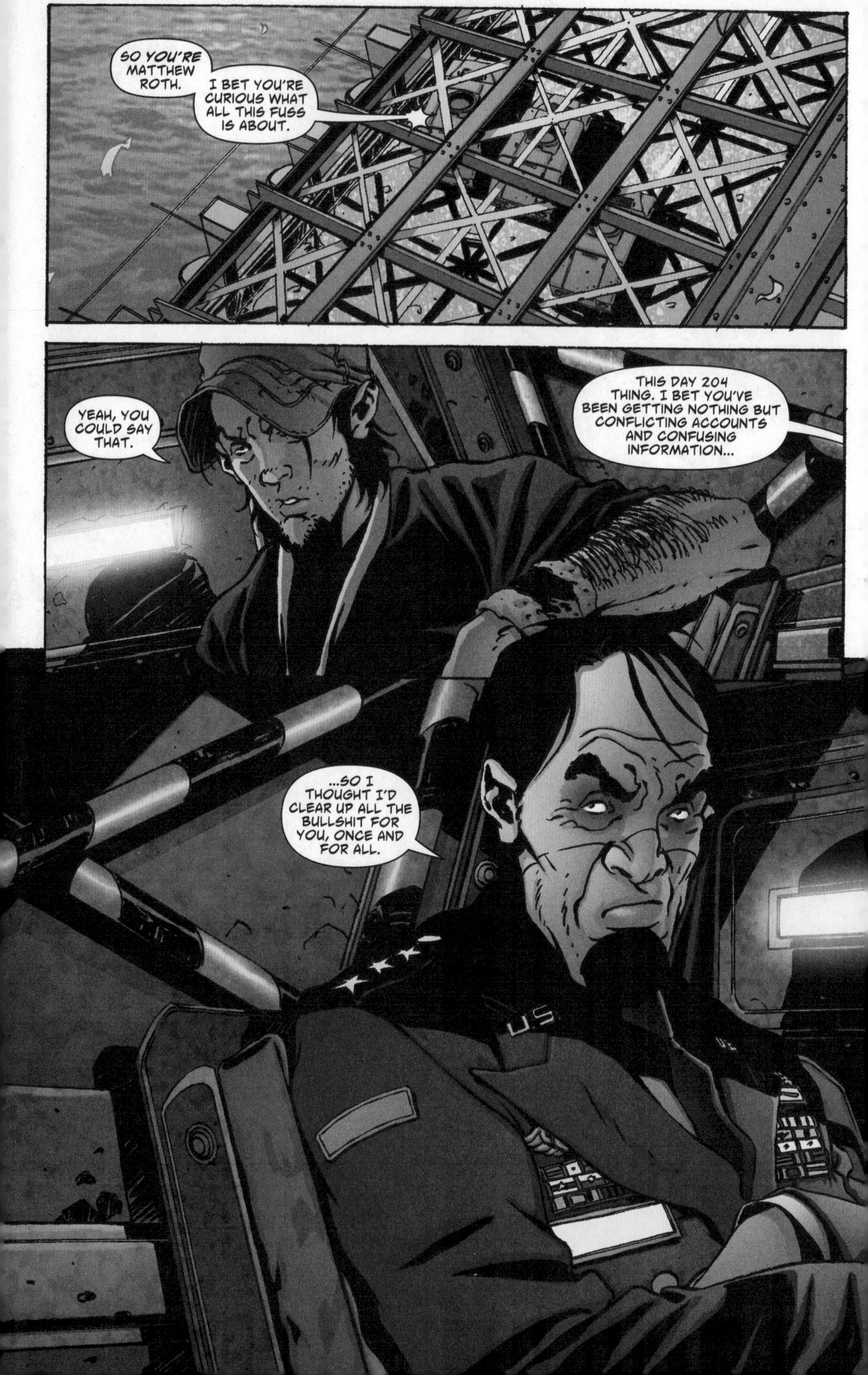
SO YOU'RE MATTHEW ROTH.
I BET YOU'RE CURIOUS WHAT ALL THIS FUSS IS ABOUT.
YEAH, YOU COULD SAY THAT.
THIS DAY 204 THING. I BET YOU'VE BEEN GETTING NOTHING BUT CONFLICTING ACCOUNTS AND CONFUSING INFORMATION...
...SO I THOUGHT I'D CLEAR UP ALL THE BULLSHIT FOR YOU, ONCE AND FOR ALL.

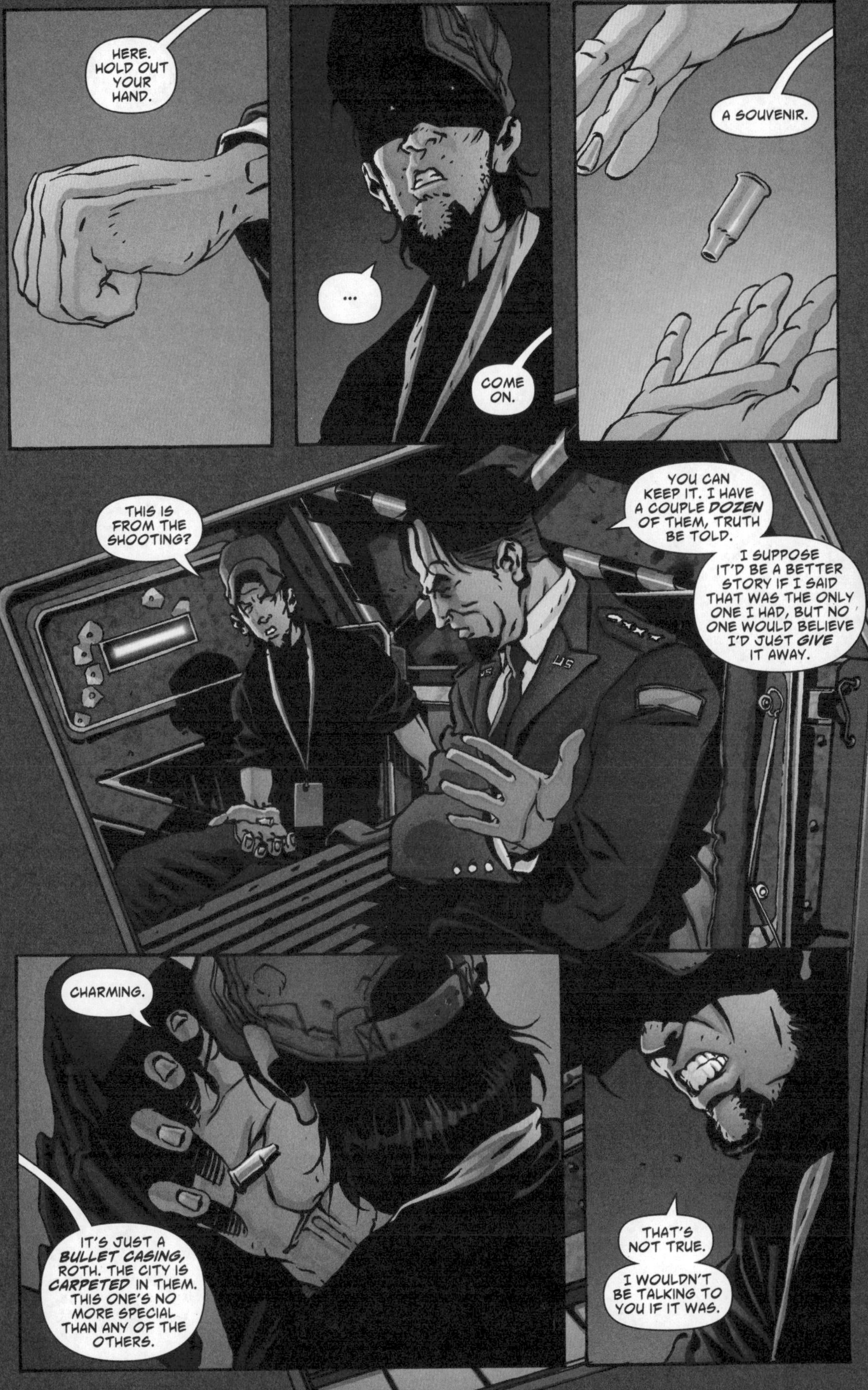
HERE. HOLD OUT YOUR HAND.
...
COME ON.
A SOUVENIR.
THIS IS FROM THE SHOOTING?
YOU CAN KEEP IT. I HAVE A COUPLE DOZEN OF THEM, TRUTH BE TOLD.
I SUPPOSE IT'D BE A BETTER STORY IF I SAID THAT WAS THE ONLY ONE I HAD, BUT NO ONE WOULD BELIEVE I'D JUST GIVE IT AWAY.
CHARMING.
IT'S JUST A BULLET CASING, ROTH. THE CITY IS CARPETED IN THEM. THIS ONE'S NO MORE SPECIAL THAN ANY OF THE OTHERS.
THAT'S NOT TRUE.
I WOULDN'T BE TALKING TO YOU IF IT WAS.

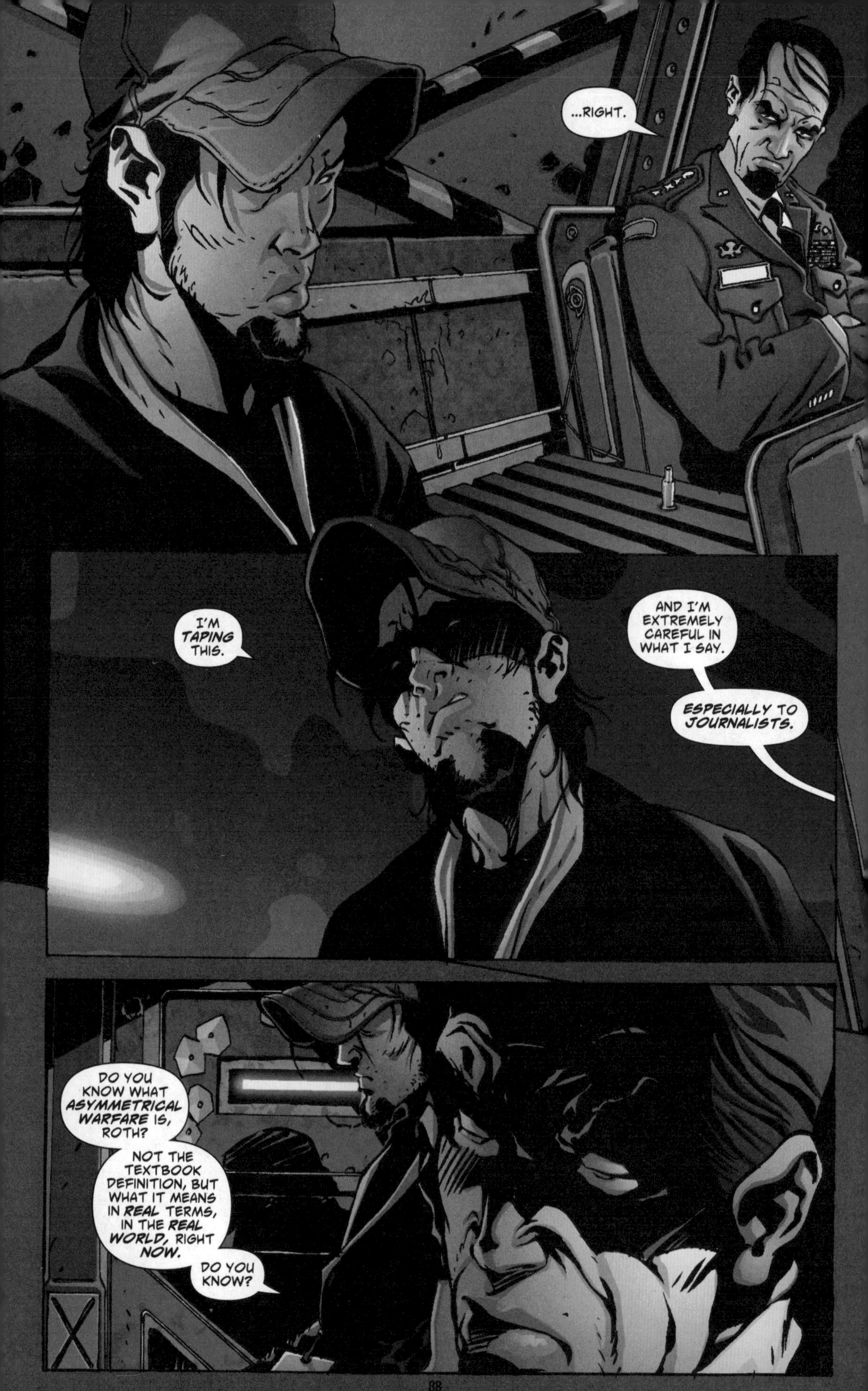
...RIGHT.
I'M *TAPING* THIS.
AND I'M EXTREMELY CAREFUL IN WHAT I SAY.
ESPECIALLY TO JOURNALISTS.
DO YOU KNOW WHAT ***ASYMMETRICAL WARFARE*** IS, ROTH?
NOT THE TEXTBOOK DEFINITION, BUT WHAT IT MEANS IN ***REAL*** TERMS, IN THE ***REAL WORLD,*** RIGHT ***NOW.***
DO YOU KNOW?

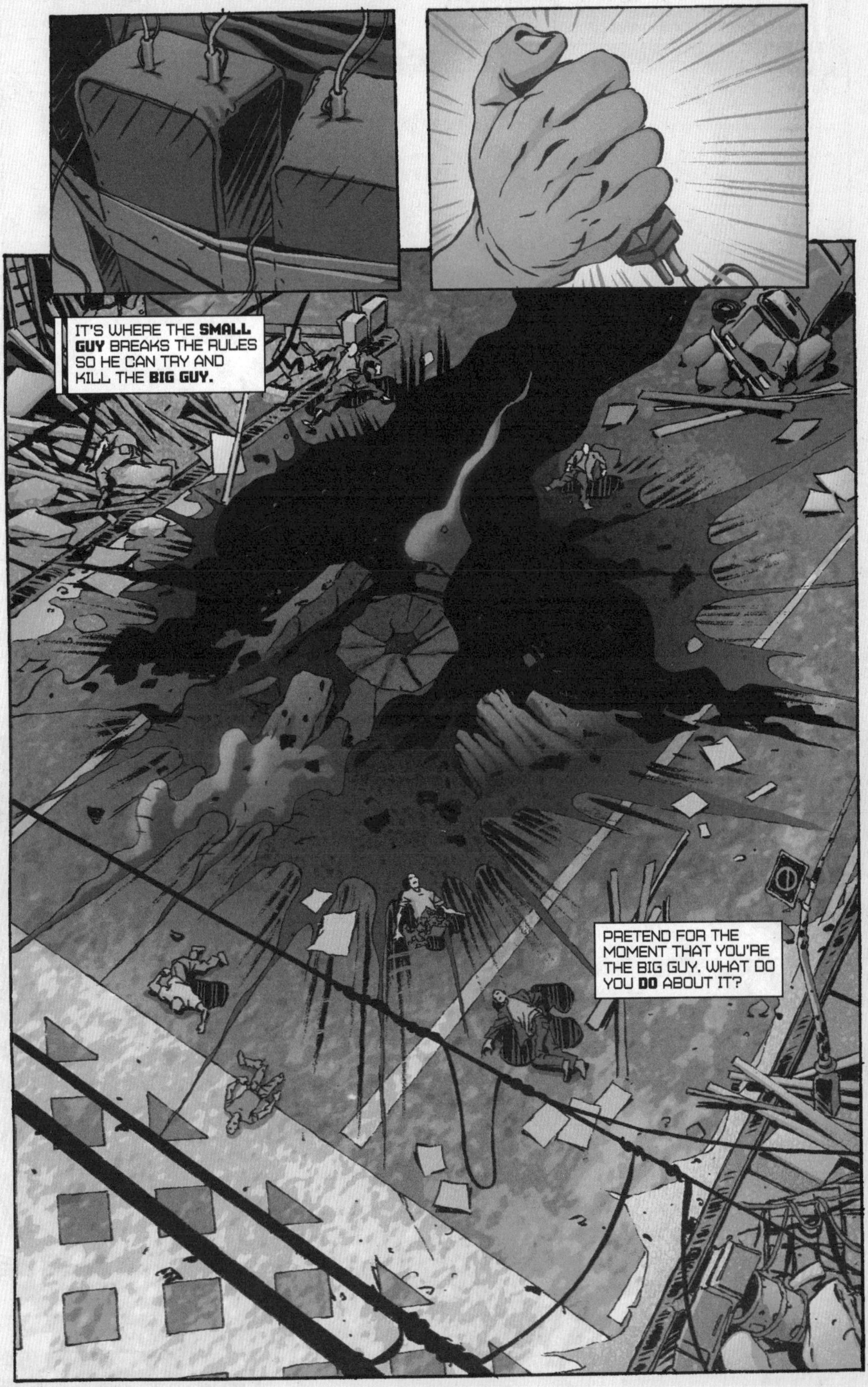
IT'S WHERE THE SMALL GUY BREAKS THE RULES SO HE CAN TRY AND KILL THE BIG GUY.
PRETEND FOR THE MOMENT THAT YOU'RE THE BIG GUY. WHAT DO YOU DO ABOUT IT?

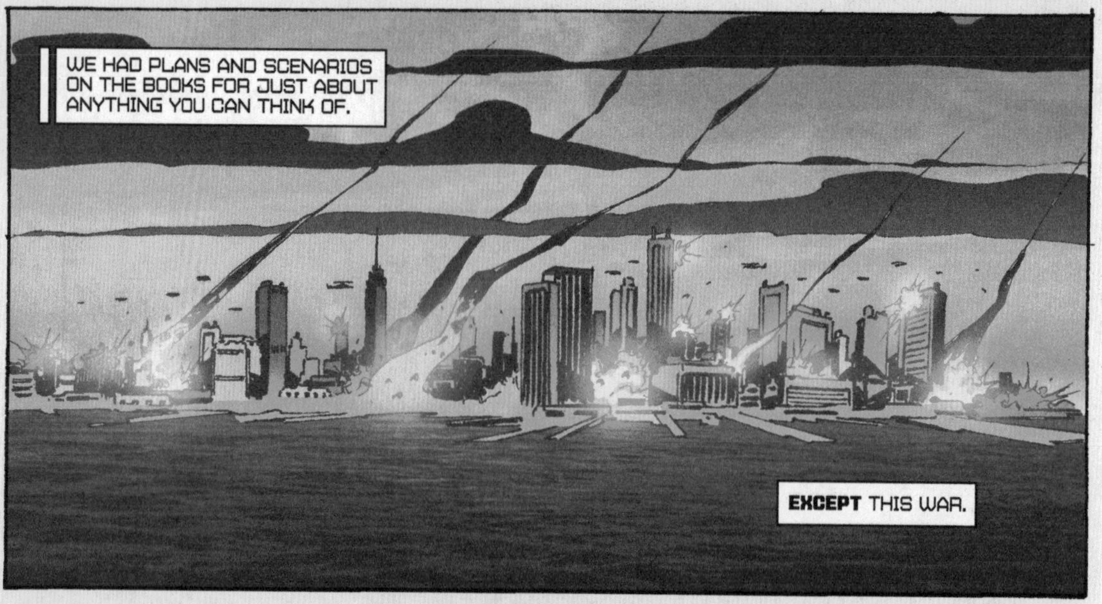
WE HAD PLANS AND SCENARIOS ON THE BOOKS FOR JUST ABOUT ANYTHING YOU CAN THINK OF.
EXCEPT THIS WAR.

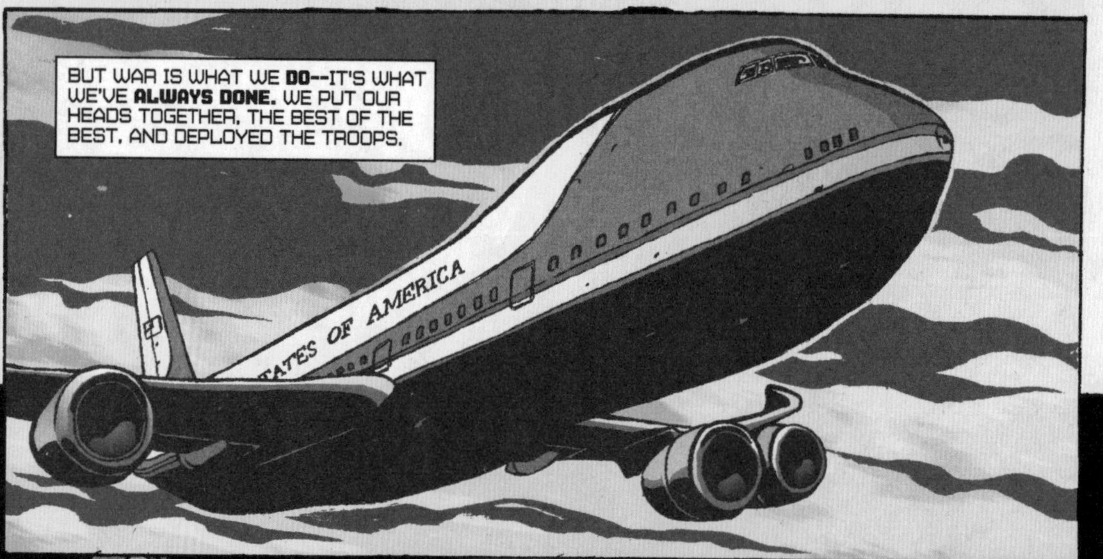
BUT WAR IS WHAT WE DO--IT'S WHAT WE'VE ALWAYS DONE. WE PUT OUR HEADS TOGETHER, THE BEST OF THE BEST, AND DEPLOYED THE TROOPS.
TATES OF AMERICA

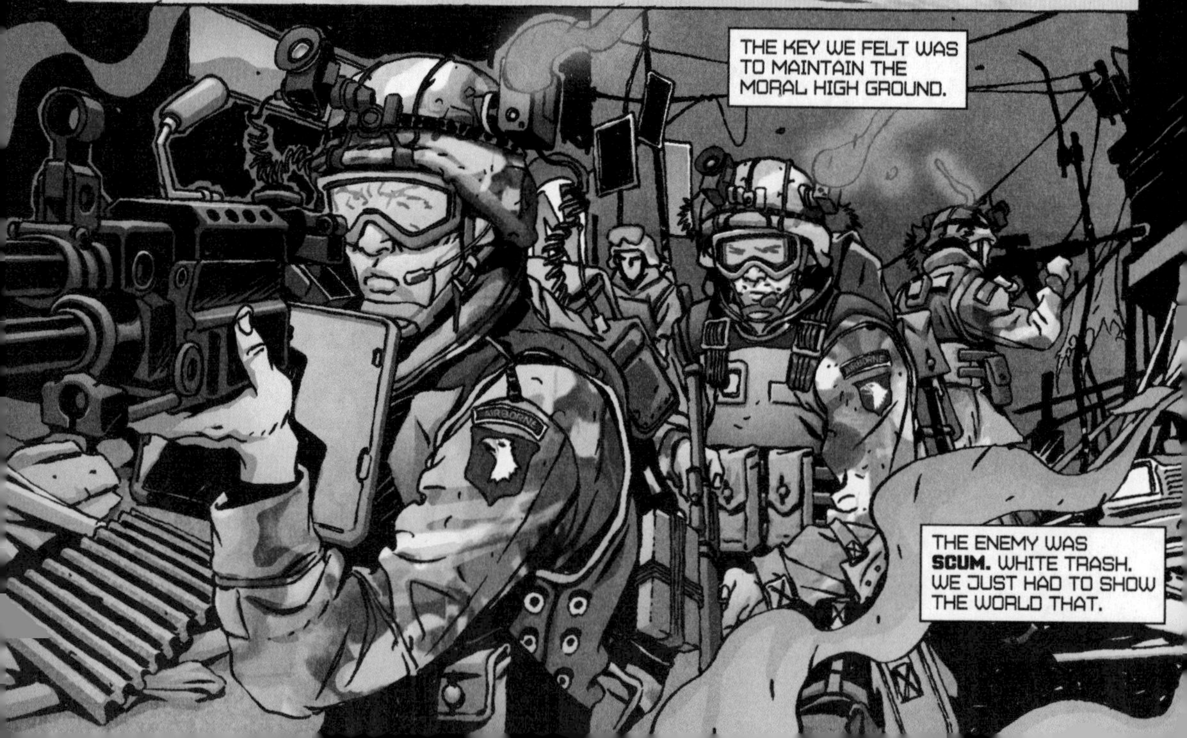
THE KEY WE FELT WAS TO MAINTAIN THE MORAL HIGH GROUND.
AIRBORNE
THE ENEMY WAS SCUM. WHITE TRASH. WE JUST HAD TO SHOW THE WORLD THAT.

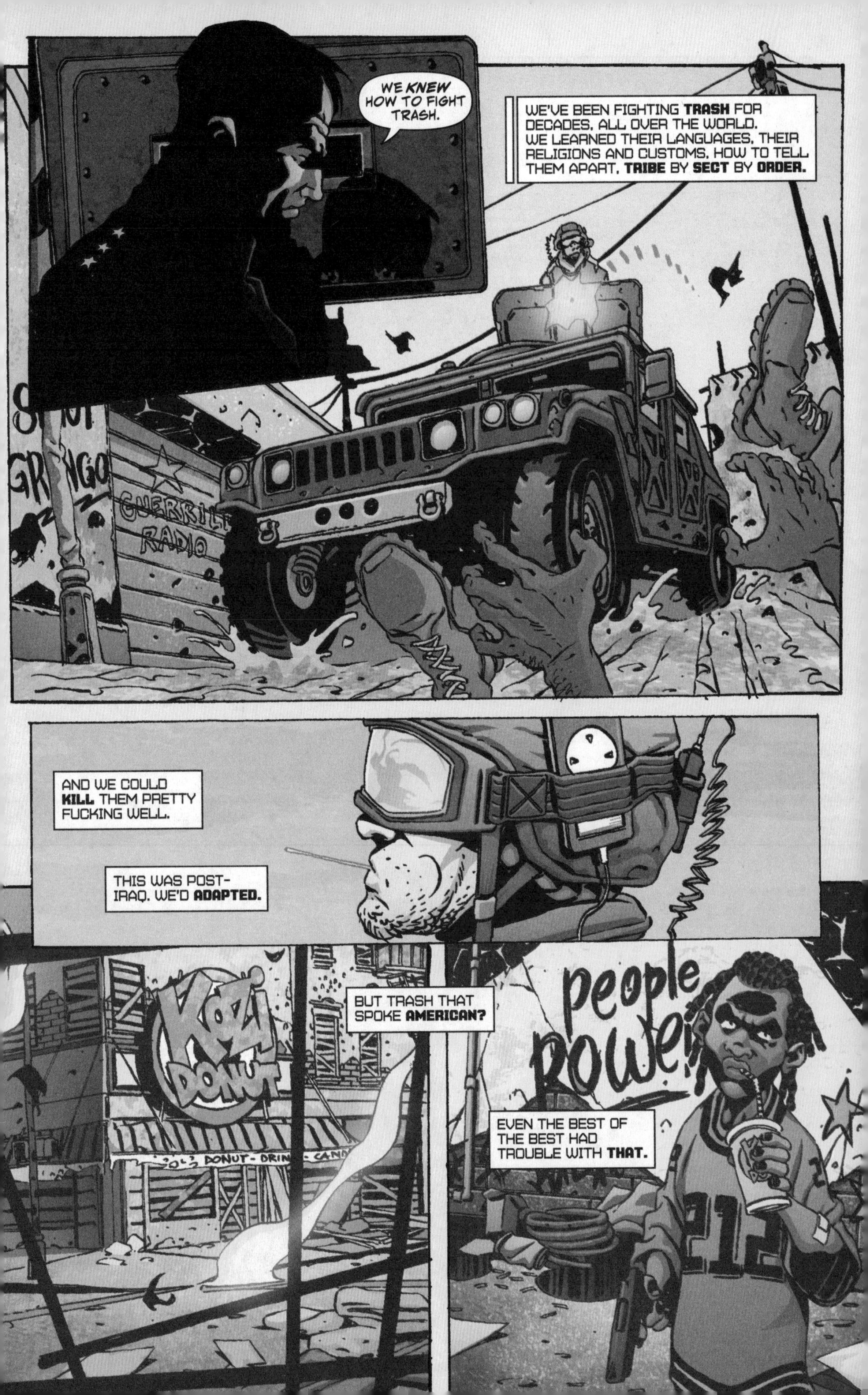
WE KNEW HOW TO FIGHT TRASH.
WE'VE BEEN FIGHTING TRASH FOR DECADES, ALL OVER THE WORLD. WE LEARNED THEIR LANGUAGES, THEIR RELIGIONS AND CUSTOMS, HOW TO TELL THEM APART, TRIBE BY SECT BY ORDER.
AND WE COULD KILL THEM PRETTY FUCKING WELL.
THIS WAS POST-IRAQ. WE'D ADAPTED.
BUT TRASH THAT SPOKE AMERICAN?
people
EVEN THE BEST OF THE BEST HAD TROUBLE WITH THAT.

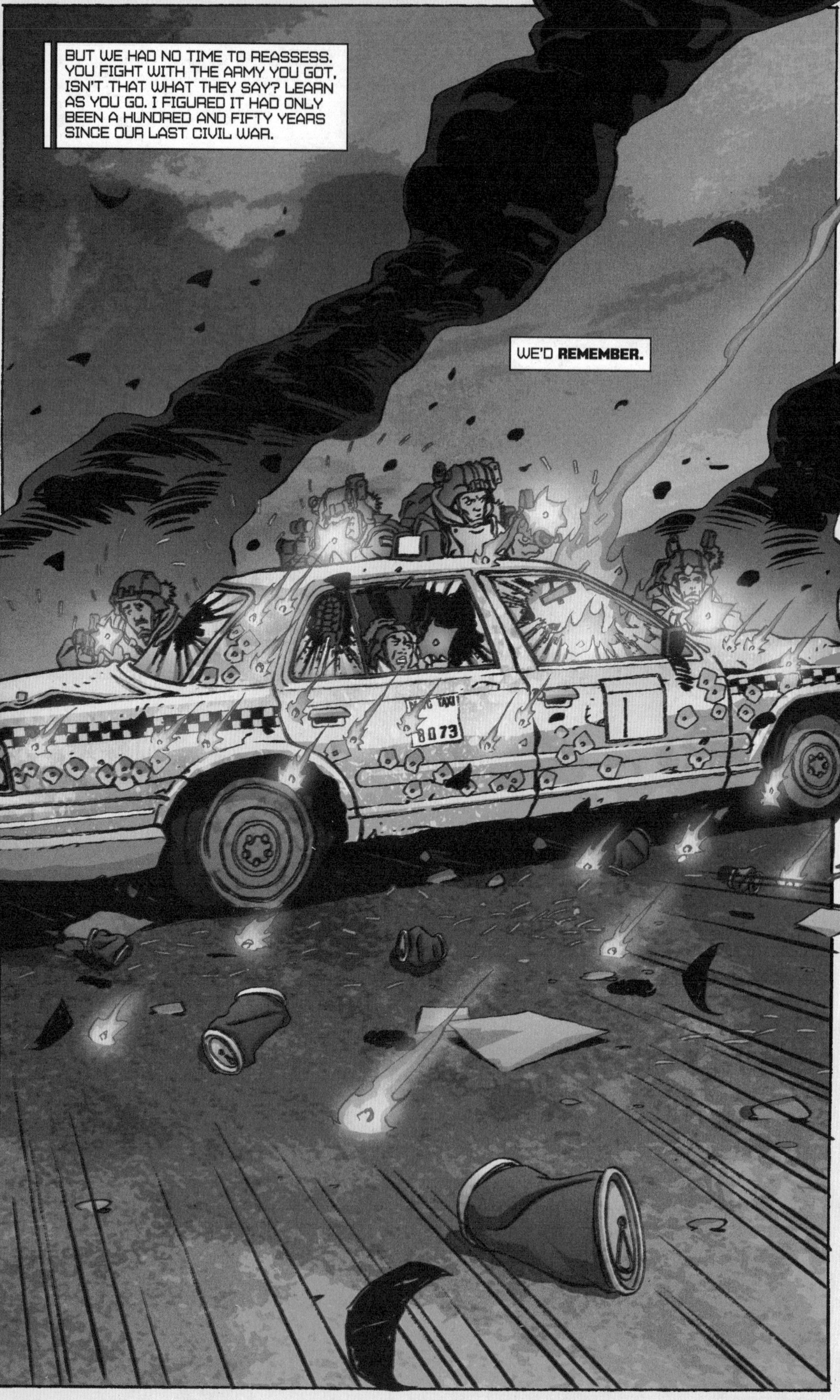
BUT WE HAD NO TIME TO REASSESS. YOU FIGHT WITH THE ARMY YOU GOT. ISN'T THAT WHAT THEY SAY? LEARN AS YOU GO. I FIGURED IT HAD ONLY BEEN A HUNDRED AND FIFTY YEARS SINCE OUR LAST CIVIL WAR.
WE'D **REMEMBER.**
8073

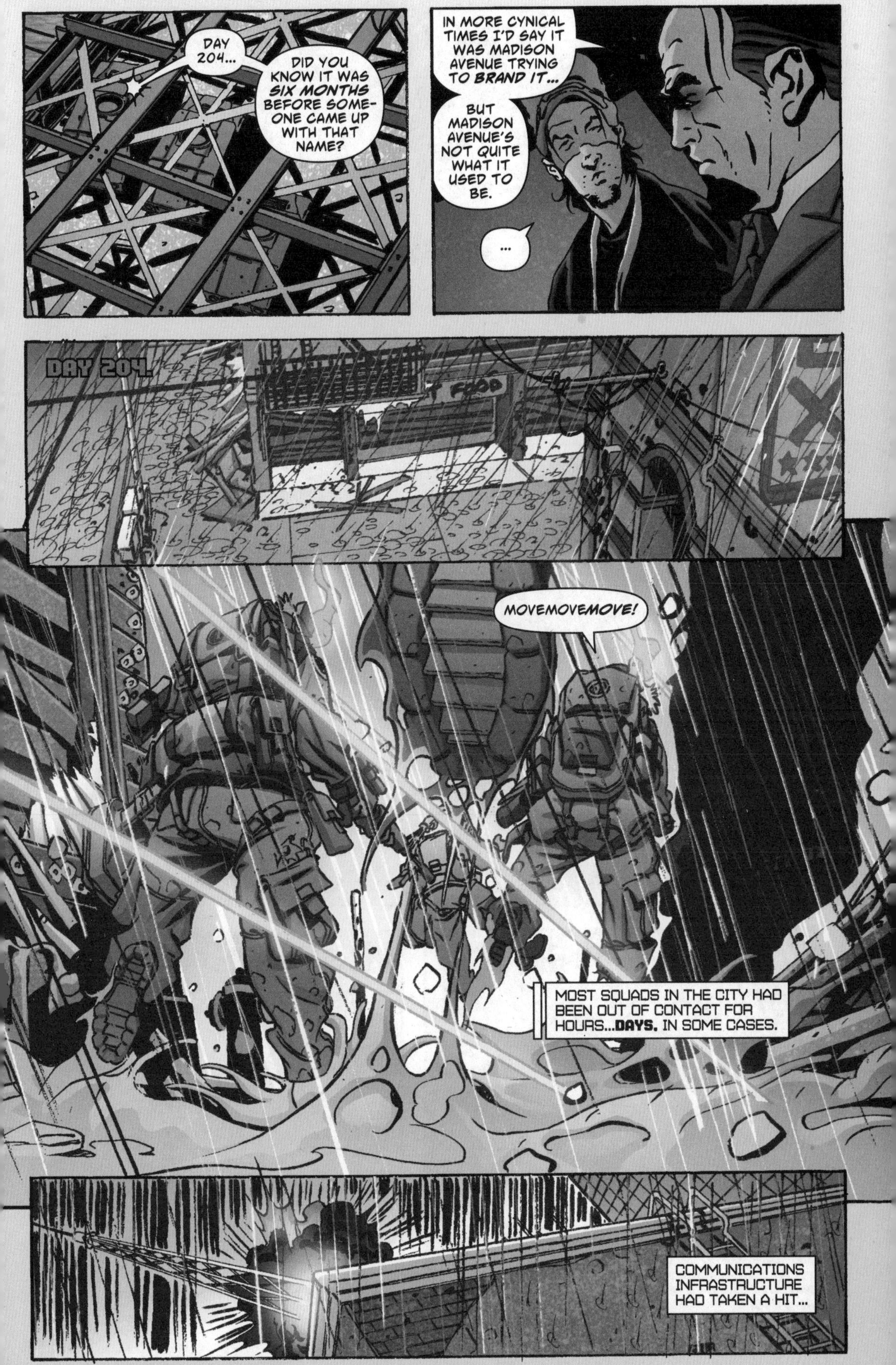
DAY 204...
DID YOU KNOW IT WAS SIX MONTHS BEFORE SOME-ONE CAME UP WITH THAT NAME?
IN MORE CYNICAL TIMES I'D SAY IT WAS MADISON AVENUE TRYING TO BRAND IT...
BUT MADISON AVENUE'S NOT QUITE WHAT IT USED TO BE.
...
DAY 204.
FOOD
MOVEMOVEMOVE!
MOST SQUADS IN THE CITY HAD BEEN OUT OF CONTACT FOR HOURS...DAYS. IN SOME CASES.
COMMUNICATIONS INFRASTRUCTURE HAD TAKEN A HIT...

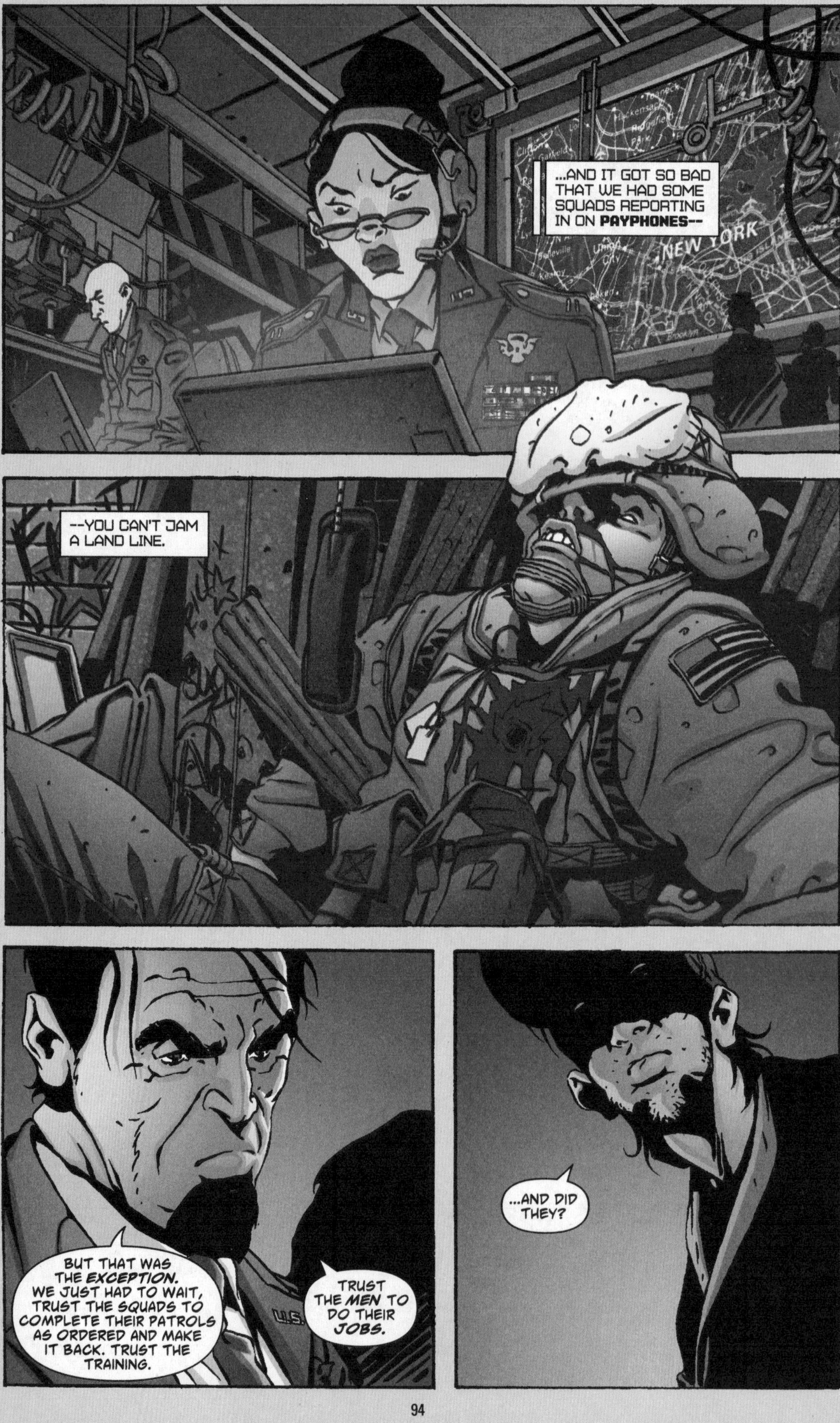
...AND IT GOT SO BAD THAT WE HAD SOME SQUADS REPORTING IN ON **PAYPHONES**--
NEW YORK
--YOU CAN'T JAM A LAND LINE.
BUT THAT WAS THE *EXCEPTION*. WE JUST HAD TO WAIT, TRUST THE SQUADS TO COMPLETE THEIR PATROLS AS ORDERED AND MAKE IT BACK. TRUST THE TRAINING.
TRUST THE *MEN* TO DO THEIR *JOBS*.
U.S.
...AND DID THEY?

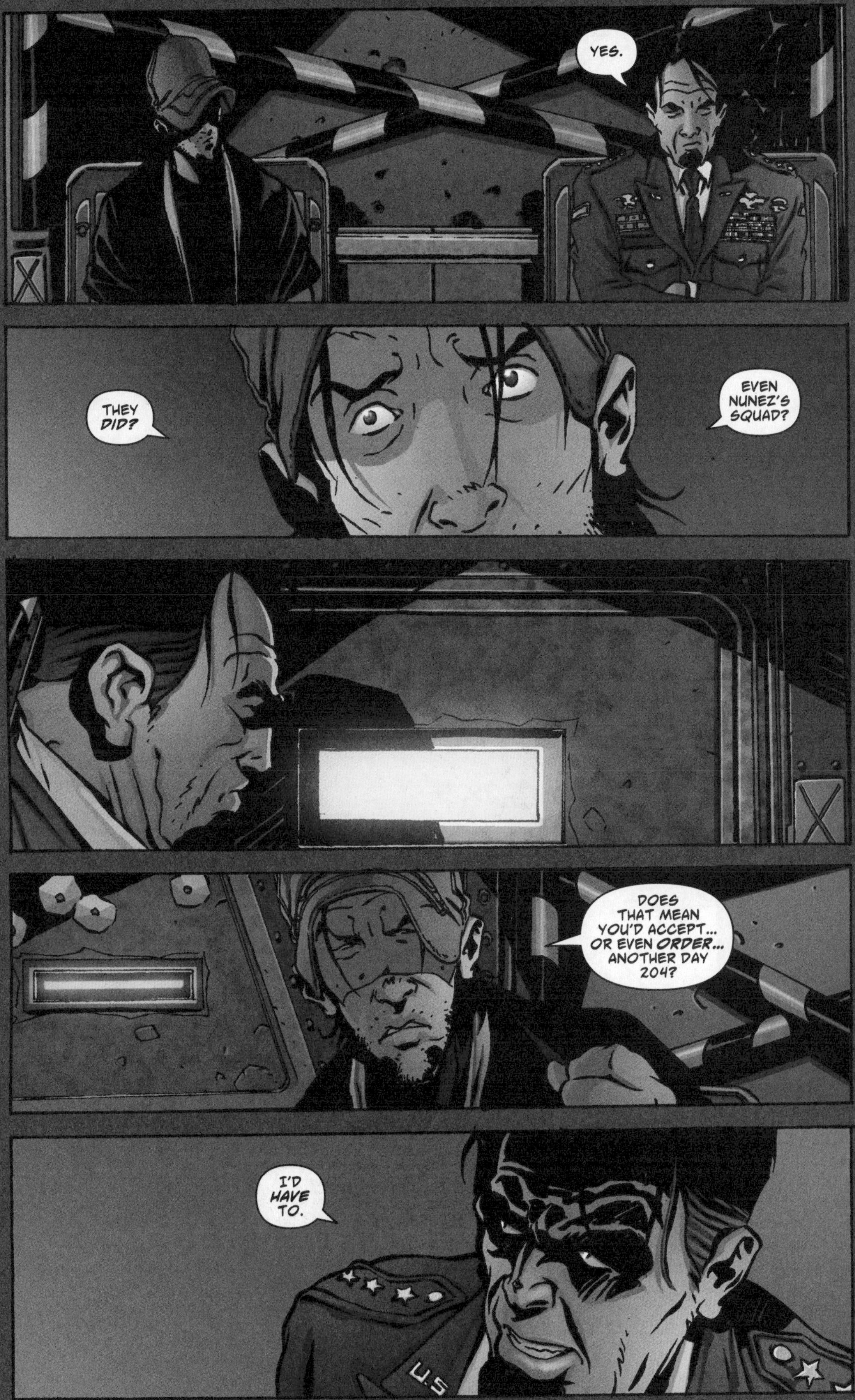
YES.
THEY DID?
EVEN NUNEZ'S SQUAD?
DOES THAT MEAN YOU'D ACCEPT... OR EVEN ORDER... ANOTHER DAY 204?
I'D HAVE TO.
U.S

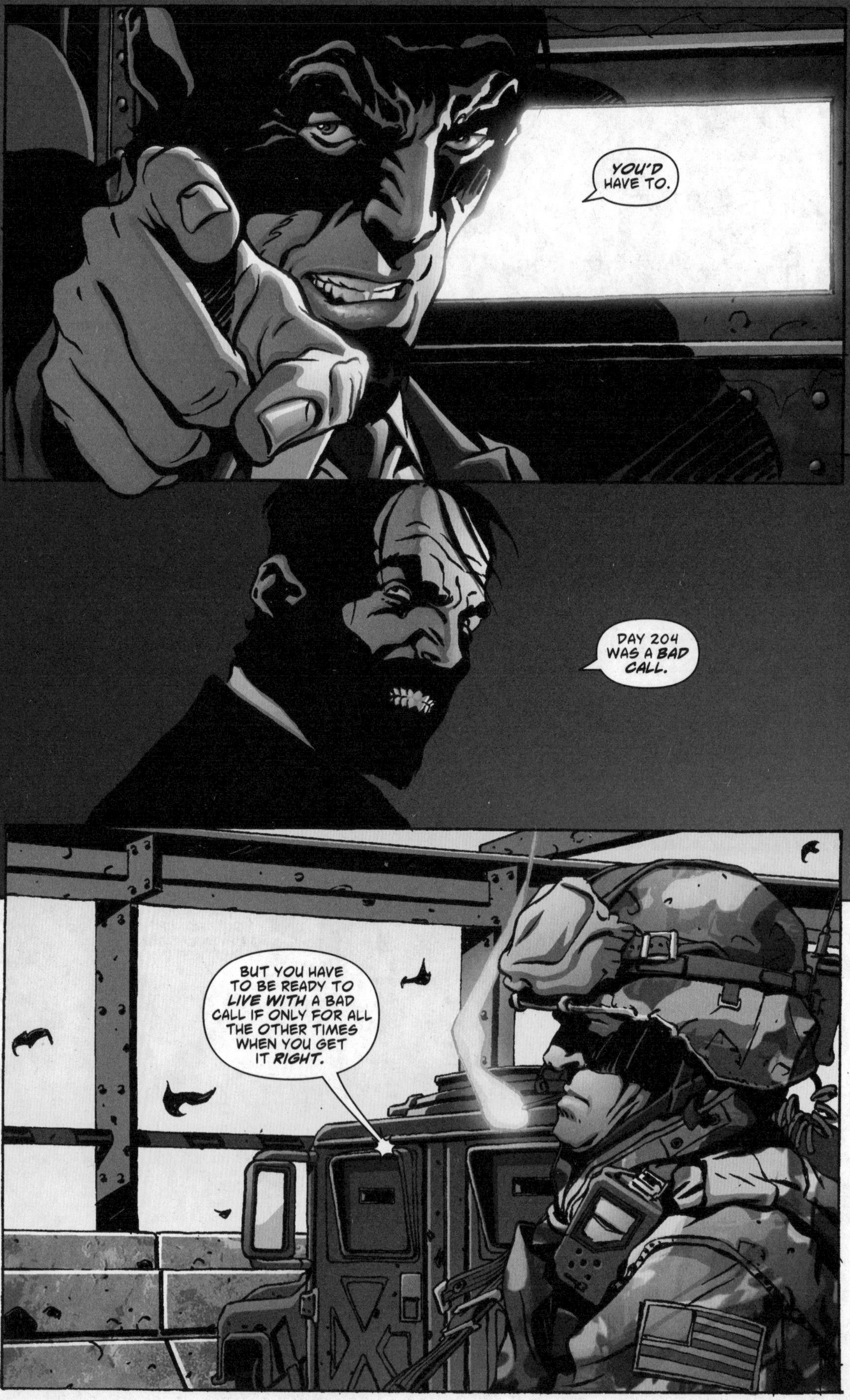
YOU'D HAVE TO.
DAY 204 WAS A BAD CALL.
BUT YOU HAVE TO BE READY TO LIVE WITH A BAD CALL IF ONLY FOR ALL THE OTHER TIMES WHEN YOU GET IT RIGHT.

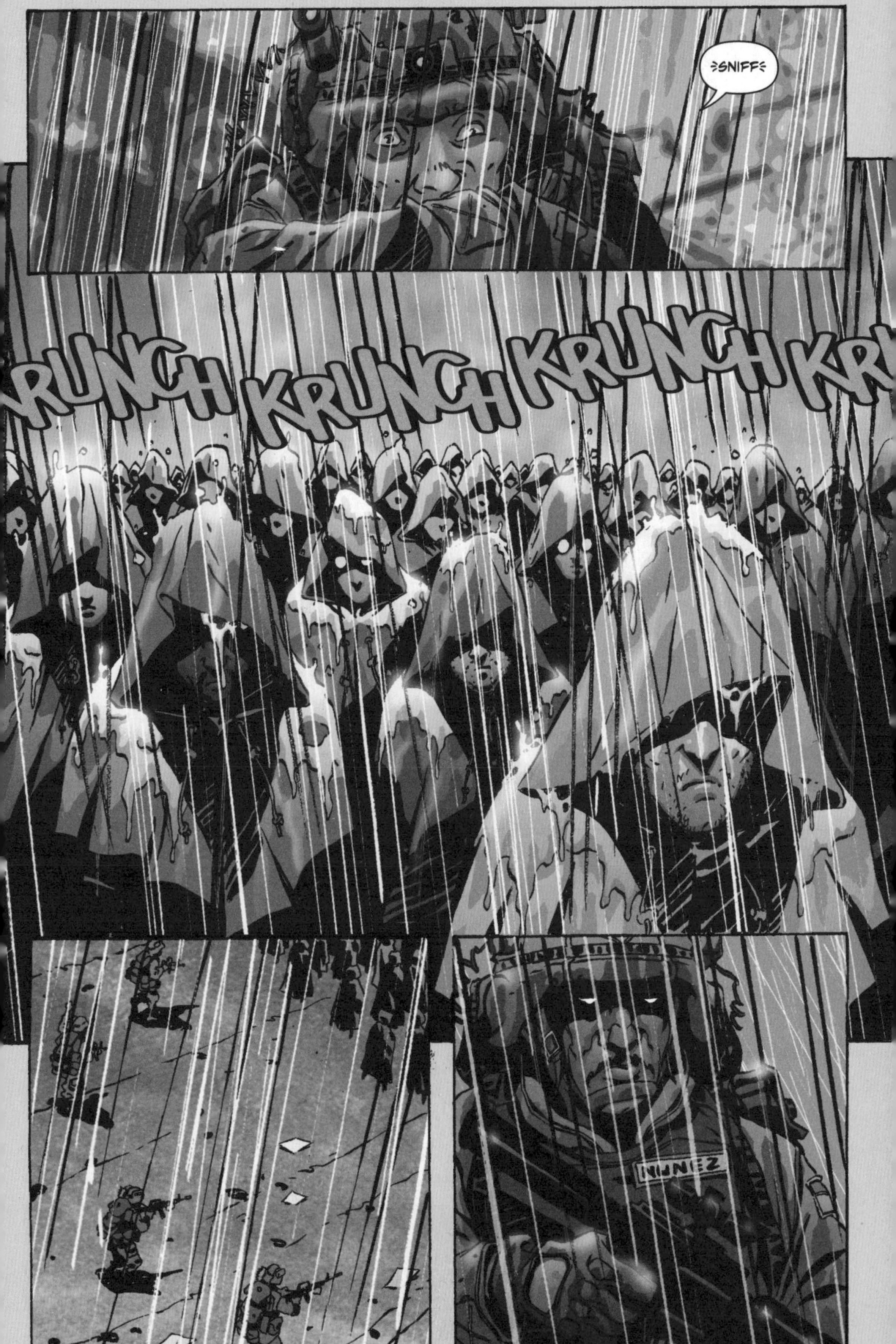

SNIFF
RUNCH KRUNCH KRUNCH KR
NUNEZ

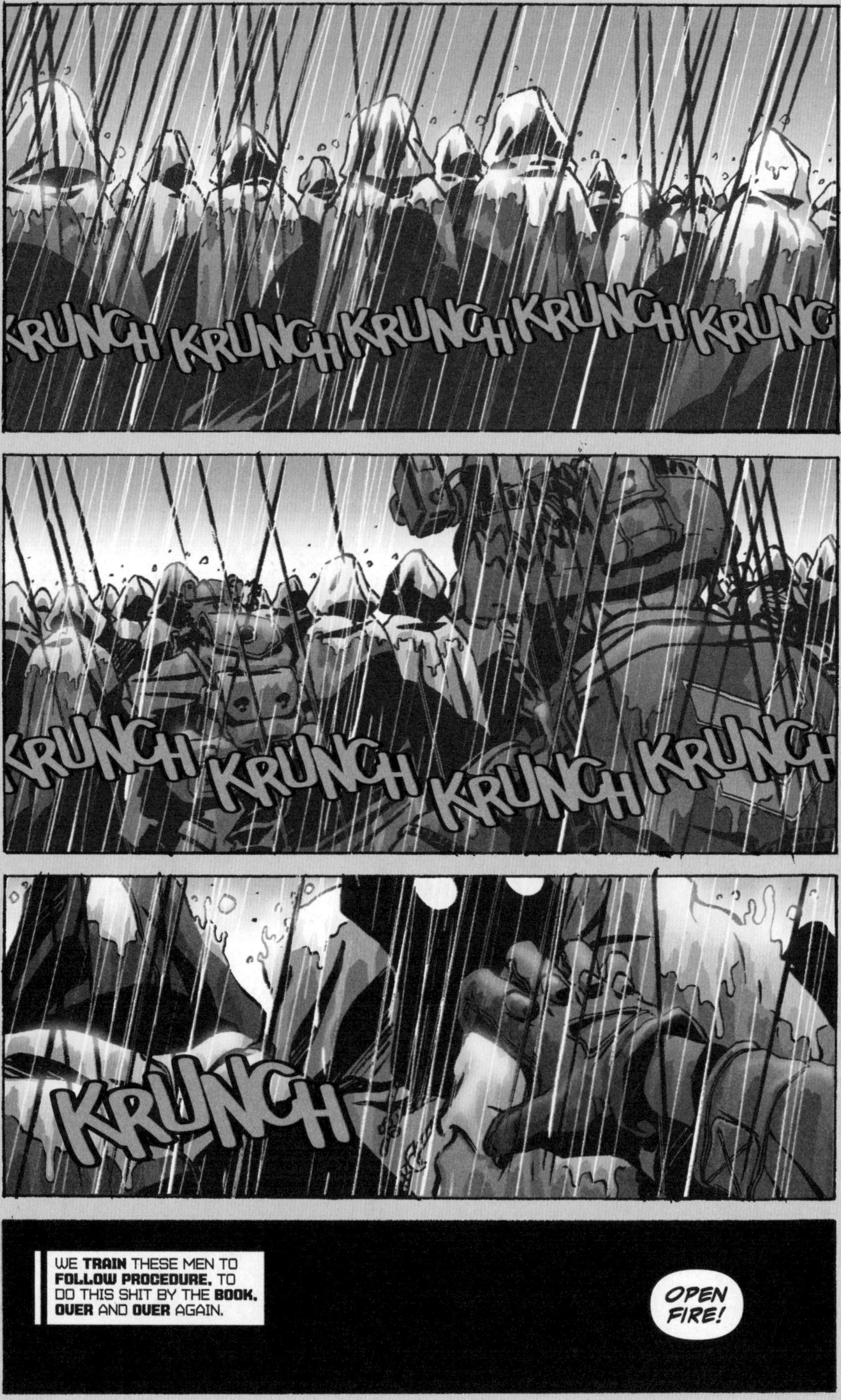
KRUNCH KRUNCH KRUNCH KRUNCH KRUNC
KRUNCH KRUNCH KRUNCH KRUNCH
KRUNCH
WE **TRAIN** THESE MEN TO **FOLLOW PROCEDURE,** TO DO THIS SHIT BY THE **BOOK, OVER** AND **OVER** AGAIN.
OPEN FIRE!

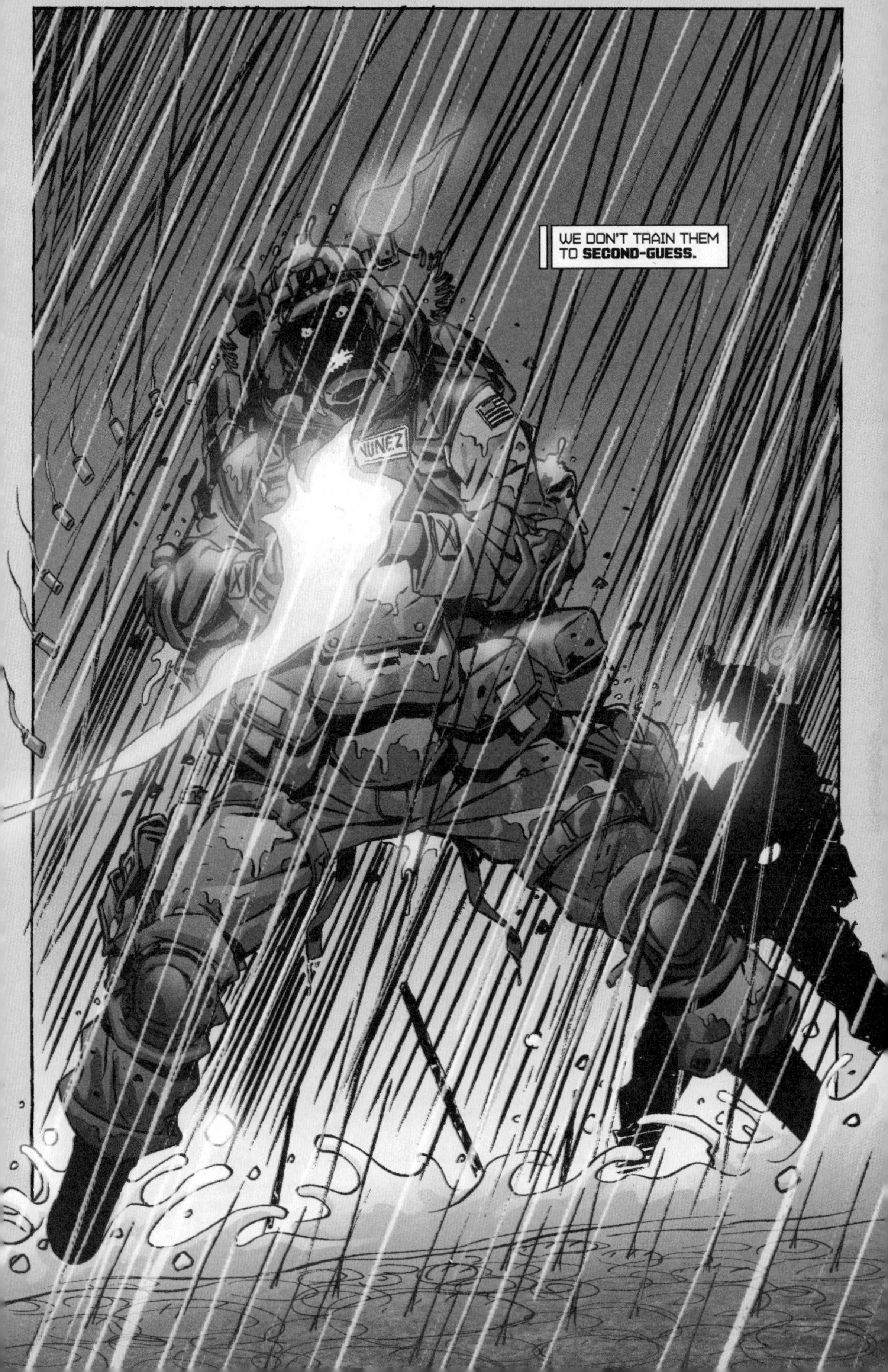
WE DON'T TRAIN THEM TO **SECOND-GUESS.**
YUNEZ

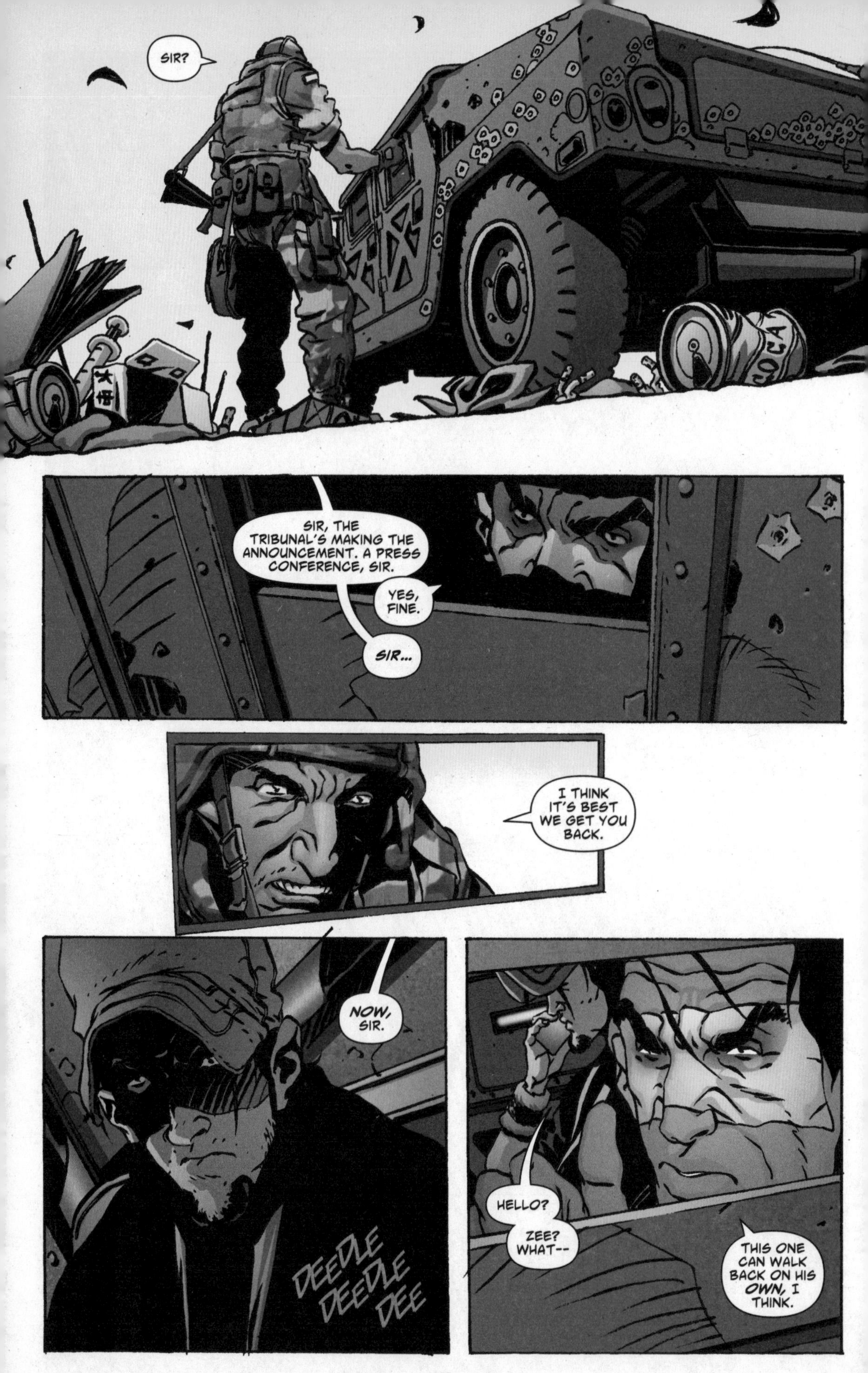
SIR?
SIR, THE TRIBUNAL'S MAKING THE ANNOUNCEMENT. A PRESS CONFERENCE, SIR.
YES, FINE.
SIR...
I THINK IT'S BEST WE GET YOU BACK.
NOW, SIR.
DEEDLE DEEDLE DEE
HELLO?
ZEE? WHAT--
THIS ONE CAN WALK BACK ON HIS OWN, I THINK.
COCA

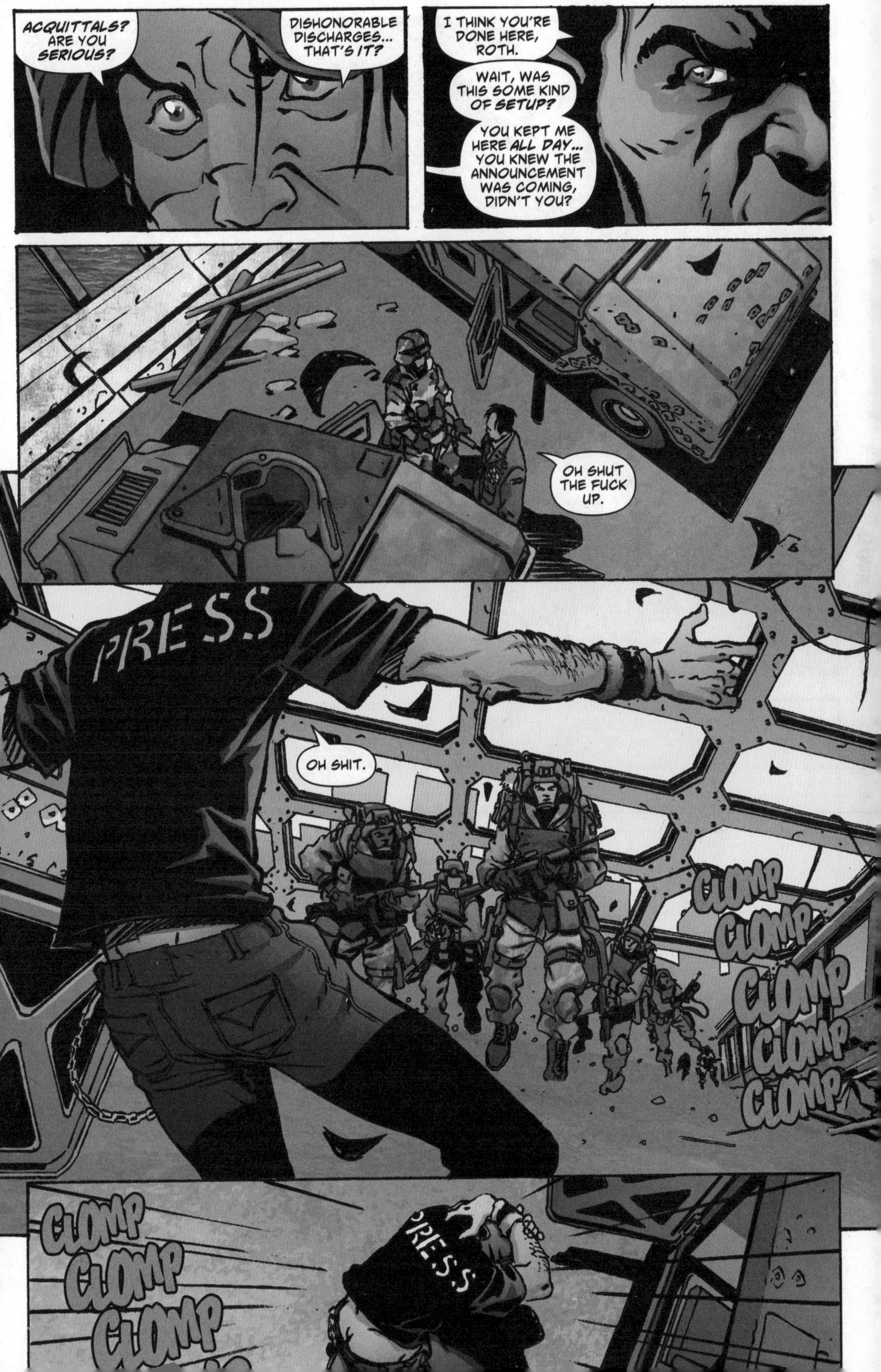
ACQUITTALS? ARE YOU SERIOUS?
DISHONORABLE DISCHARGES... THAT'S IT?
I THINK YOU'RE DONE HERE, ROTH.
WAIT, WAS THIS SOME KIND OF SETUP?
YOU KEPT ME HERE ALL DAY... YOU KNEW THE ANNOUNCEMENT WAS COMING, DIDN'T YOU?
OH SHUT THE FUCK UP.
PRESS
OH SHIT.
CLOMP CLOMP CLOMP CLOMP CLOMP
CLOMP CLOMP CLOMP
PRESS

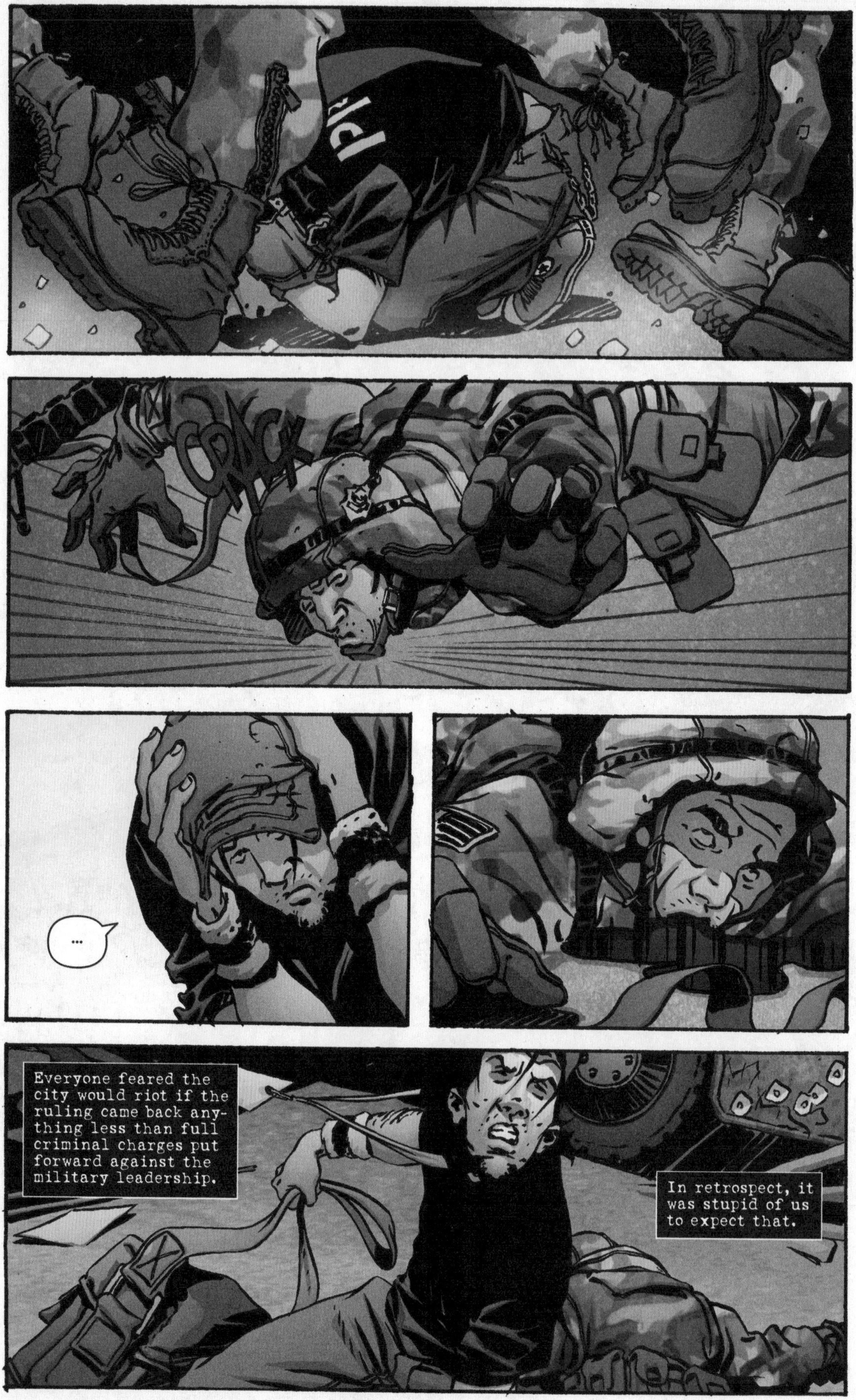
CRACK
...
Everyone feared the city would riot if the ruling came back anything less than full criminal charges put forward against the military leadership.
In retrospect, it was stupid of us to expect that.

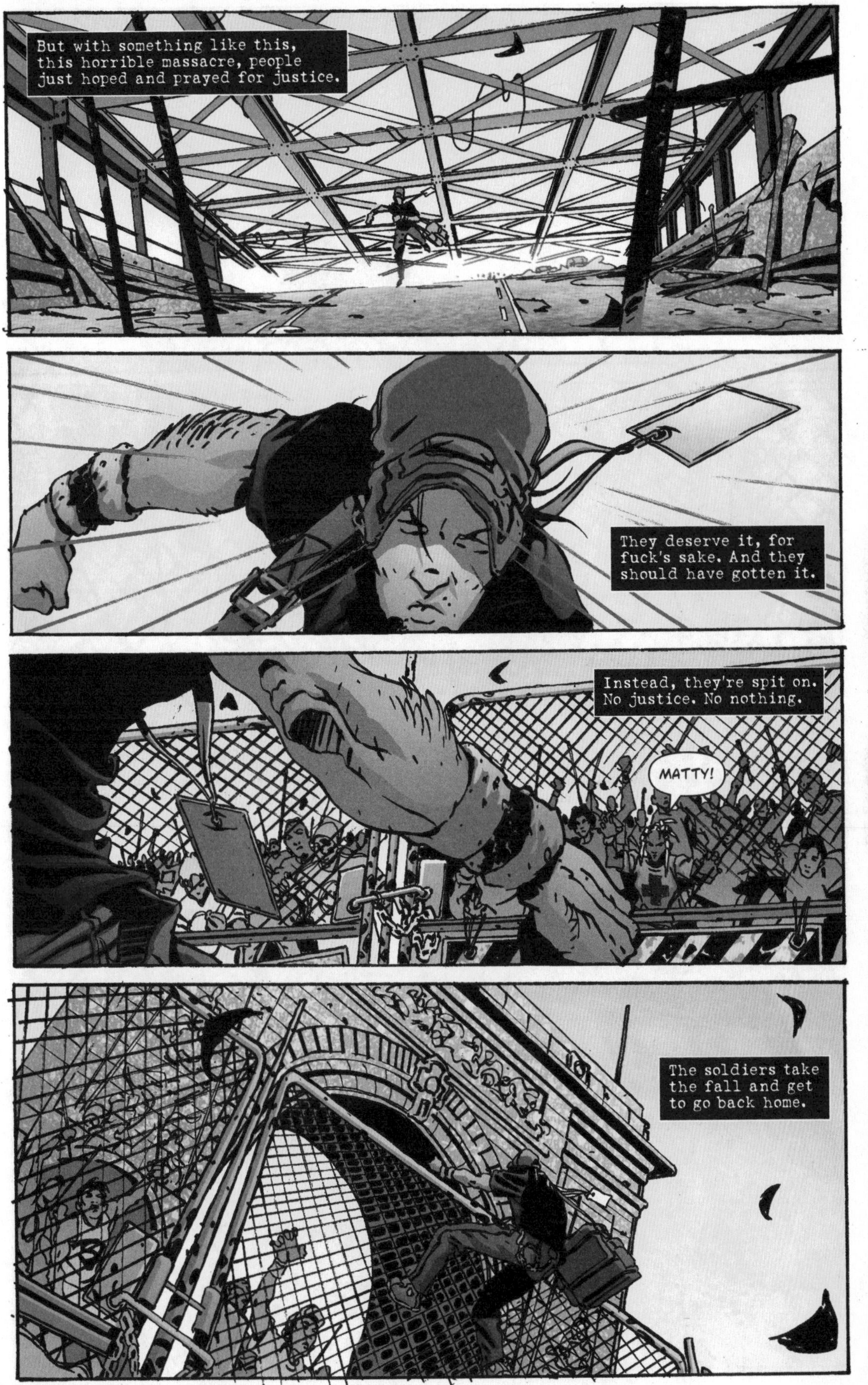
But with something like this, this horrible massacre, people just hoped and prayed for justice.
They deserve it, for fuck's sake. And they should have gotten it.
Instead, they're spit on. No justice. No nothing.
MATTY!
The soldiers take the fall and get to go back home.

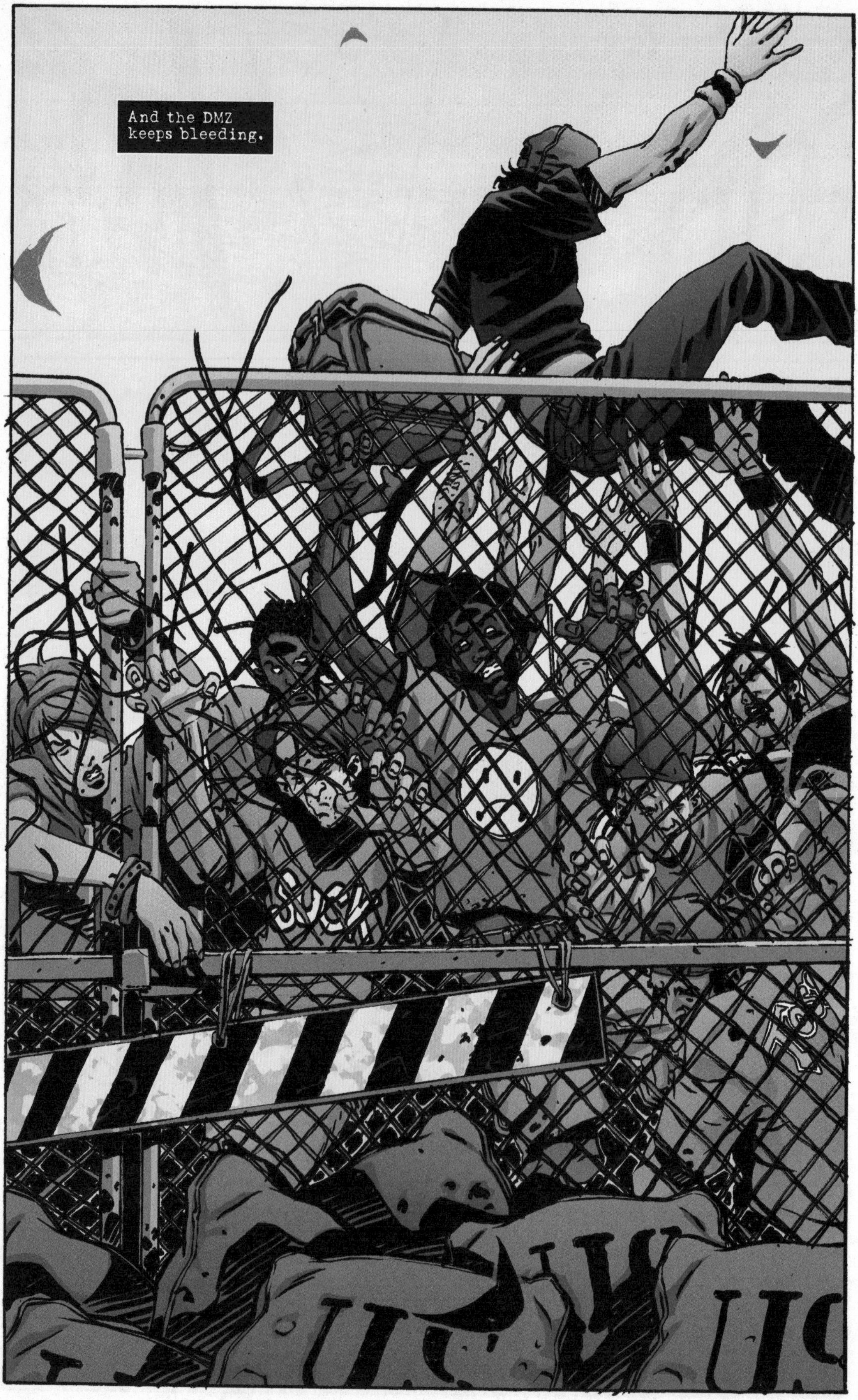
And the DMZ keeps bleeding.

CHAPTER FIVE

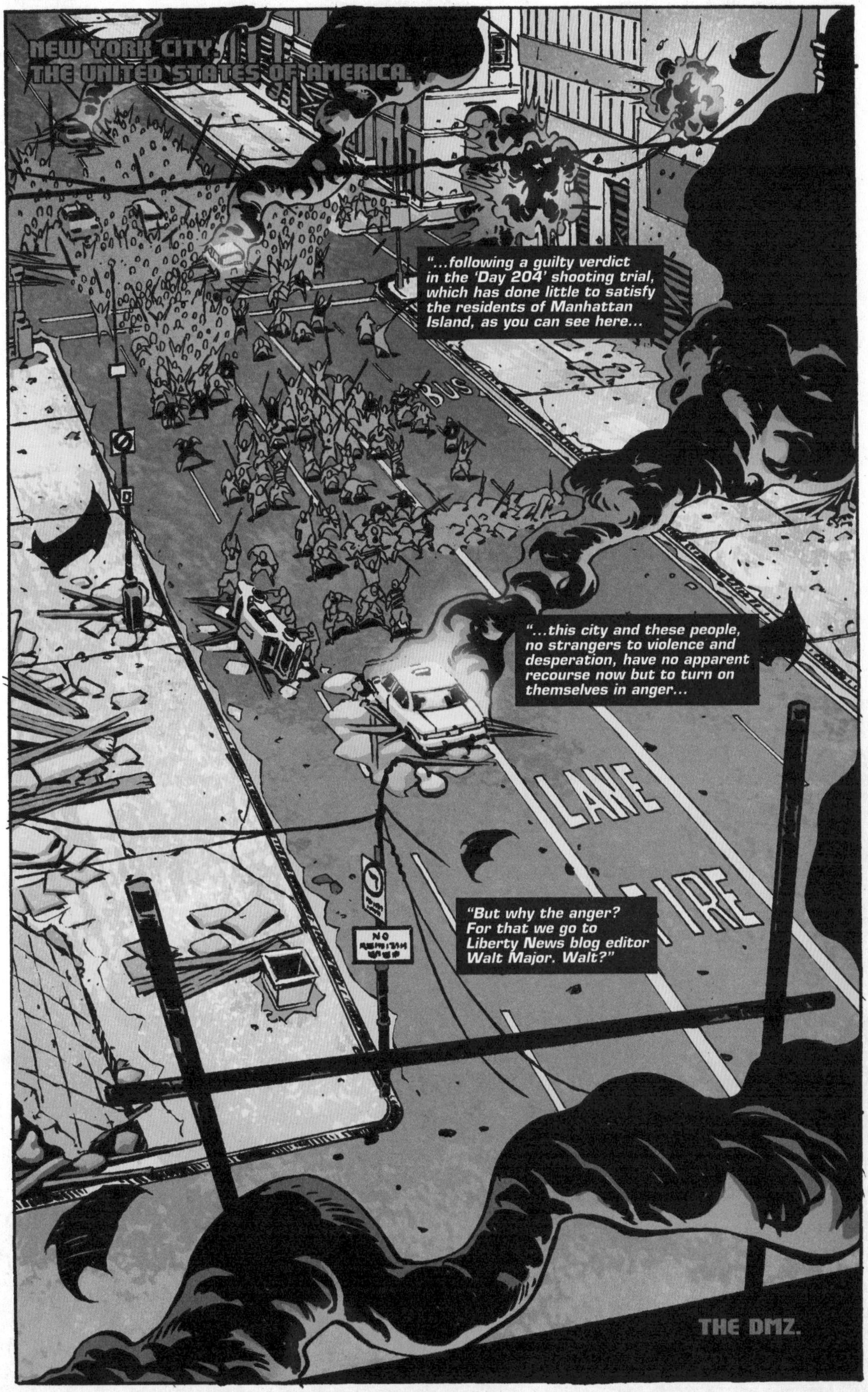
NEW YORK CITY,
THE UNITED STATES OF AMERICA.
"...following a guilty verdict in the 'Day 204' shooting trial, which has done little to satisfy the residents of Manhattan Island, as you can see here...
BUS
"...this city and these people, no strangers to violence and desperation, have no apparent recourse now but to turn on themselves in anger...
LANE
"But why the anger? For that we go to Liberty News blog editor Walt Major. Walt?"
NO
THE DMZ.

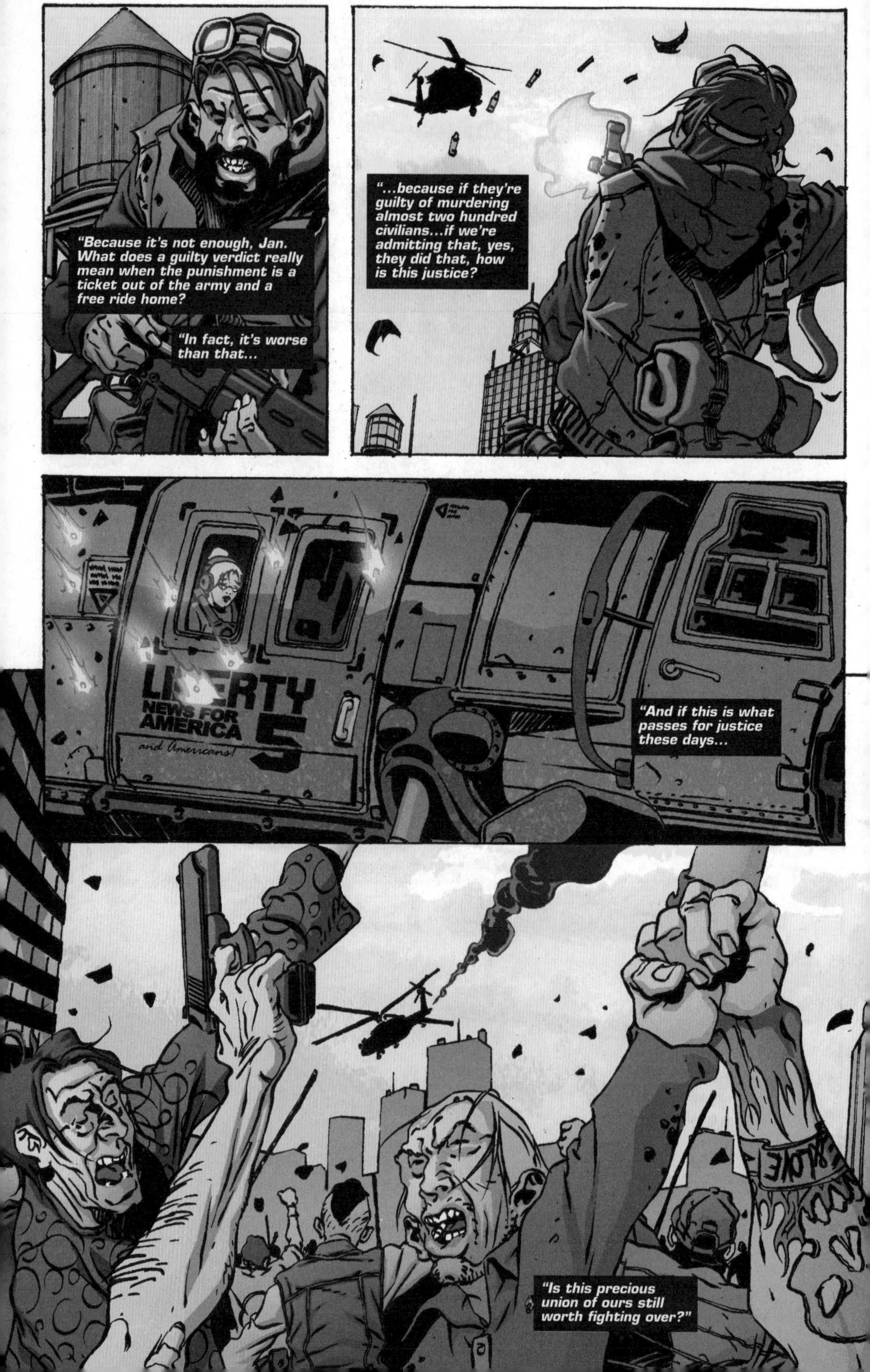
"Because it's not enough, Jan. What does a guilty verdict really mean when the punishment is a ticket out of the army and a free ride home?
"In fact, it's worse than that...
"...because if they're guilty of murdering almost two hundred civilians...if we're admitting that, yes, they did that, how is this justice?
NEWS FOR AMERICA
5
and Americans!
"And if this is what passes for justice these days...
"Is this precious union of ours still worth fighting over?"

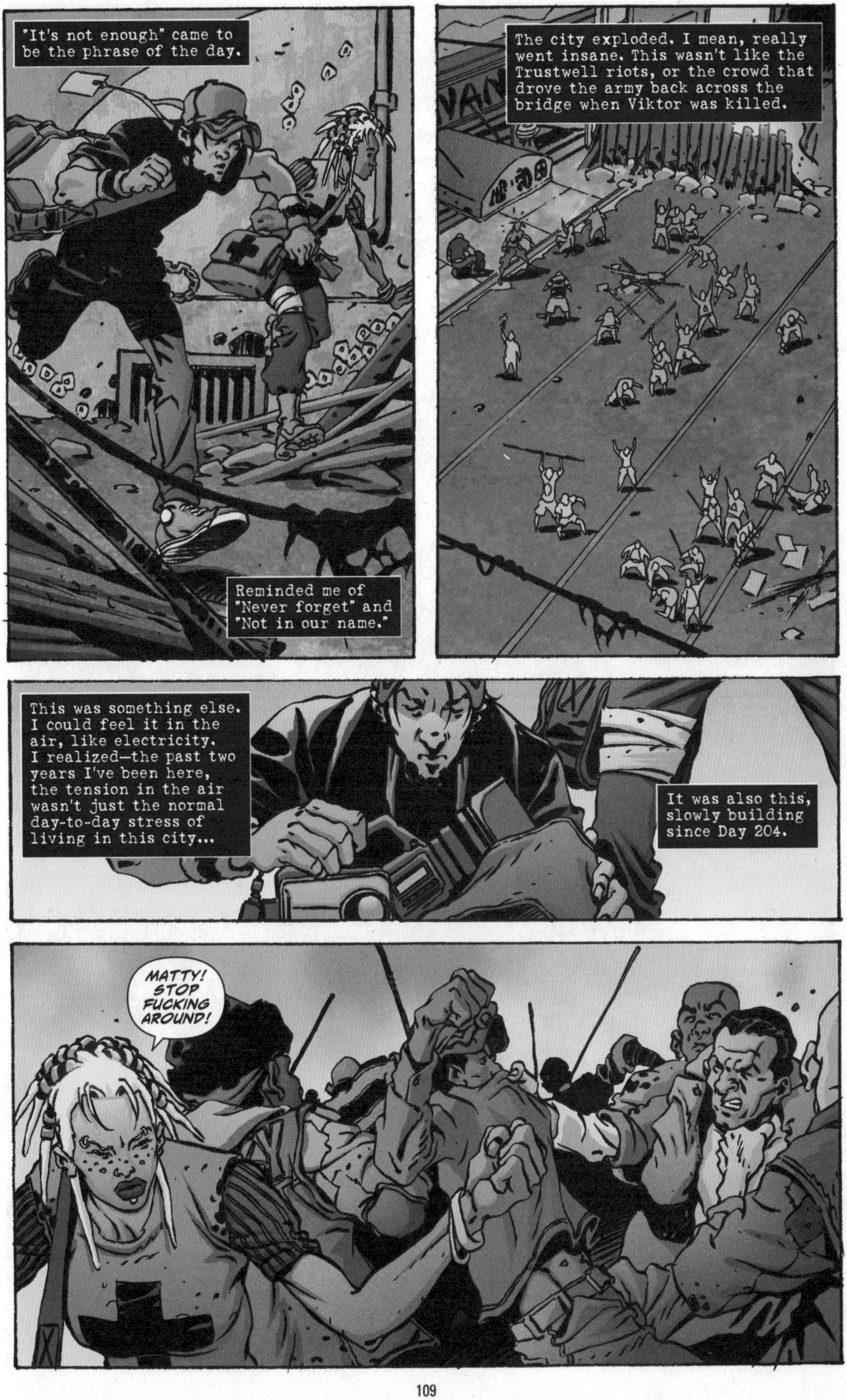
"It's not enough" came to be the phrase of the day.
Reminded me of "Never forget" and "Not in our name."
The city exploded. I mean, really went insane. This wasn't like the Trustwell riots, or the crowd that drove the army back across the bridge when Viktor was killed.
This was something else. I could feel it in the air, like electricity. I realized—the past two years I've been here, the tension in the air wasn't just the normal day-to-day stress of living in this city...
It was also this, slowly building since Day 204.
MATTY! STOP FUCKING AROUND!

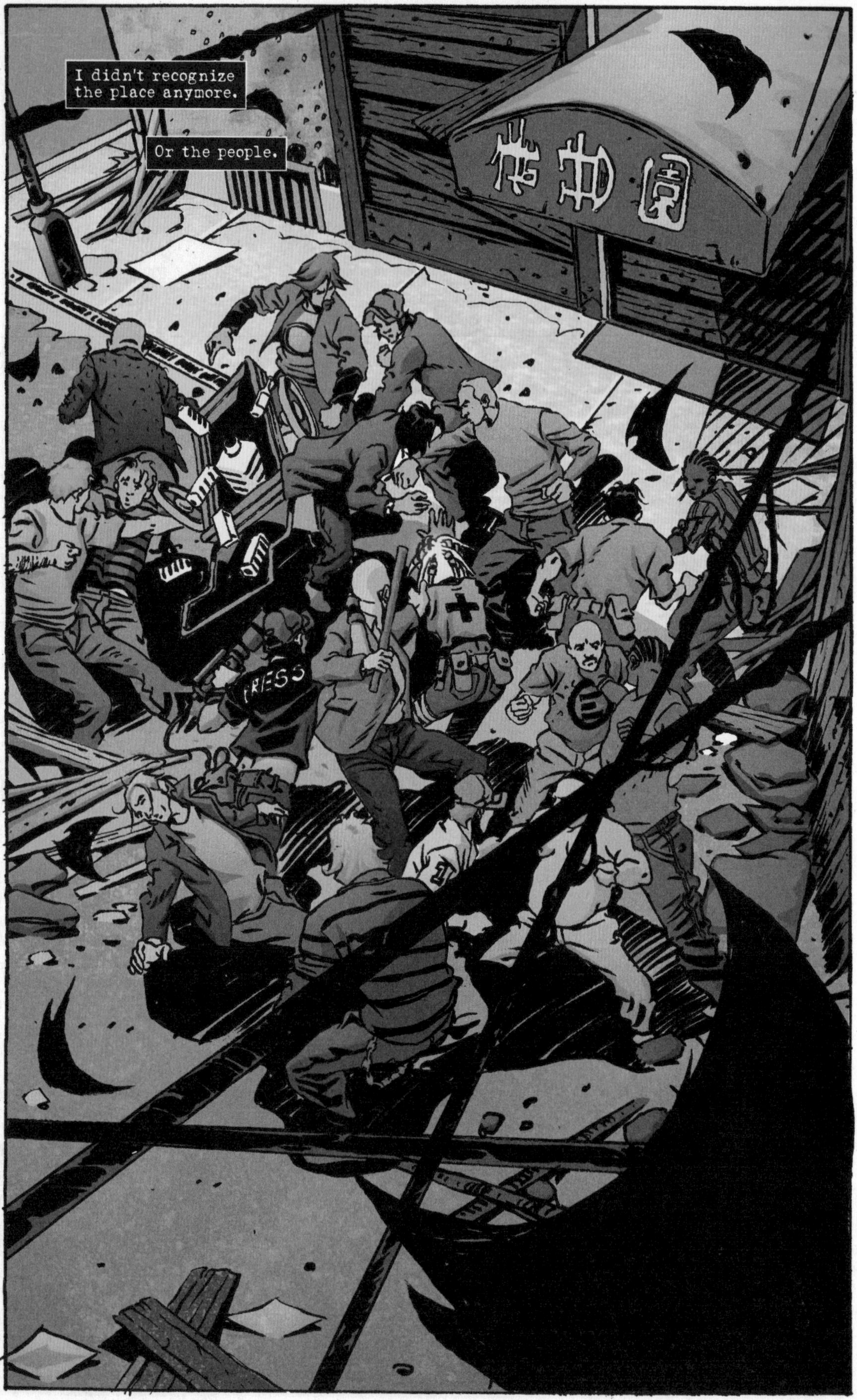
I didn't recognize the place anymore.
Or the people.

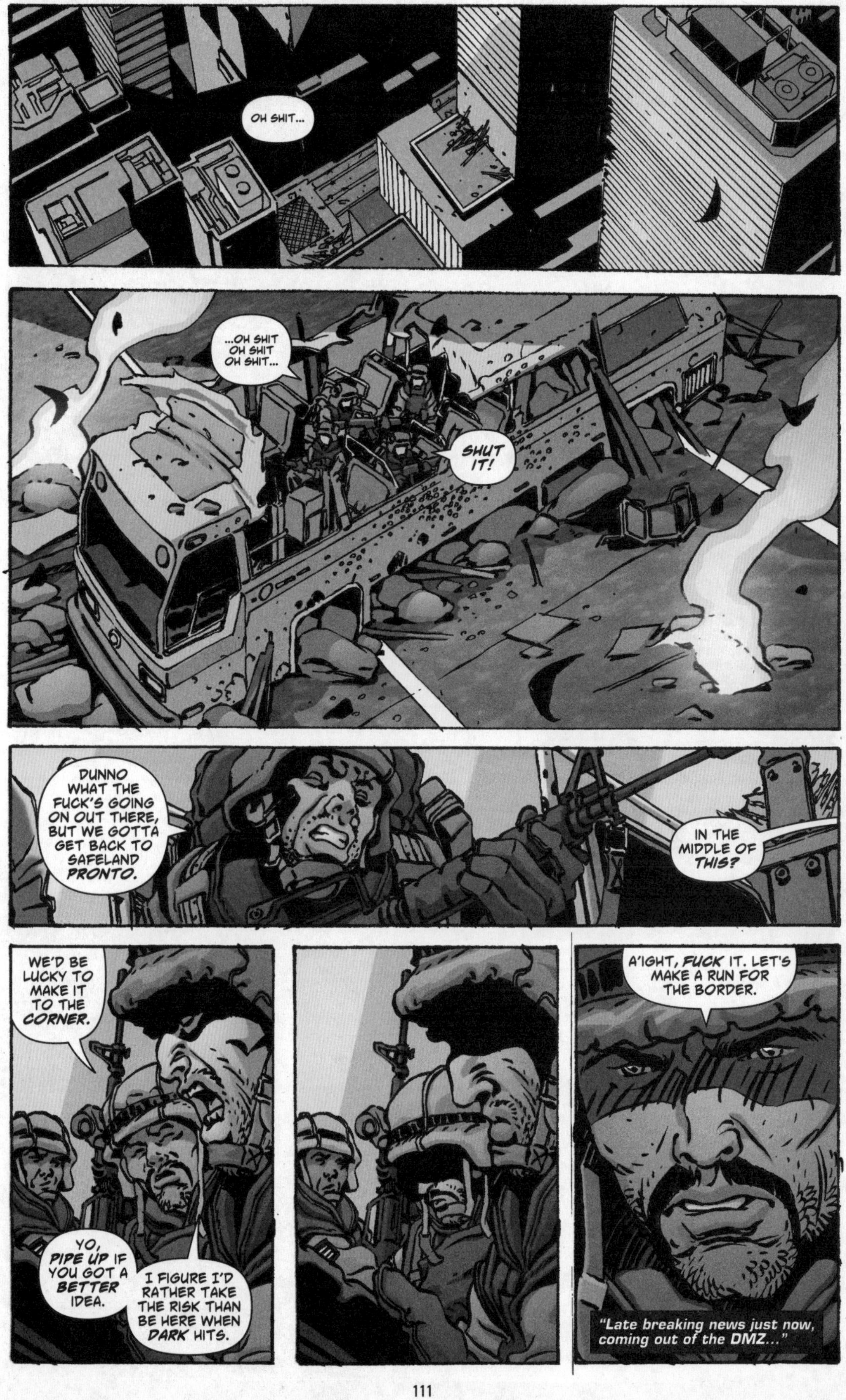
OH SHIT...
...OH SHIT OH SHIT OH SHIT...
SHUT IT!
DUNNO WHAT THE FUCK'S GOING ON OUT THERE, BUT WE GOTTA GET BACK TO SAFELAND PRONTO.
IN THE MIDDLE OF THIS?
WE'D BE LUCKY TO MAKE IT TO THE CORNER.
YO, PIPE UP IF YOU GOT A BETTER IDEA.
I FIGURE I'D RATHER TAKE THE RISK THAN BE HERE WHEN DARK HITS.
A'IGHT, FUCK IT. LET'S MAKE A RUN FOR THE BORDER.
"Late breaking news just now, coming out of the DMZ..."

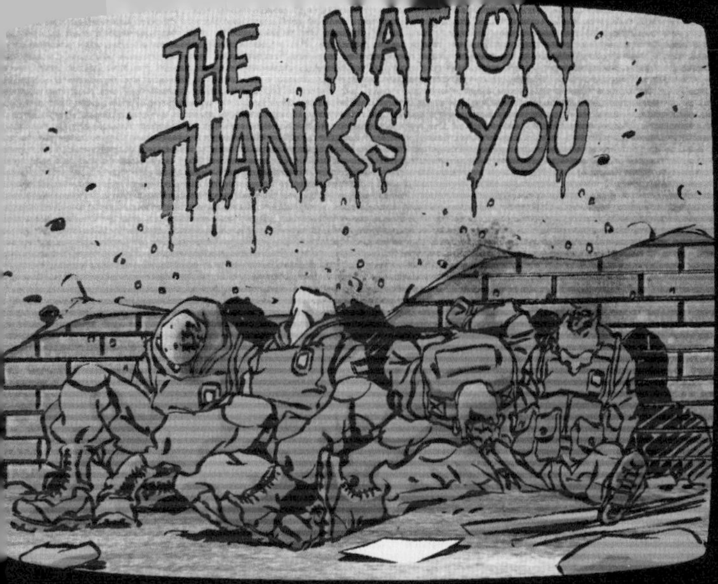
THE NATION THANKS YOU

"...five U.S. soldiers seen here, apparently the victims of torture and assassination at the hands of what experts claim is the 'Nation of Fearghus,' a violent hate-group known to operate within the city of Manhattan.

"These still images were emailed into Liberty News moments ago, and the identity of these heroic soldiers is being withheld pending identification.

"The riots following the 'Day 204' verdict enter their fifth hour, and with dusk approaching and nighttime to follow soon after, the death toll associated with this latest unrest threatens to skyrocket.

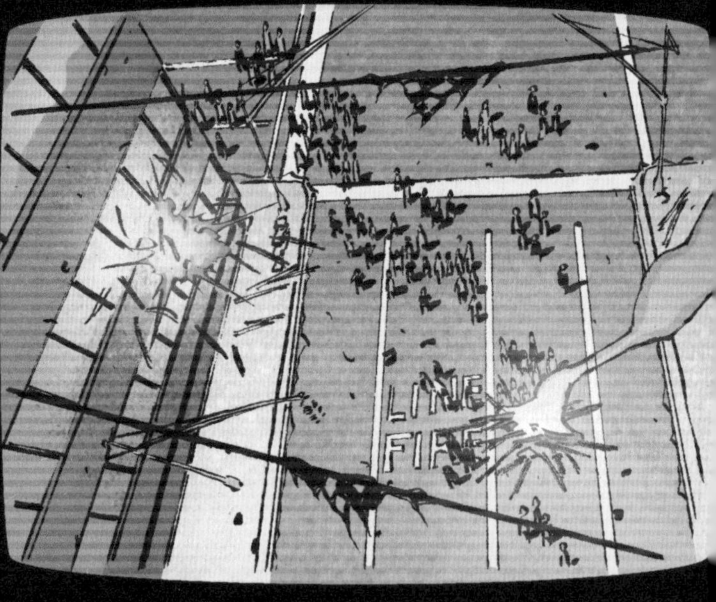

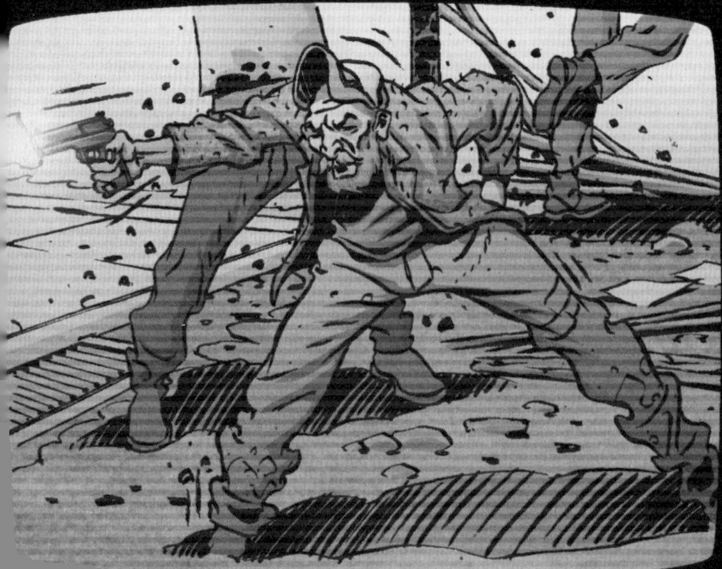

"The United States military remains helpless to intervene, and the various militant factions within the city show no desire to police themselves.

"A tragic ending to a tragic story."

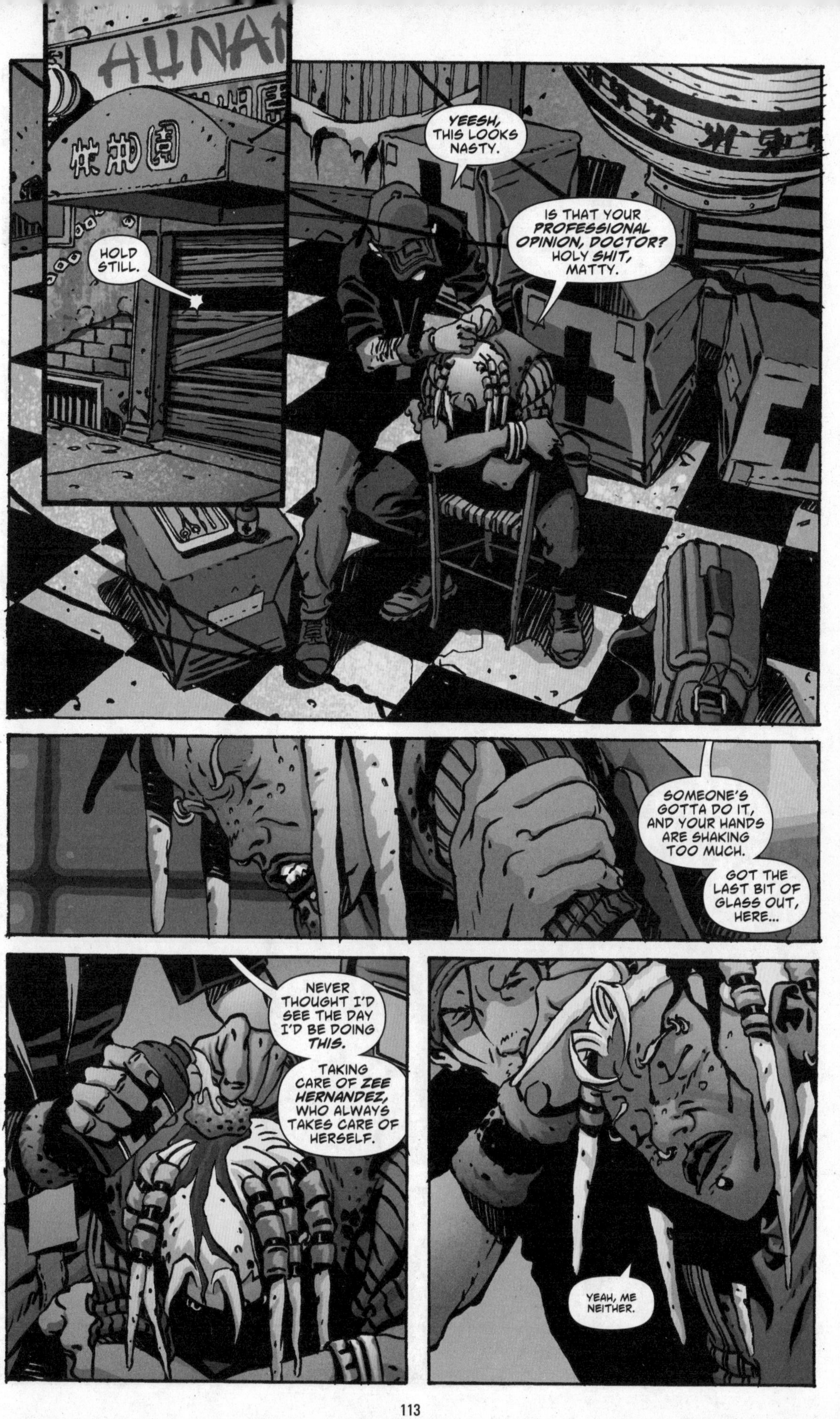
HUNAN
YEESH, THIS LOOKS NASTY.
HOLD STILL.
IS THAT YOUR PROFESSIONAL OPINION, DOCTOR? HOLY SHIT, MATTY.
SOMEONE'S GOTTA DO IT, AND YOUR HANDS ARE SHAKING TOO MUCH.
GOT THE LAST BIT OF GLASS OUT, HERE...
NEVER THOUGHT I'D SEE THE DAY I'D BE DOING THIS.
TAKING CARE OF ZEE HERNANDEZ, WHO ALWAYS TAKES CARE OF HERSELF.
YEAH, ME NEITHER.

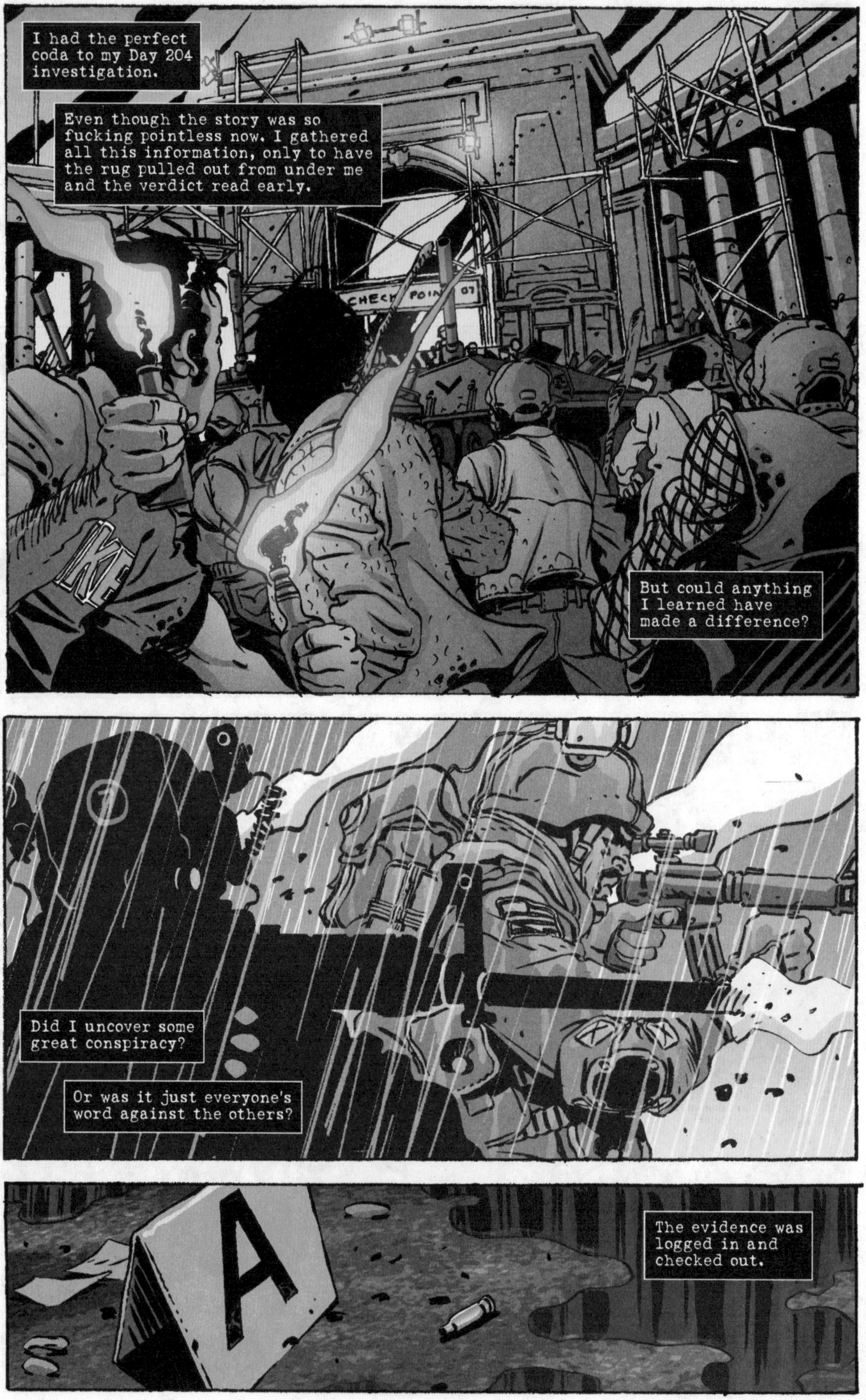
I had the perfect coda to my Day 204 investigation.
Even though the story was so fucking pointless now. I gathered all this information, only to have the rug pulled out from under me and the verdict read early.
But could anything I learned have made a difference?
Did I uncover some great conspiracy?
Or was it just everyone's word against the others?
The evidence was logged in and checked out.

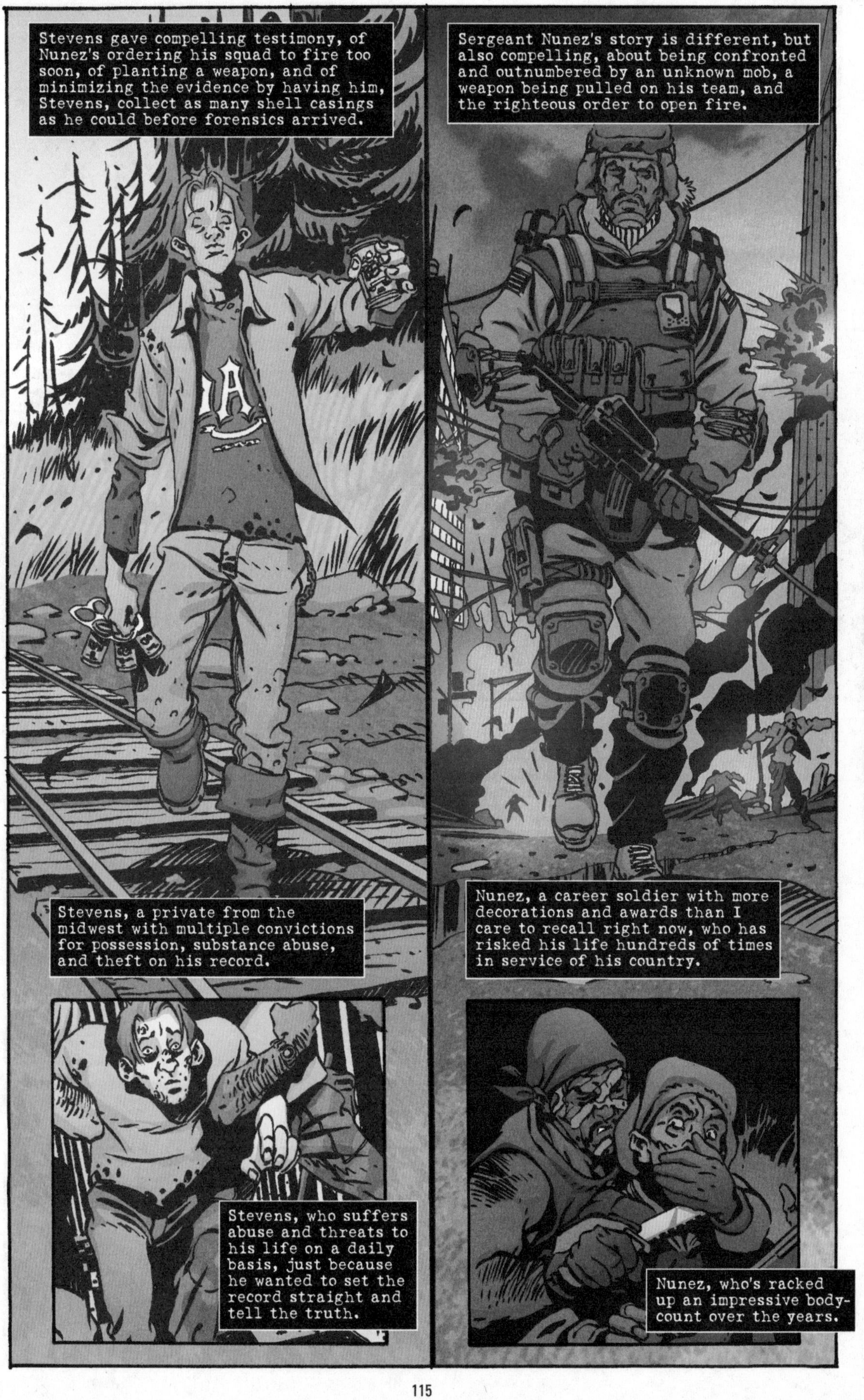

Stevens gave compelling testimony, of Nunez's ordering his squad to fire too soon, of planting a weapon, and of minimizing the evidence by having him, Stevens, collect as many shell casings as he could before forensics arrived.
Sergeant Nunez's story is different, but also compelling, about being confronted and outnumbered by an unknown mob, a weapon being pulled on his team, and the righteous order to open fire.
Stevens, a private from the midwest with multiple convictions for possession, substance abuse, and theft on his record.
Nunez, a career soldier with more decorations and awards than I care to recall right now, who has risked his life hundreds of times in service of his country.
Stevens, who suffers abuse and threats to his life on a daily basis, just because he wanted to set the record straight and tell the truth.
Nunez, who's racked up an impressive body-count over the years.

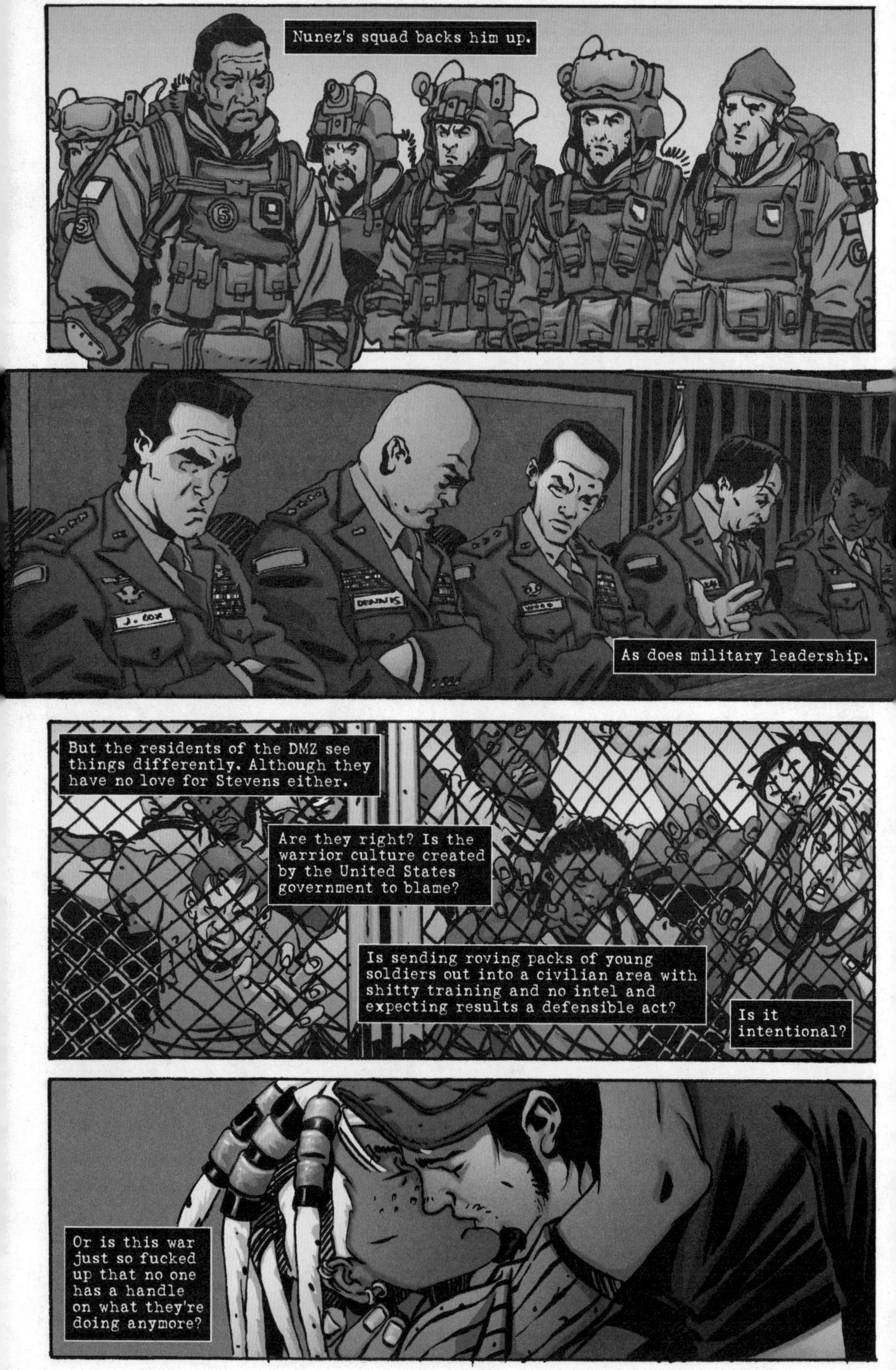
Nunez's squad backs him up.
As does military leadership.
But the residents of the DMZ see things differently. Although they have no love for Stevens either.
Are they right? Is the warrior culture created by the United States government to blame?
Is sending roving packs of young soldiers out into a civilian area with shitty training and no intel and expecting results a defensible act?
Is it intentional?
Or is this war just so fucked up that no one has a handle on what they're doing anymore?

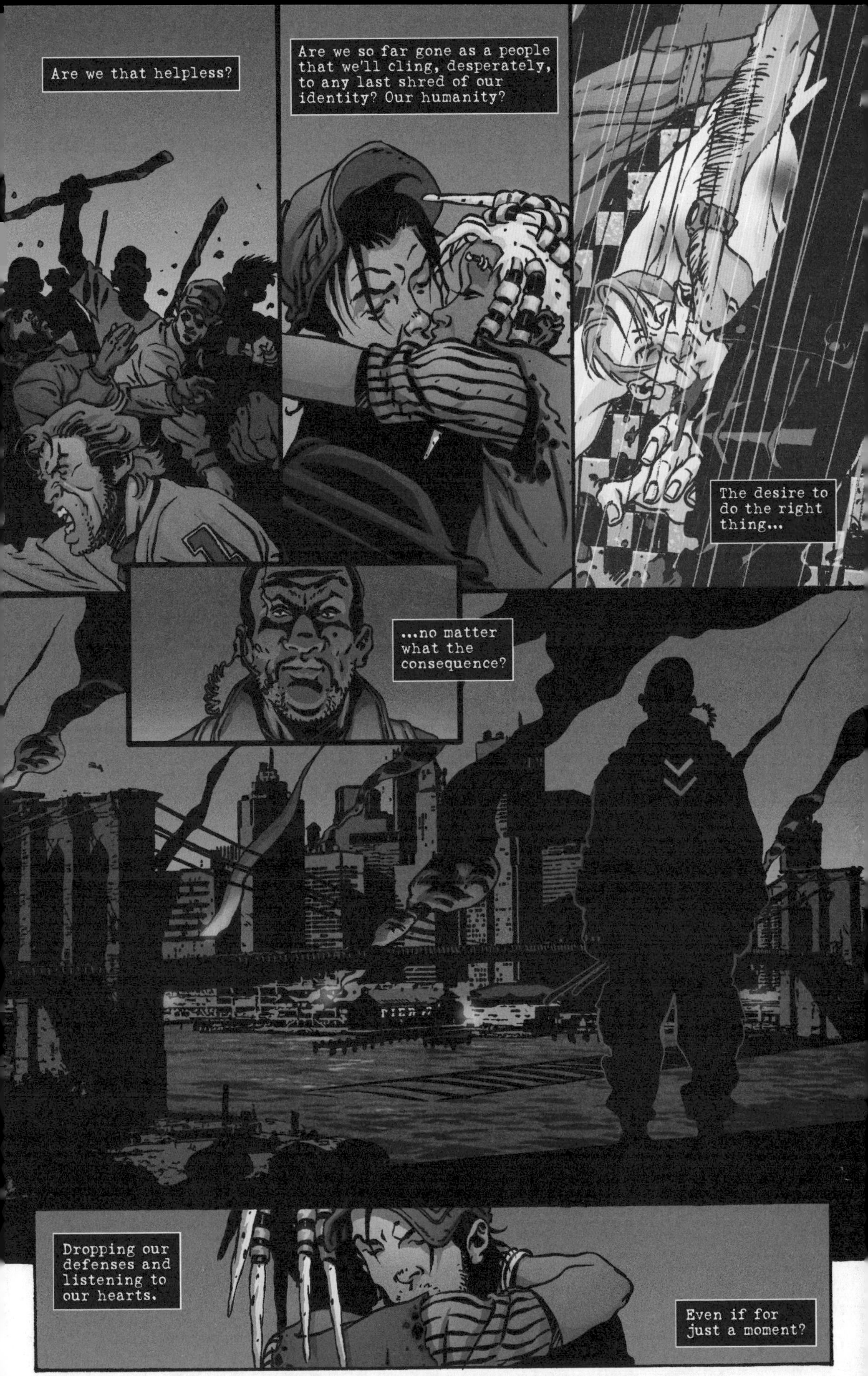
Are we that helpless?
Are we so far gone as a people that we'll cling, desperately, to any last shred of our identity? Our humanity?
The desire to do the right thing...
...no matter what the consequence?
PIER 17
Dropping our defenses and listening to our hearts.
Even if for just a moment?

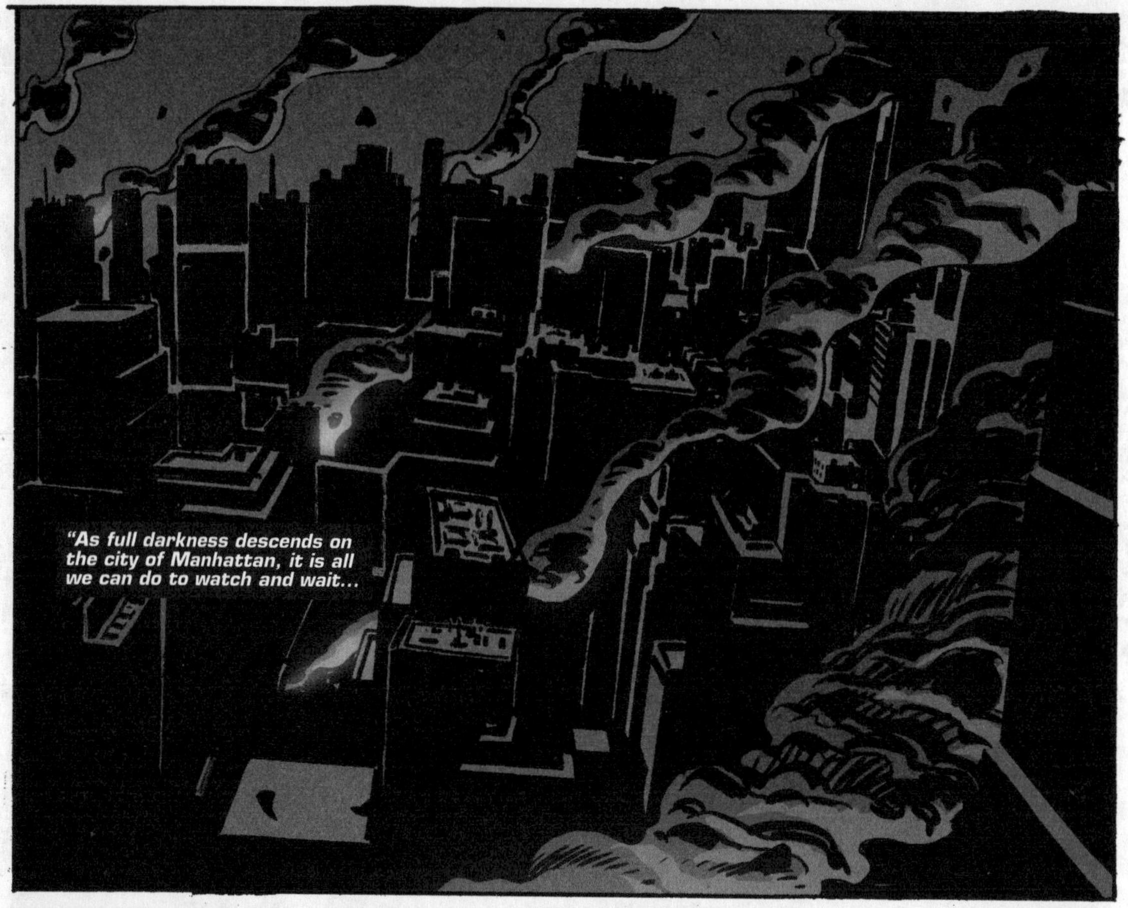
"As full darkness descends on the city of Manhattan, it is all we can do to watch and wait...

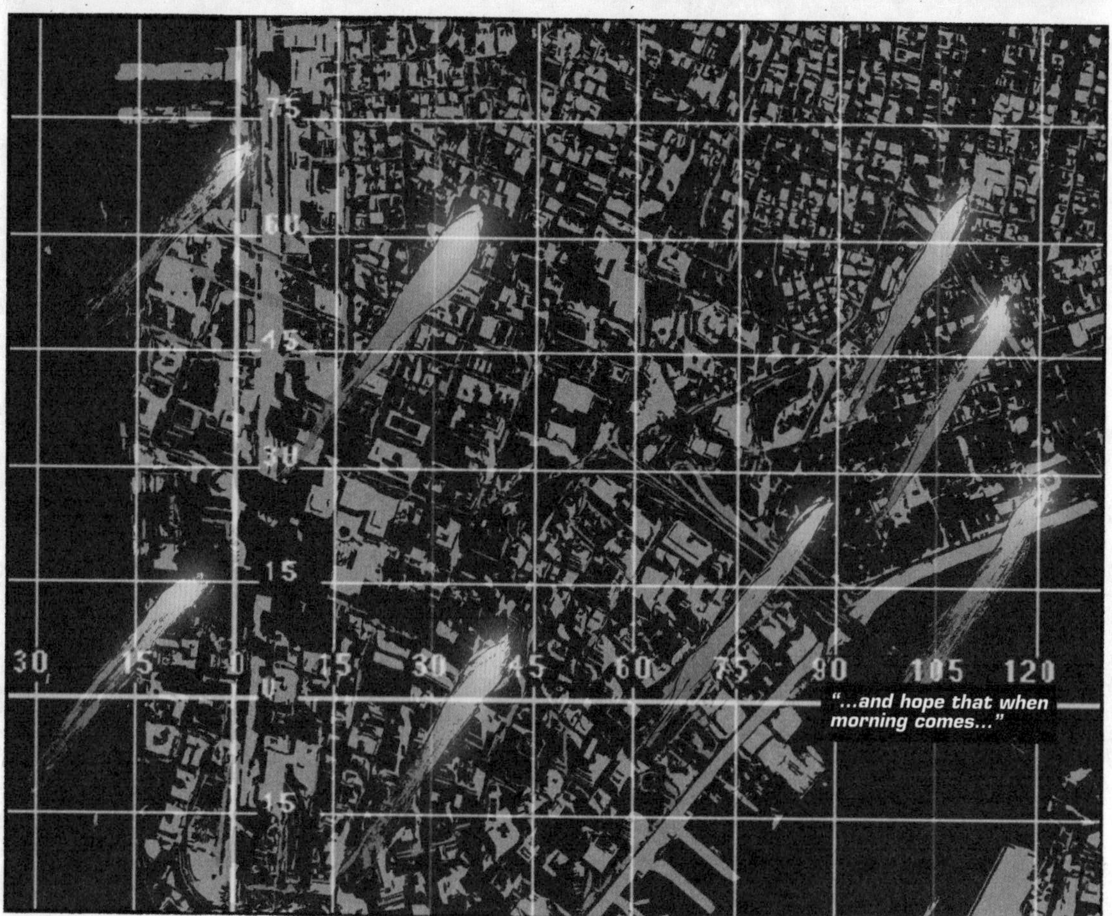
"...and hope that when morning comes..."

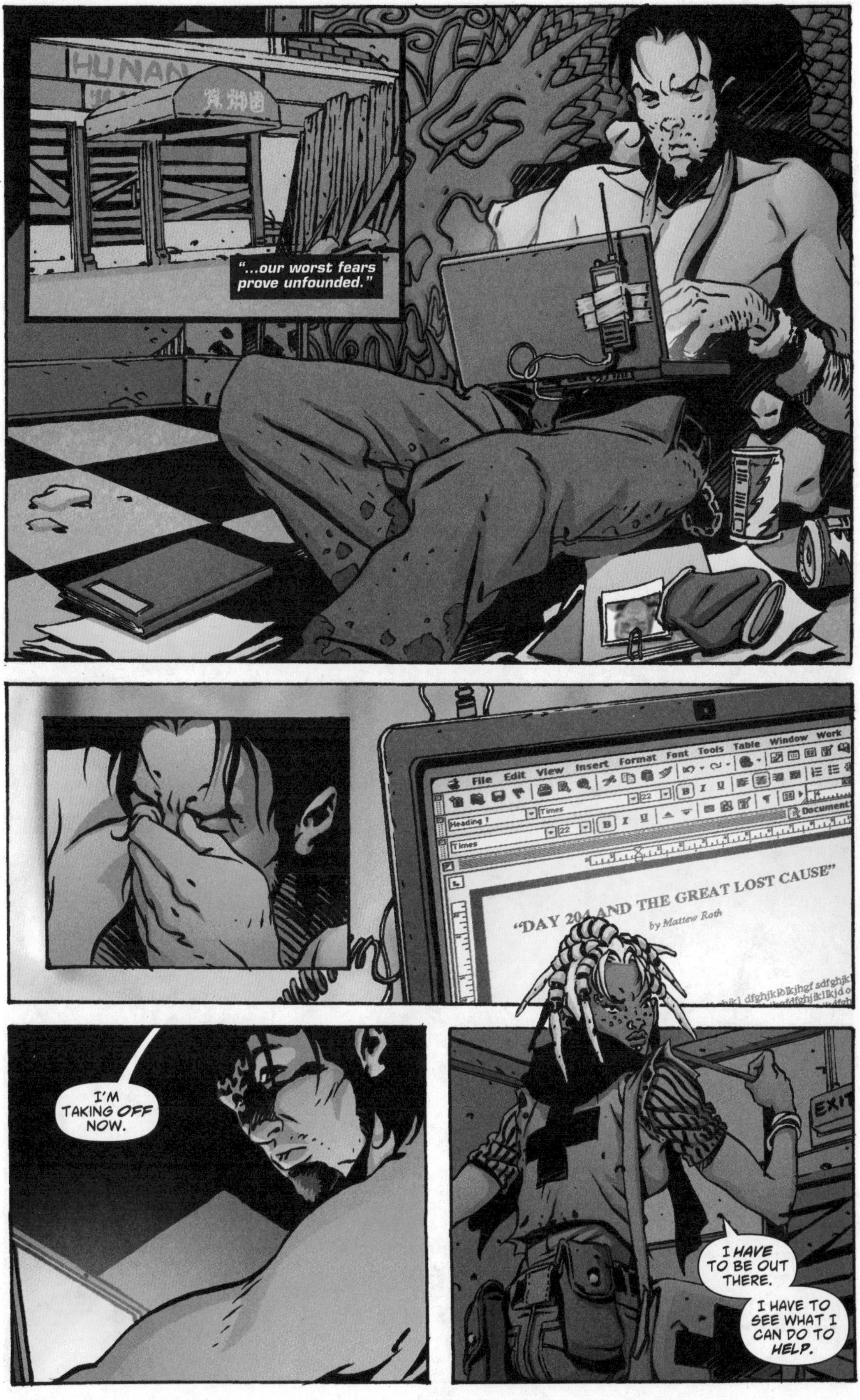
HUNAN
"...our worst fears prove unfounded."
File Edit View Insert Format Font Tools Table Window Work
"DAY 204 AND THE GREAT LOST CAUSE"
by Mattew Roth
I'M TAKING OFF NOW.
EXIT
I HAVE TO BE OUT THERE.
I HAVE TO SEE WHAT I CAN DO TO HELP.

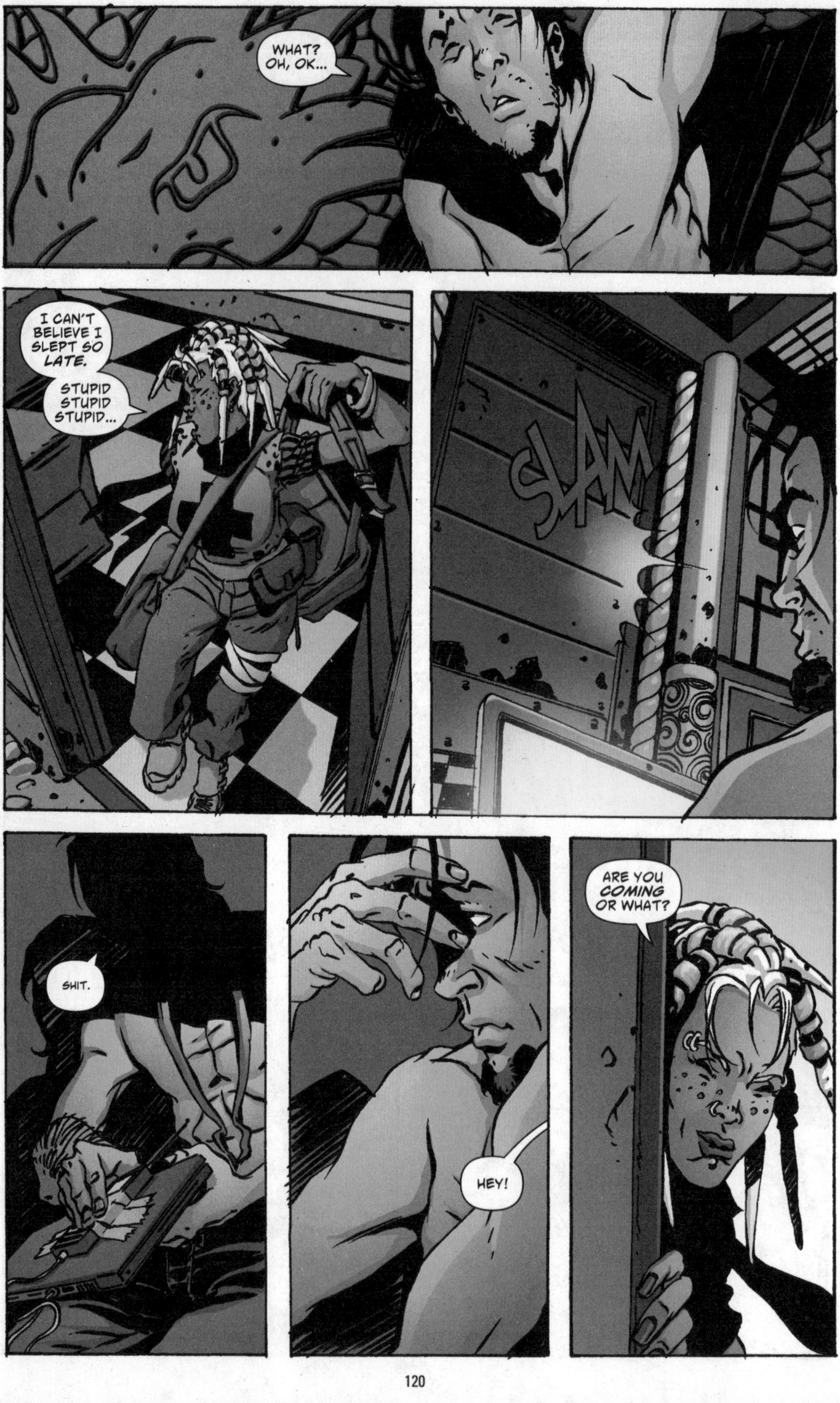
WHAT? OH, OK...
I CAN'T BELIEVE I SLEPT SO LATE.
STUPID STUPID STUPID...
SLAM
SHIT.
HEY!
ARE YOU COMING OR WHAT?

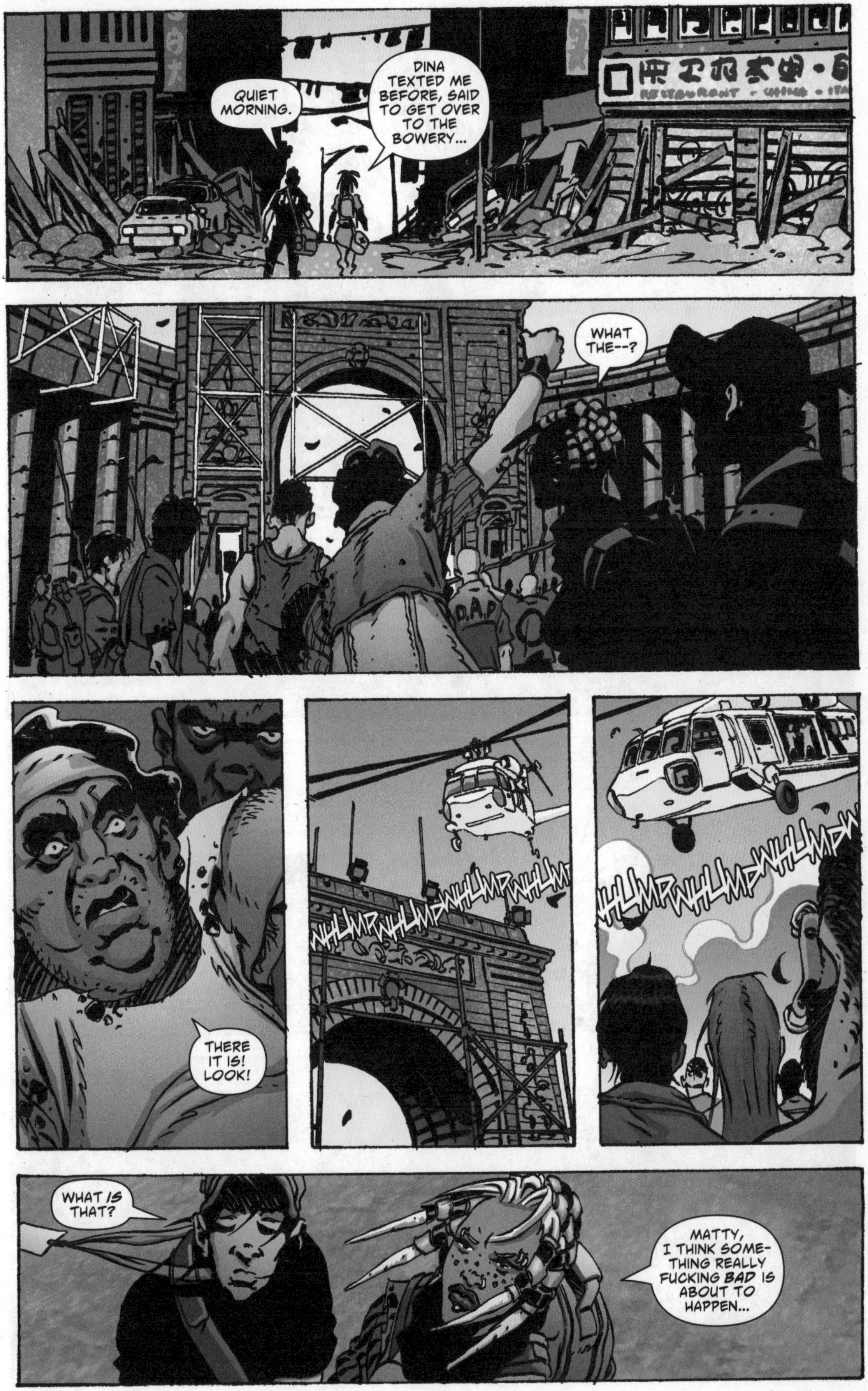
QUIET MORNING.
DINA TEXTED ME BEFORE, SAID TO GET OVER TO THE BOWERY...
RESTAURANT · CHINA
WHAT THE--?
D.A.P.
THERE IT IS! LOOK!
WHUMPWHUMPWHUMP
WHUMPWHUMPWHUMPWHUMP
WHAT IS THAT?
MATTY, I THINK SOME-THING REALLY FUCKING BAD IS ABOUT TO HAPPEN...

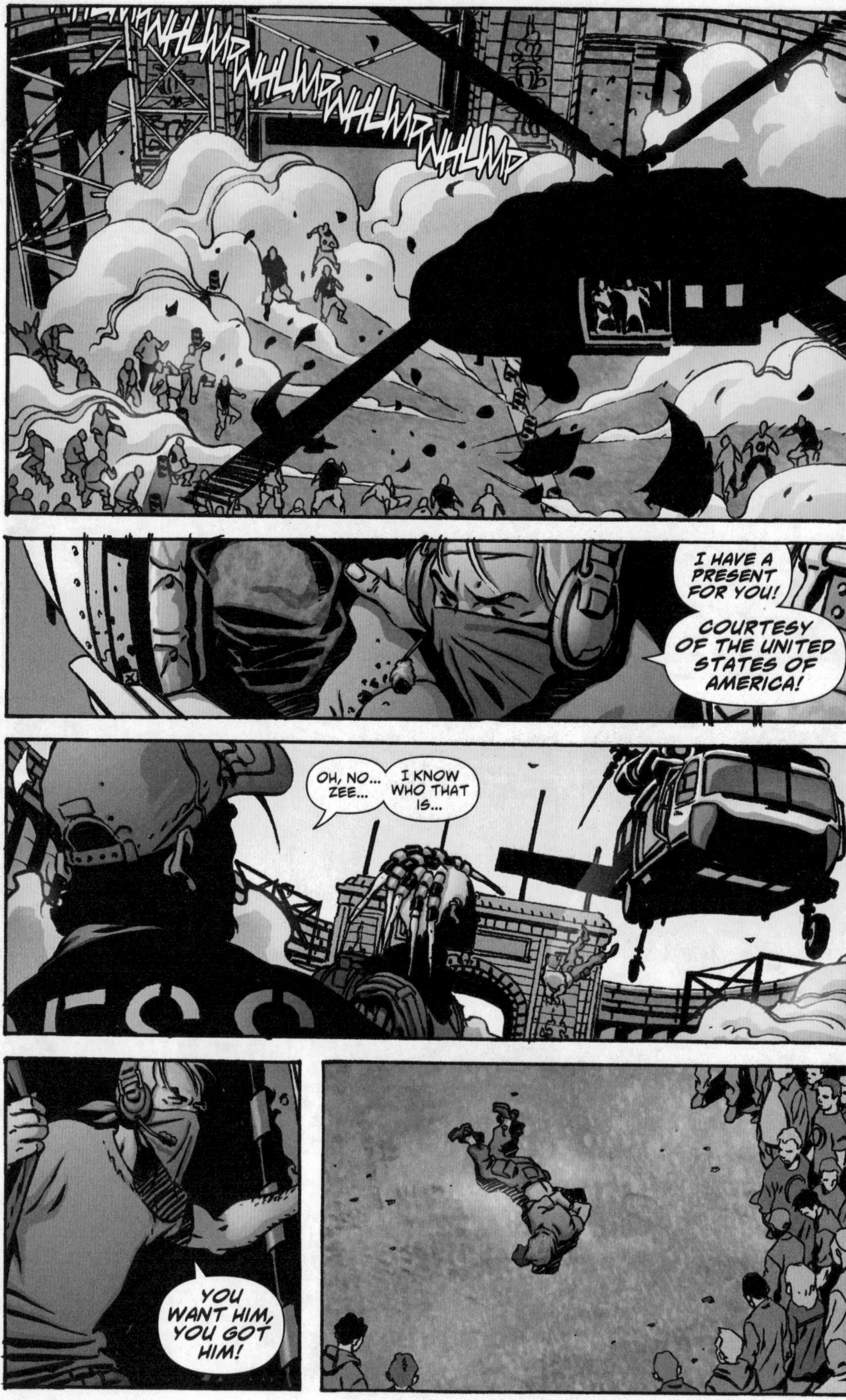
WHUMP WHUMP WHUMP WHUMP WHUMP
I HAVE A PRESENT FOR YOU!
COURTESY OF THE UNITED STATES OF AMERICA!
OH, NO... ZEE...
I KNOW WHO THAT IS...
YOU WANT HIM, YOU GOT HIM!

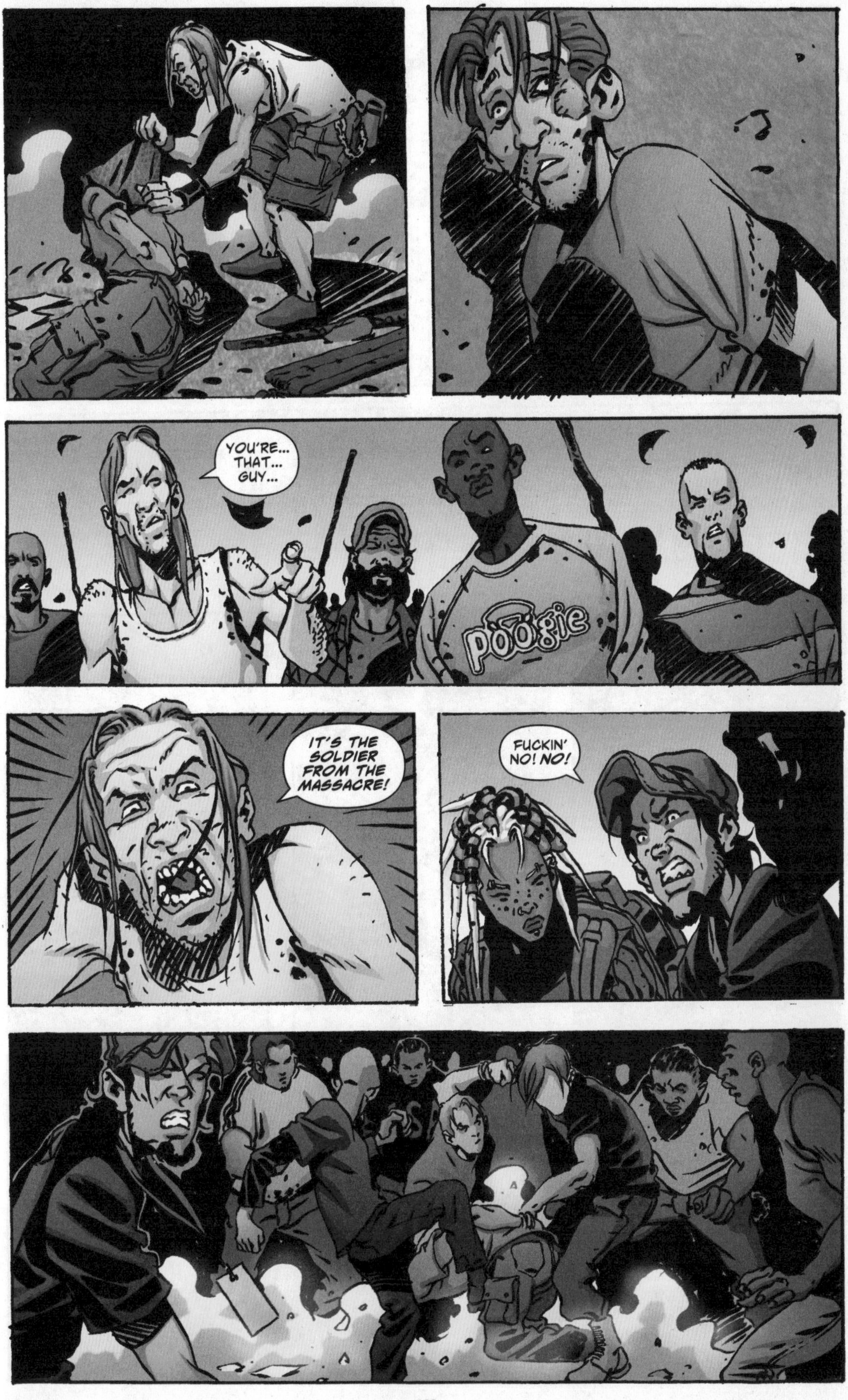
YOU'RE... THAT... GUY...
IT'S THE SOLDIER FROM THE MASSACRE!
FUCKIN' NO! NO!

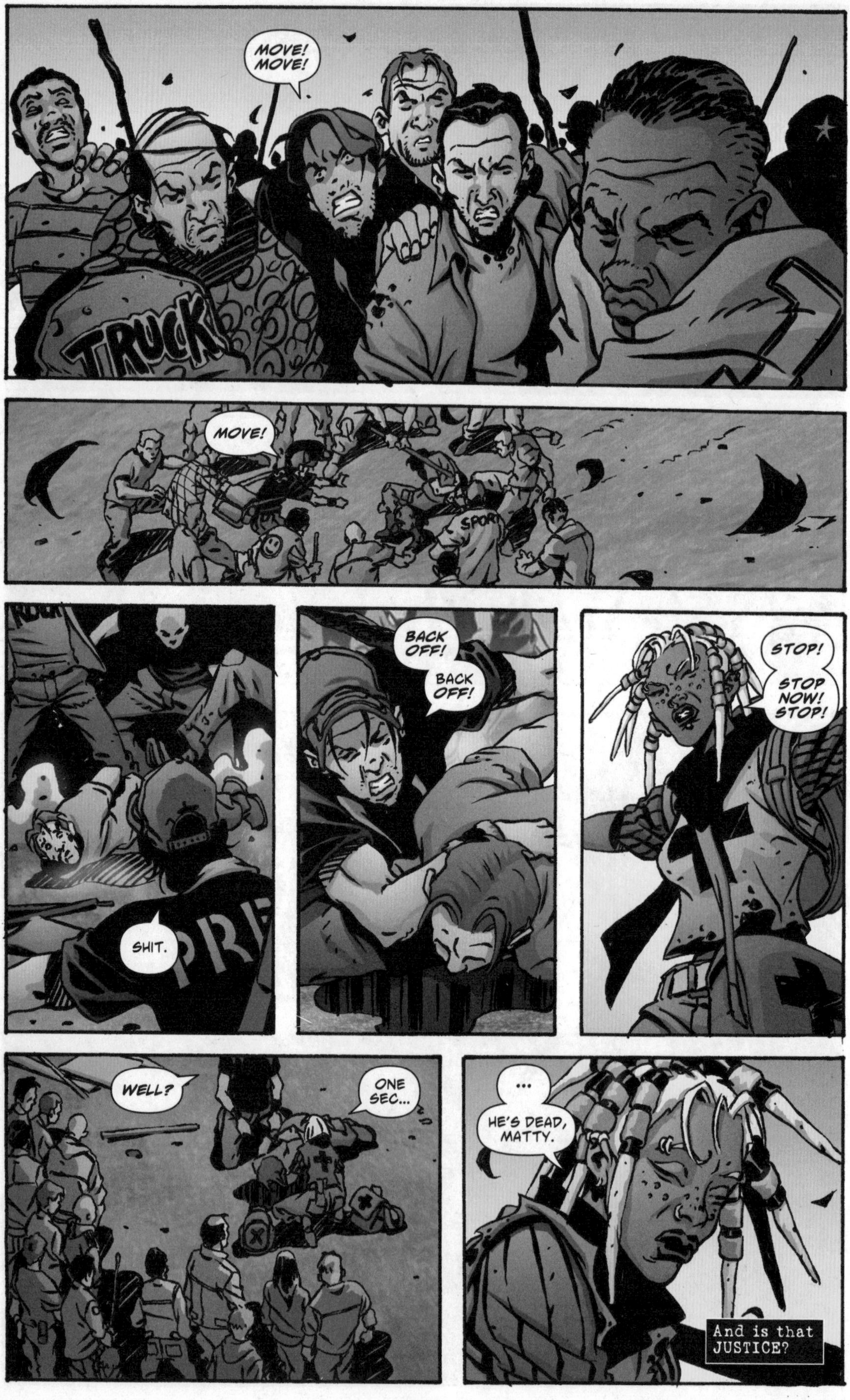

MOVE! MOVE!
MOVE!
TRUCK
SPORT
BACK OFF!
BACK OFF!
SHIT.
STOP!
STOP NOW! STOP!
WELL?
ONE SEC...
...
HE'S DEAD, MATTY.
And is that JUSTICE?

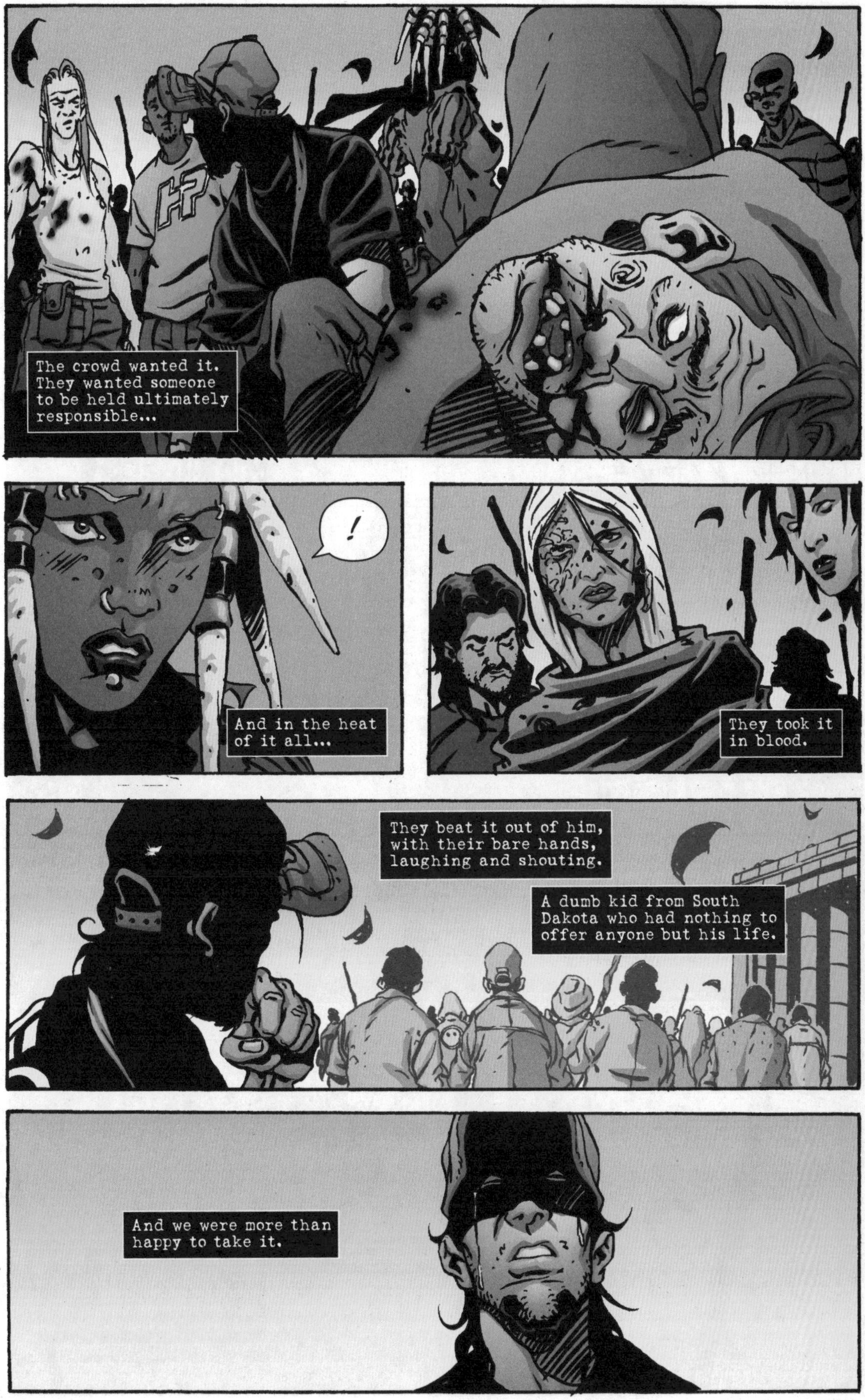
The crowd wanted it. They wanted someone to be held ultimately responsible...
!
And in the heat of it all...
They took it in blood.
They beat it out of him, with their bare hands, laughing and shouting.
A dumb kid from South Dakota who had nothing to offer anyone but his life.
And we were more than happy to take it.

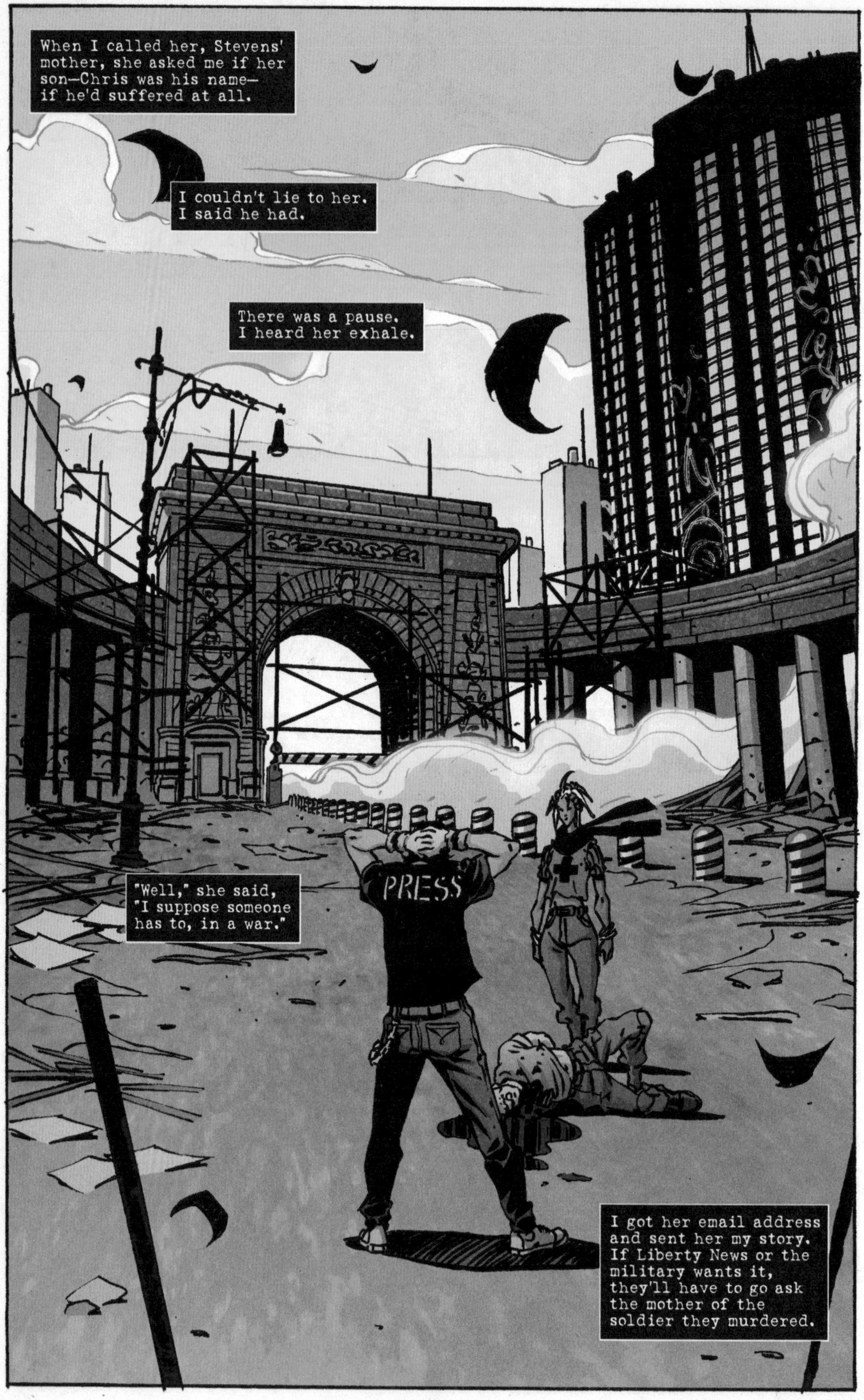
When I called her, Stevens' mother, she asked me if her son—Chris was his name—if he'd suffered at all.
I couldn't lie to her. I said he had.
There was a pause. I heard her exhale.
PRESS
"Well," she said, "I suppose someone has to, in a war."
I got her email address and sent her my story. If Liberty News or the military wants it, they'll have to go ask the mother of the soldier they murdered.

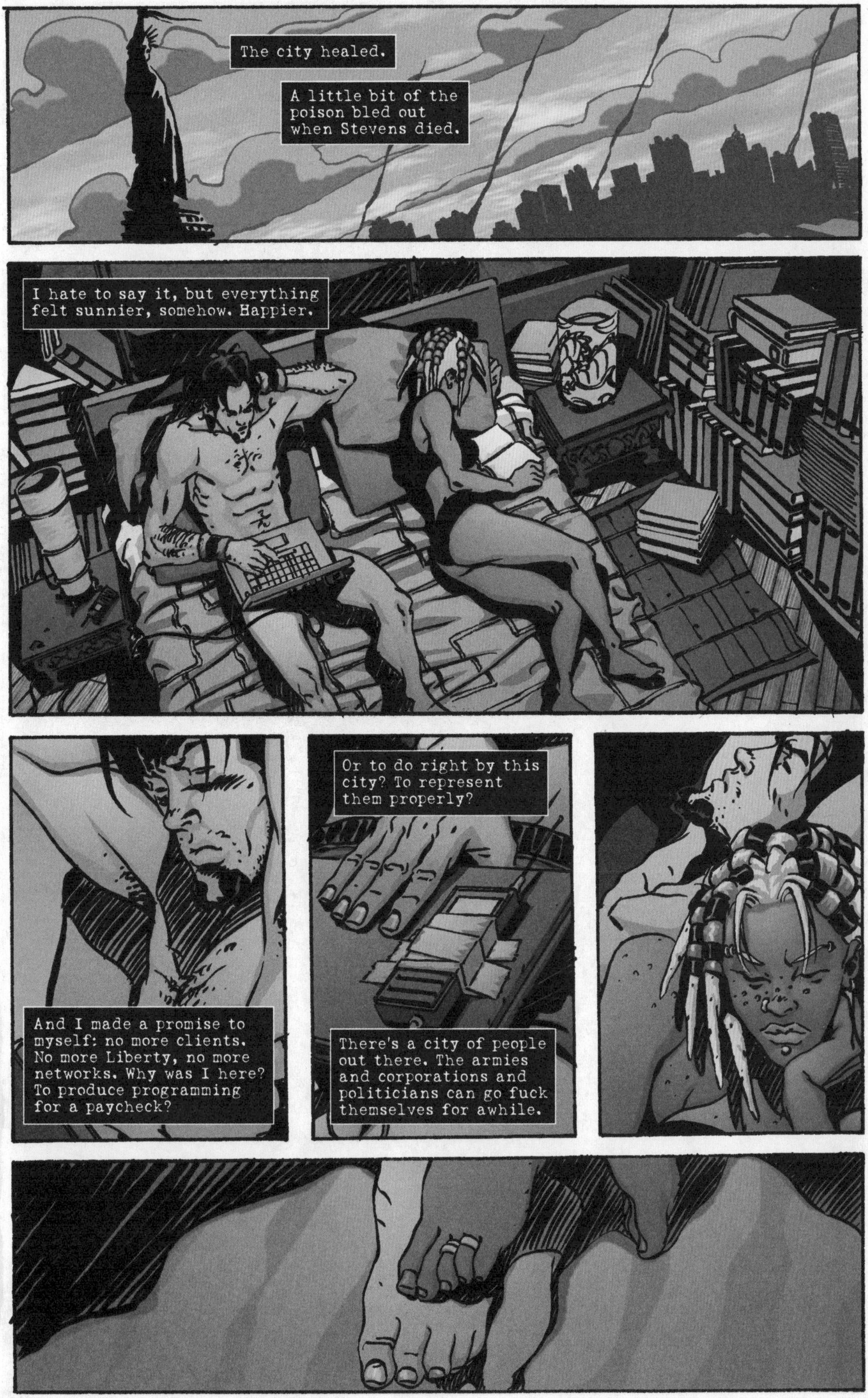
The city healed.
A little bit of the poison bled out when Stevens died.
I hate to say it, but everything felt sunnier, somehow. Happier.
And I made a promise to myself: no more clients. No more Liberty, no more networks. Why was I here? To produce programming for a paycheck?
Or to do right by this city? To represent them properly?
There's a city of people out there. The armies and corporations and politicians can go fuck themselves for awhile.

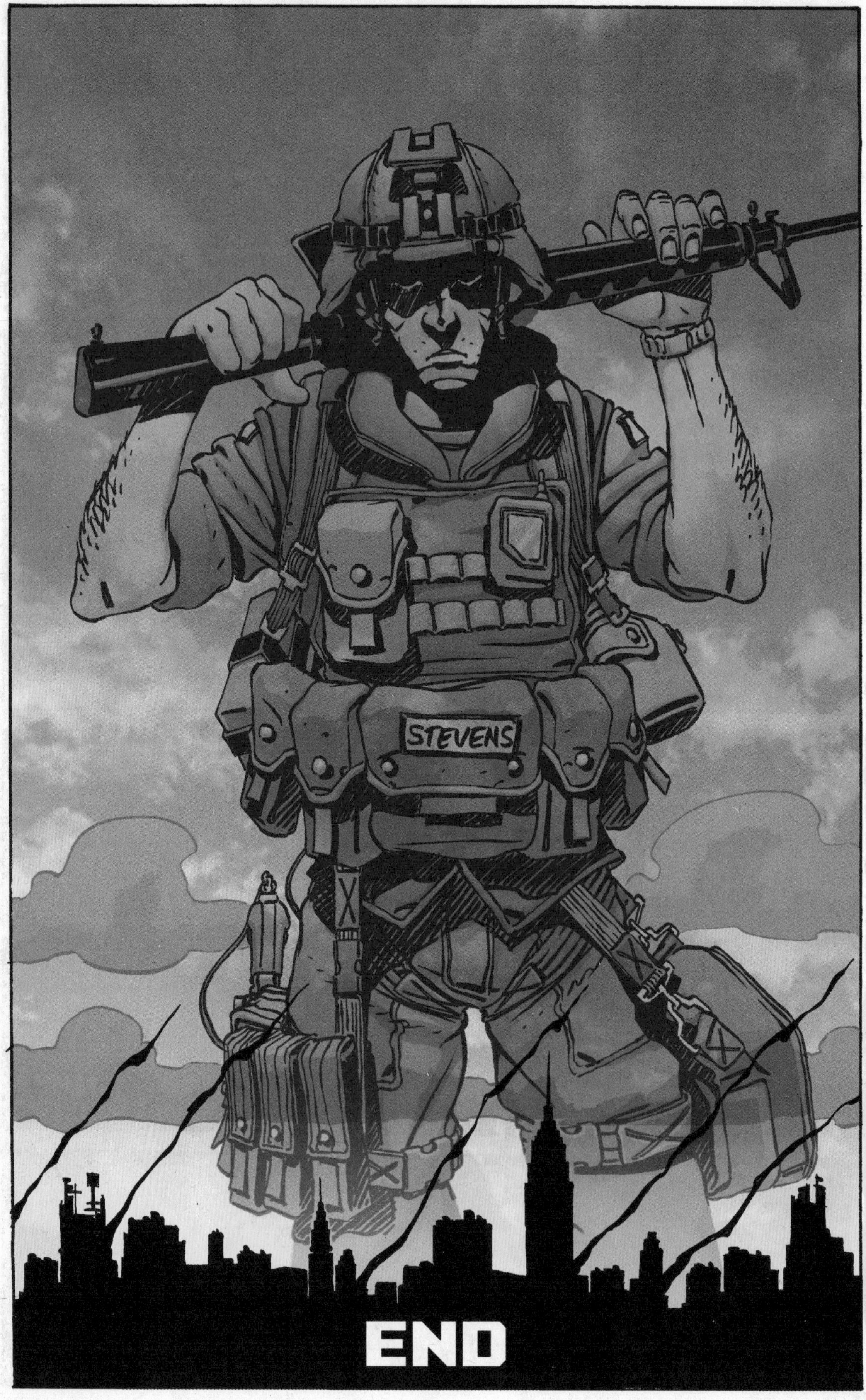
STEVENS
END